If You C.... ../ w uir.
Long Enough

Exploring the Pyrenees

Steve Cracknell

for Veronica

First published in 2008 at Lulu.com
All rights reserved
Third edition © 2016 Steve Cracknell

Published by lulu.com

Designed and produced by the author

ISBN 978 1 4710 6911 6

Website and blog: www.pyreneanway.com
Éditions françaises : voir www.GR10pyrenees.com

Contents

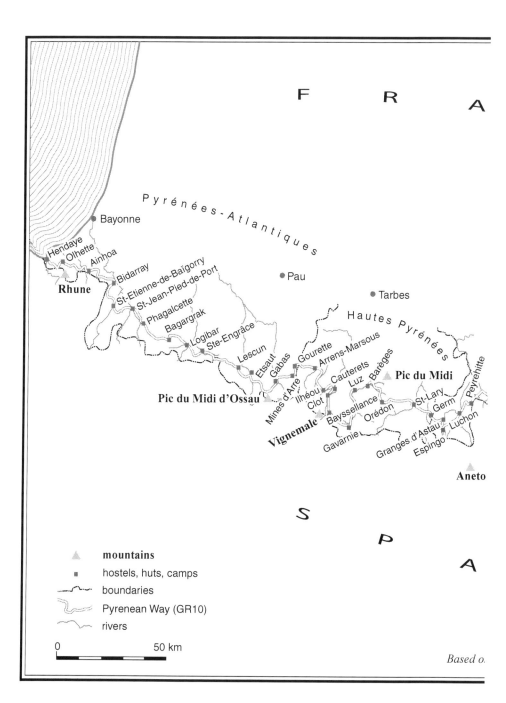

F R A

Pyrénées-Atlantiques

• Bayonne

Hendaye
Olhette
Ainhoa
Bidarray
Rhune
St-Etienne-de-Baïgorry
St-Jean-Pied-de-Port
Phagalcette
Bagargrak
Logibar
Ste-Engrâce

• Pau

• Tarbes

Hautes Pyrénées

Lescun
Etsaut
Gabas
Gourette
Arrens-Marsous
Mines d'Arre
Ilhéou
Cauterets
Luz
Barèges
Pic du Midi
Pic du Midi d'Ossau
Clot
Peyrehitte
Vignemale
Bayssellance
Orédon
St-Lary
Germ
Gavarnie
Granges d'Astau
Luchon
Espingo

Aneto

S

P

A

▲ **mountains**

▪ hostels, huts, camps

⌒ boundaries

⌒ Pyrenean Way (GR10)

⌒ rivers

0   50 km

Based o...

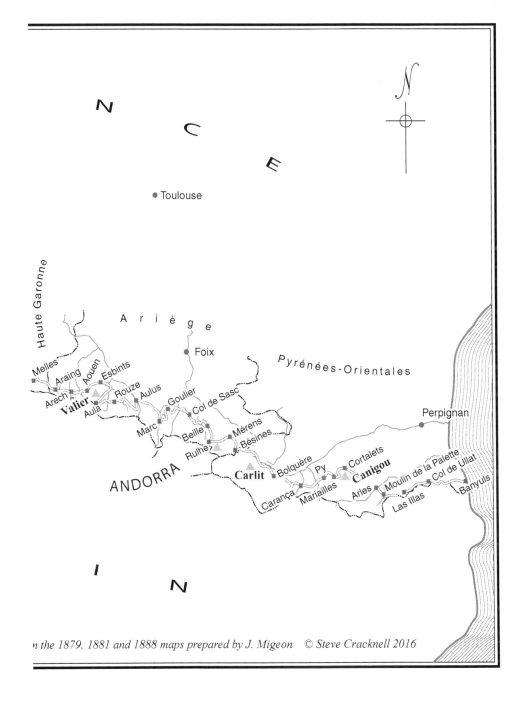

N
C
E

N

● Toulouse

Haute Garonne

A r i è g e

● Foix

Pyrénées-Orientales

Melles
Araing
Aouen
Esbints
Arech
Rouze
Aulus
Valier
Aula
Marc
Goulier
Col de Sasc
Beille
Mérens
Bésines
Rulhe
Perpignan
Carlit
Bolquère
Py
Cortalets
Canigou
Moulin de la Palette
Col de Ullat
Carança
Mariailles
Arles
Las Illas
Banyuls
ANDORRA

I
N

n the 1879, 1881 and 1888 maps prepared by J. Migeon   © Steve Cracknell 2016

vii

Notes

There are several guides to the Pyrenean Way (GR10) notably including Cicerone's *The GR10 Trail: Coast to Coast through the French Pyrenees* by Paul Lucia. However, for those who can manage a little French, the definitive guide is published by the Fédération Française de Randonnée Pédestre (FFRP), the French Ramblers' Association. The four books in the Traversée des Pyrénées series contain all the information you really need and nothing superfluous. Beware, however: no guide can be completely up to date.

Spellings: In a zone where the languages are as interwoven as the mountains and valleys there are often several different names for the same locality. I have used the versions given on the 1:25,000 IGN maps, preferring the French when there are alternatives as this is the version which has the widest distribution.

Cover photos: Hendaye, Bidarray, lac d'Aumar and lac d'Aubert, Vignemale, Esbints.

Acknowledgements

Many people have participated in the creation of this book, but above all I would like to thank Veronica Yuill for her numerous suggestions. Lucie Morice, who has translated the text into French, also made many comments which have enabled me to improve this edition. Thanks to Claude for painstakingly dissecting my photos and helping me to classify the plants. Thanks also to Paolo Mazzei for identifying the reptiles. His excellent website 'Amphibians and Reptiles of Europe' http://www.herp.it/ is worth the detour. I am much obliged to Marie Broll for the cover artwork.

And, to all those walkers and others I met on the mountains and in the valleys – whose names I have disguised – *un grand merci et bonne continuation*.

*De même que les médecins ont des stéthoscopes pour
mieux ausculter leurs patients, les randonneurs
possèdent le sentier GR 10 quand ils veulent scruter
le coeur des Pyrénées.*

Just as doctors have stethoscopes better
to examine their patients, walkers have the
GR10, the Pyrenean Way, when they wish to
examine the heart of the Pyrenees.

Pierre Minvielle

Prologue

My path leads to the east but I head west, down the beach to the Atlantic, a large yellow rucksack on my back, hairy white legs picking their way between discarded bikini tops.

I ask one of the sunbathers to take my photo, explaining my project. Before she has had time to reply, a young man dashes out of the water and strides towards us.

He asks me: 'What do you want?'

He looks at the woman without saying anything but I can read his thoughts: 'What do you want me to do with him?'

He is about to snatch the camera out of my hands when the woman grabs his arm. I explain for a second time that I would like a photograph of the start of my walk to the Mediterranean, a highly improbable excuse. Finally he calms down a little and follows me suspiciously to the water's edge. Still in a bad temper, he takes the camera.

Taking off my walking boots and wading into the water, I fill up a tiny shampoo phial, pose for the photo, and then meander barefoot to a bar for a cooling beer, squeezing the hot sand between my toes.

How long will it take me to get to the Mediterranean? I'm sure to get lost, but will I get seriously, dangerously lost? I don't know: I have never walked a long-distance path before, though the idea has been maturing for several years.

From where I live, in the vine-growing Corbières near Carcassonne, I can see the Pyrenees. On a clear day, I can make out the characteristic incisor profile of Mount Canigou. In winter, dentine white with snow, it bites into the heavens. In summer it is blue-grey, shimmering. Even when it is invisible, it is still there in my mind, palpable despite the haze.

Four years ago, I started walking in the foothills, meeting people with bulging rucksacks and serious suntans whenever I ventured on to the long-distance paths. The idea of walking the whole length of the Pyrenees gradually crept into my mind. And now I am sitting on the terrace of a bar in the seaside resort of Hendaye, about to set off.

But, despite my preparations and even before taking the first step I feel lost. Why is it so important to me? What am I looking for? I think of Alice in Wonderland, searching for her path and the moment when she meets the Cheshire Cat.

Alice went on. 'Would you tell me, please, which way I ought to go from here?'
'That depends a good deal on where you want to get to,' said the Cat.
'I don't much care where – ' said Alice.
'Then it doesn't matter which way you go,' said the Cat.
'– so long as I get somewhere,' Alice added as an explanation.
'Oh, you're sure to do that,' said the Cat, 'if you only walk long enough.'
Alice felt that this could not be denied, so she tried another question. 'What sort of people live about here?'

Lewis Carroll, *Alice's Adventures in Wonderland*

Like Alice I would like to know more about my new mountain neighbours: their history, their way of life, their values. Although I have read extensively about the Pyrenees, my mind is disordered. It is as if I have been collecting stamps and storing them in a box instead of putting them in an album. To have a meaningful collection, I need to classify them, put them in the correct order and identify any gaps. I hope that my journey will provide me with the missing elements.

I ask myself why I want to do it. For the challenge? A middle-aged man ludicrously trying to convince himself that he is still young. No, it is not just that; the explanation is too easy. I *need* to walk. Not just for a couple of hours, but day after day, though I don't quite know why. I hope to stumble on some kind of an answer before I arrive at the other end of the range.

In practical terms, the guide books tell me that I have a choice of three routes. The shortest is the *Haute Route Pyrénéenne*. It marches directly towards the watershed between France and Spain, and stays there. It only takes 40 days or so to exchange the bustling waves of the Atlantic for the torpid blue of the Mediterranean. But it makes no concessions to comfort and is technically difficult – if you decide to take in Aneto, the highest peak, you will need crampons, an ice axe, and no fear of heights, which rules me out.

The second possibility is the Spanish *Gran Recorrido 11* which sticks to the southern slopes and is well served by hostels. It is reasonably straight, but very exposed to the sun. More importantly my command of the language is very poor. I haven't got beyond the present tense in Spanish. The GR 11 belongs to the future.

So I have decided to walk the French Pyrenean Way, the GR10, described in my guide book as a *trait d'union* – a hyphen – between the Atlantic and the Mediterranean. As hyphens go this one is rather long and not at all straight. Changing valleys once or even twice a day, it snakes up minor passes but shuns the highest peaks of the range, passing through countryside which is sometimes rugged, sometimes bucolic, but rarely banal. At the end of the day it makes a detour to sniff out a meal and a bed.

The first problem, I have been warned, is that the path doesn't exist on any map, even though some of them have a continuous red line running from west to east. Landslides, unhelpful landowners, and even the FFRP, the French Ramblers' Association, create diversions, for worse or for better. In addition, in some areas there are several different official routes, never mind the unofficial ones. Even estimates of its length vary wildly: 700km, like walking from London to Edinburgh? Or 866km, London to Aberdeen? I don't have the time to do it all in one year. I'll start tomorrow and see how far I get.

I

In the Basque country – Hendaye to Gabas

Hendaye to Olhette

In the morning, I check that my bottle of sea water is not leaking. Then I put on a pair of odd socks – for luck – and set out towards the east, perfumed with summer-smelling sun cream. At first the path is bordered by palms, fig trees, and cacti but as soon as it leaves town, the vegetation changes dramatically, as if the moderating effect of the Gulf Stream only stretches as far as the urban limits. The English Cotswolds appear: sweet chestnut and beech trees, foxgloves in purple flower, pasture for sheep and cattle, and country mansions conspicuously defended by barking dogs. The houses are, however, clearly Basque, as is the temperature.

At Biriatou a few kilometres outside Hendaye I catch up with a man in the process of repacking his rucksack.

'GR10?' I ask.

'Yes,' he replies, in French.

'How many kilos?'

'Twelve.'

'Me too.'

I can't see how I could get away with less. Spare clothing, food, water. In the heat I drink three litres of water a day. I take a slug of the already tepid liquid.

My fellow walker is in his 60s. He is thin, very thin, with every detail of his leg muscles visible – like a Da Vinci anatomical drawing; it is as if his skin has been shrink-wrapped around him. These are not body-builder's all-for-show muscles, plump and fleshy; they are dense, rigid, almost additional bones. We are both going to be staying in Olhette this evening.

I continue up the ferny hillside overlooking the meandering Bidassoa river which forms the frontier here. During the Spanish civil war, I have read, this was a favoured observation point for watching the fighting on the other side. Safe in their ring-side seats, protected by a line on a map, the French spectators came here to experience death *live*.

At the top of the hill the path turns east, descends again along the edge of the forest and around a small hillock, and then tumbles directly into a street of shops. This is not a flashy out-of-town shopping mall: the buildings are crumbling disgracefully. Nor is there any of the infrastructure normally associated with shops: no domestic housing, no schools, no doctors, no town hall. No town, in fact. Just thirty or so emporiums, with a few tacky fairground stalls and restaurants. A row of decaying teeth with rotting meat stuck between them. The shop windows are stacked high with boxes and cartons with felt-tip prices scrawled on them: primarily strong alcohol and cigarettes but also just about every kind of bric-a-brac imaginable.

I have crossed the border by a few metres. Here, what little difference there is between the two countries has been distilled, concentrated, and regurgitated. French *pastis* is a top seller. Imported into Spain to benefit from lower taxes, it is quickly whisked off back to its homeland. Here, cigarettes cost half what they do in France. Long-legged dolls in frozen flamenco insist that Spain starts here, at the Col d'Ibardin, 1000km away from their Andalusian origins. Gadgets made in Hong Kong complete the range of knick-knacks on sale. The smell of hot oil and candy floss fills the air. Yet this tawdry setting attracts thousands of shoppers every year, their buses and cars winding slowly up the hillside; careering down again packed to the gunwales with inflammables, a disaster waiting to happen.

I pass through quickly. The path wanders down the hill again, into France and then turns, climbing. It is hot, suffocatingly hot, even under the trees. In the dappled shade I almost trip over a small stone post, inscribed 'R 18'. I walk around it and look carefully at each face, but there is nothing more to explain its purpose. Nevertheless it must be one of them. I've been looking out for them all morning, and although I must have been close to several, this is the first I have noticed. It must be a frontier marker. According to all accounts, there are 602 of them. The first marker is on the banks of the Bidassoa just upstream from Hendaye, and the last is hidden in a cave on the Mediterranean coast.

I've always thought that the Pyrenees were a natural frontier but in the cool of yesterday evening I ambled through Hendaye up the river Bidassoa and back in time, to the Île des Faisans, and discovered a period when the logic wasn't so clear.

On the French side grimly efficient industrial estates give way to leafy suburban gardens. On the Spanish side the bank is lined with rows of apartment blocks. In the middle is an anonymous island covered with rough scrub and self-seeded trees. The only indication of the importance of the site is a plain monument in a small clearing. Why did the French prime minister and his Spanish counterpart choose what must have been a desolate spot for their meeting? I have difficulty imagining them in their best court clothes jumping into boats still smelling of fish from the morning's catch, in order to negotiate the future of the two countries. The island, and hence the monument which might enlighten me, is inaccessible.

Disappointed, I continue upstream to a bridge where a series of notices explains all. In the 17th century most of the island was covered by a mansion with bridges linking it to both banks of the river. Velázquez decorated the Spanish half. So it was in this sumptuous building that the future of Europe was decided, not in some anonymous clearing.

The 1659 treaty itself is a fascinating document. It starts with a half-baked history lesson: 'The Pyrenean mountains, which in ancient times divided the Gauls and the Spanish, will from now on again become the division between the two kingdoms' and continues on the same vague lines. The treaty was so loosely worded that it wasn't until 1868 that it was even possible to mark out an agreed frontier on the ground (the 602 markers). It is a frontier which defies geographical logic and even preserves a Spanish enclave within France. It doesn't even follow the watershed for one-third of its length.

Yet, like some arranged marriages where the husband and wife care little for each other, have affairs, frequent rows, and longer wars, it somehow worked. In much the same way, in fact, as the marriage between the 21-year-old Louis XIV and his Spanish cousin Marie-Thérèse; the contract for their marriage also formed part of the treaty.

In recognition of its historical importance, the Île des Faisans was made into a condominium: it is jointly owned by the two countries. It is administered by France from 12 August to 11 February and by Spain for the other six months of each year.

***

Faded red paint on one side of the frontier marker indicates that the Venta Inzola is not far away. The *venta* itself is a long building with a string of outhouses nestling at the head of the valley. There is a bicycle shed, a small terrace, wooden picnic tables, and a concrete platform running down one side. It looks rather like a disused but well-maintained railway station, but the topography of the area rules this out. A dirt track disappears to the south into Spain; to the north the only access is by the Pyrenean Way. A chalked sign announces that the establishment is closed this week but normally postcards, drinks, snacks, and souvenirs are on sale.

This is more like it. The shops at the Col d'Ibardin may claim to be part of the *venta* tradition but Inzola really looks like the *venta* of my imagination: a smuggler's haunt, part of Basque folklore. On another occasion while staying in the Spanish Basque country I met Iñaki, an 'unemployed smuggler' as he described himself. He had followed in the tracks of his father and grandfather, both metaphorically and literally, taking sheep and cows across the border.

'That was when Franco was in power,' he said. 'You needed special permits to import livestock.'

He continued: 'It was much more dangerous going to fetch the animals than bringing them back. On the way out you could be shot if the frontier guards thought you were a terrorist. But on the way back the animals always made so much bloody noise nobody could mistake you for an outlaw. You might be arrested but you didn't risk anything more.'

His greatest claim to fame was 'importing' televisions in 1982.

I asked him: 'Why televisions? Spain wasn't really that backwards, was it?'

'*Colour* televisions,' he explained. 'In 1982, when the World Cup was held in Spain, everybody wanted a new telly. They were practically unobtainable in Spain, or else they were very expensive. So I drove across the border on a dirt track and came back with a van full of tellies bouncing from side to side.'

Despite occasional opportunities like that, semi-professional smugglers have been in decline since the Second World War. At the same time the prospects for amateurs have increased. The *ventas* transformed themselves into grocers, tobacconists, cafés, bars, and restaurants. But the tidal wave of the European single market has left these shopkeeper buccaneers all but shipwrecked and it is only the differential taxes which make their trade economically viable. That, and the tradition of a Sunday trip into the countryside.

Leaving the *venta* behind me, I trudge up the hill. I am overtaken by an old man.

'Is this the way to Olhette?' I ask.

'Yes. Just, tag along with me,' is the reply as he strides off. I struggle to keep up, quickly overheating.

'The Venta Inzola is closed this week,' I call after him, desperately hoping to slow him down, 'but it doesn't look as though it can do much trade anyway.'

'You're wrong, usually it is full of people.'

'What food like?' I gasp.

'Very good. Pilar grills the meat on a wood fire. And a meal only costs 15€.'

The roller-coaster path crosses yet another watershed. I can now see houses in the distance.

'Where come today?'

'Olhette. I'm just doing a little circuit for the afternoon. And you?'

'Hendaye. GR10.' Finally, he slows his pace and we stroll down to the hostel.

A single-storey, stone-built structure, the hostel has recently been renovated. Mature plane trees provide shade for the immaculate, juicy lawn. Scattered around is an impressive collection of nostalgia – wickerwork beehives, an impossibly clean, red-painted plough with a white coulter, a cider press, and a wooden sledge with a long pole designed to be drawn by horses. At the back of the house are traditional haystacks, like shaggy-topped mushrooms, somewhat the worse for wear, only for show. The only things which are in their natural place are the *lauzes*, thin stone slabs which mark the edge of the garden, creating a low fence. Inside, the dining room is bestrewn with horseshoes, stirrups, and cow bells. Strings of garlic and peppers hang from the ceiling.

My feet divested of boots and socks, I ask the owner for a drink and, wiggling my toes, sip it in the garden contemplating the outrageously contrived decoration. With a beer in one hand and my feet propped up on a packing case, it is unambiguously *perfect*.

The walker I met in Biriatou arrives shortly after me.

'I always walk slowly,' he comments. 'I'm Paul. *Comment tu t'appelles?* – what's your name?'

Haystacks in the garden of the hostel in Olhette

Paul has silvery grey hair and glasses to match. His old-fashioned look and slightly protruding top lip remind me of the onetime British Prime Minister John Major, though the resemblance stops there. He is wearing a dark blue flannel tee-shirt with a turned-down collar, two buttons at the front, and red and white striped hems – the kind of tee-shirt you could buy in the 1970s and wear for 30 years without it fading. His beige shorts have turn-ups and ironed creases. He takes his boots off and replaces them with shockingly modern white trainers.

Later, we are called for dinner in a converted barn and sit down at the table. Paul almost disappears. Like a child, his head barely pokes up over the table top, though I hadn't noticed that he was especially small. I look to see if he has been given a particularly low chair, but no, it is the same as mine. Then I realise that he is bent over forwards. Carrying a rucksack must be good for his spine, I guess.

We both eat greedily. Paul has just retired. With 30 years of long-distance walking behind him, he is much more experienced than I am, though he has not done the Pyrenean Way before. He speaks with a hint of pride in his voice; I listen attentively. Is that why I want to walk to the Mediterranean? To have a tale to tell? To feel just that bit superior? In any case, we are both hoping to reach the Pic du Midi d'Ossau before 4 July.

After dinner I saunter down the road in search of the centre of the village but there doesn't appear to be one. The houses are spread over a large area and are named, not numbered. They are immense, built of stone, with half-timbered façades, the wood often painted red.

Despite the troubled times which the Basque country has witnessed, the architecture suggests peace and prosperity over a long period. There are no run-down hovels. Only the houses of the rich survive, I conclude.

I was wrong. I turned the question over in my mind while walking but it was only later that I discovered the explanation. In fact these houses were the norm in the Basque country. They survived because the *etxe* – the house, the land, the furnishings… everything – had to be passed down to the eldest child – male or female.

Astonishingly, in the Basque country, a woman who inherited the *etxe* really was the head of the household and had considerable power. Not the kind of power attributed by men sitting comfortably in a public bar: 'All this talk of feminism is ridiculous. My wife wears the trousers… By the way, I must be going or she'll get the rolling pin out…' No. Not only was she the official guardian of the *etxe*, but also the *etxe* was deeply rooted in Basque culture, representing the soul of the family, generations past and generations to come.

In principle, the occupants of the *etxe* would be an old couple, a young couple (the eldest child and spouse), any unmarried children of either couple, and the servants. The farm was worked by the household in common.

So this is why the houses are so imposing. It is as if the house is living and the family members are merely visiting. The rules of inheritance also meant that the land was kept as a single viable unit, the whole system creating and maintaining a stable society.

A stable society? At the expense of those who didn't fit in. An eldest child couldn't marry another eldest child. They each had obligations to different *etxe*. Where would they live? And younger children who married younger children were semi-outcasts. As long as the population was only growing slowly the difficulties could be accommodated; the towns and the fishing industry could take up the surplus. This is no longer the case, but although society has changed, the landscape is still marked by these ancient footprints.

***

I return to the hostel warmed by the last embers of the disappearing sun, to hear shrieks of laughter and splashes coming from below in the woods. Half hidden in the twilight, two naked men are showering themselves in the river. Shortly afterwards one of them appears, dressed in a furry black pyjama suit, shaking droplets from his hair.

'*Bonsoir.* Do you think that I could have some water please?' he asks.

'I'll show you the tap. Are you camping by the river?'

'Yes. We've just arrived from Hendaye. We are knackered. My friend is out of condition so it took rather longer than expected, with all the stops.'

They have taken 12 hours, nearly twice the time given in the *FFRP Guide.* They are each carrying 20kg.

Olhette to Ainhoa

I set out just as the sun is rising over the hills, in the direction of La Rhune. Its name means 'pasture' but it is the first hill of any significance, though only 950m high at the summit. The grassy slopes are dissected by small streams, their shallow rounded valleys emphasised in the shade cast by the low sun, like a vast green sheet being shaken out, billowing in the wind. A red-and-white striped television mast caps the rocky crag at the top of the hill.

My first encounter of the day is with a foal: long white legs, a light brown coat, and a white star between its eyes. Its mane and tail are soft and fluffy. I approach it cautiously but it skips off ahead to rejoin its mother and the others. They are a curious collection. Some piebald, some a stunning chestnut, some grey. Pottoks, I conclude, in all their diversity.

The path levels out two-thirds of the way up the flank of La Rhune and skirts around it. Shortly afterwards I arrive at a level crossing. In a reversal of the usual roles, I am walking on the flat and it is the railway which is climbing, to the summit. The view from the top is said to stretch from the Atlantic coast to the high peaks of the Pyrenees, a panorama which has earned it three Michelin stars.

I hate Michelin stars. Any sense of awe which might be offered by a cathedral, a historic monument, or even a view is shattered by sharing it with a crowd. And three Michelin stars guarantee a crowd: the train carries over 350,000 visitors a year. On the other hand the train itself is just right. Its electric engines don't pollute and don't make much noise; the restored wooden carriages merely creak. What noise there is, from the cogs on the train chewing into the rack between the tracks, is concentrated into a few minutes as the train passes by.

On an interpretive panel sited near to the crossing, the names Espagne (Spain) and Pyrénées-Atlantiques have been defaced. EHE has been scrawled over them in felt tip, and the word Euskara has been cut into the surface. EHE stands for Euskal Herrian Euskaraz. Euskara is the Basque language.

The path descends between scattered *etxe* to the village of Sare – Sara in Basque. Here, wherever the name is written in capitals, the

As have horizontal bars across their apex, like little berets to keep the sun off.

SĀRĀ

'Why are there lines over the As? Are they pronounced differently?' I ask in the tourist office.

'No. They are pronounced exactly like any other A. It's just the way we write them round here.'

Written down, the Basque language certainly looks very strange, full of Ks and Xs. It disdains the letters C, Q, V, W, and Y but revels in stacking consonants together in tooth-breaking combinations. One of the reasons it looks so odd is that it is completely different from any other living language. It is not even part of the Indo-European family. Also, it has stayed more or less in one place for a very long time whilst the other European languages around it were on the move or, in some cases, simply dying out.

A leaflet in the tourist office tells me that there are about 650,000 Basque speakers, of whom 90% live on the Spanish side of the border. In the French Basque country, where state schools have always favoured French over Basque, young people are much less likely to know the language than their elders.

Which brings us back to Sare. It is here that the first bilingual state school classes were created in 1983.

'*Saran astia*' as the saying goes: in Sare one takes one's time, and it is only half past ten. So I leave my rucksack slumped tiredly in the cool shade of the tourist office and skip out under the stone arches into the sun. The white walls have already warmed up and are beginning to redistribute excess heat into the streets.

I buy a small *gâteau basque* – it resembles a Derbyshire Bakewell pudding – at a stall from a young woman who suggests I visit the Basque cake museum, or the Basque house museum, or the prehistoric grotto (and museum). But I reject them all and wander around the streets. Just opposite the cake stall is a panel evoking the visit of the Empress Eugénie in 1859. (She was Spanish; the extravagant fandango she danced on the top of La Rhune scandalised the court.) Also the long-disappeared tramway, the time when 6000 spectators came to watch *pelote* being played for two whole days, and the wonderful 'authenticity' of the town.

So is Basque identity in France just a kind of quaint folklore, kept alive to entertain tourists? One Basque, a beret. Two Basques, a game of *pelote*. Three Basques, a choir? History recycled to placate a few hotheads? Nothing more than the splashes from the cauldron boiling on the other side of the Bidassoa. Or is it an important force?

Perhaps I have the beginnings of an answer to my question. Sometime after finishing the GR10 I spent three months exploring the Spanish Basque country. The walls of the villages were covered in slogans demanding independence, and professionally executed murals – evidently officially sanctioned – protesting about the 'political prisoners' locked up in Spanish and French jails: 'Here they torture every day', 'Free our prisoners', 'Amnesty'.

The key moment, however, came when I entered a down-at-heel shop in the fishing village of Elantxobe. Inside, I asked the timid woman behind the counter if there was a local paper.

'If you really want to know what is happening here you should read *Gara*,' she told me.

So I bought a copy. She seemed excessively pleased. The newspaper read like the graffiti on the walls. I thought: if this ordinary middle-aged shopkeeper identifies with what *Gara* says, the Spanish Basques are heading for independence. In comparison, Basque identity north of the border is a mere chimera.

But that was much later. Let's go back to Sare and our famished walker.

I eat a lazy lunch washed down with a bottle of wine, accompanied by the sound of Basque spoken at the next table, and then totter unevenly down the cobbled street to the river. The stone walls which line the road shimmer in the heat. Beyond them, the pale yellow corn stubble is all that remains after the annual shave; but in other fields the maize bristles are still a vigorous deep green. My boots sink into the squishy tarmac and I regret the time passed in the relative cool of the morning in Sare. I could have been near my destination by now.

My left foot starts to hurt. It feels as if I have a hairline fracture precisely at the middle and on the left side of the fourth metatarsal. It has felt like that for a year now, but my doctor insists that I wouldn't be able to walk at all with a fractured bone, so I don't pay it much attention.

At the top of a small hill there is an isolated but imposing *venta* dedicated to tiles – floor tiles, roof tiles, wall tiles, bath tiles, nothing but tiles. More tarmac takes me down laboriously to the completely unremarkable Pont du Diable. Normally, Devil's bridges have at least one incredible feature. Some span an immeasurably deep chasm, which no stone mason's scaffolding could possibly have bridged. Some are so delicate that they can only be held in place by some magical exception to the normal laws of gravity. Here the devil has contented himself with an ordinary concrete slab bridge across a lazy river. I suppose the devil must have off-days like the rest of us.

I arrive at my destination, Ainhoa, under a veiled sky in mid-afternoon. Ainhoa, like Sare, is officially one of 'the most beautiful villages of France'. As in Sare, the houses in the centre of the village are imposing three-storey structures. On my left each storey jetties a little further into the street. The woodwork is painted either ox-blood red or a dark green, as if inspired by the local wine and the bottles it comes in. The spaces between the timbers are brilliantly whitewashed. On the other side of the street the façades are mostly plainer: traditionally Basque houses keep their backs to the wind so that they have a plain west façade and a more decorative eastern side. Whether they faced or had their backs to the high street was of no consequence.

Motor cars and lorries are trundling noisily up and down a high

Ainhoa

street lined with even more cars. The Japanese mulberry trees and decorative flower pots seem surprisingly resistant to the pollution. In the square at the south end of the road I discover some banana trees with their green hands stretching towards a sun fast disappearing behind the clouds, and I head for a hotel.

'The room costs 45€,' says the receptionist.

'Don't you have anything cheaper?' I ask.

'Yes but without a bath and there is no view.'

'I'll take it.'

'It's in the attic on the top floor. No 10,' she says, handing me the key.

This is the second time I have stayed in a hotel and the second time I have been offered room no 10.

I am lying on the bed when I hear a soft 'plup' sound in the distance. It repeats at irregular intervals so I get dressed and head in the direction of the noise. The source of the sound, the village *fronton*, is an area of tarmac about the size of a tennis court, with uncomfortable stone benches on one side and a smooth high stone wall at one end. There are two teams of two young men, each equipped with what looks like an oversize table tennis bat. They are hitting the ball – called, like the game, the *pelote* – against the wall, taking care to respect the white painted lines which divide up the court, but beyond that I cannot make out under what circumstances one round finishes, or indeed who has won. There are only a handful of spectators, so I assume this is a practice and not the real thing.

Paul arrives later and we eat together again. I study him, trying to work out how he fits together. When he sits up straight, he has the build and aerodynamics of a professional cyclist. I ask him, and he confirms that he goes cycling from time to time but not seriously. He orders a glass of wine at the beginning of the meal but only takes a couple of timid sips whilst eating. Then, after polishing off his dessert, he raises the glass to his lips and downs it in greedy slurps. He doesn't drink much water either.

'I only get through a litre a day,' he says. 'People tell me it's not enough, but I don't feel dehydrated.'

My dessert is ice cream flavoured with *piment d'Espelette*, a kind of hot pepper grown locally and named after a neighbouring village. Threaded onto strings, it can be seen hanging from beams in grocers and private houses throughout the Basque country. On the Scoville scale it is classified as level four (out of ten), somewhere between Hungarian and Cayenne.

Licking the ice cream cautiously off my spoon I have the impression that I am eating a plain vanilla ice cream but then I swallow it and suddenly fire breaks out on the back of my tongue. But the fire is quenched as soon as it has started and I am left confused. I have another spoonful. Cold, hot, fire, ice. Crazy food! Capsaicin, the active ingredient in pepper, is powerful stuff but soluble in milk fat.

Hence the affinity of curry and yoghurt, and *piment d'Espelette* and ice cream.

Replete, I go to bed early.

Ainhoa to Bidarray

It rained heavily during the night and is still drizzling as I unlock the front door and let myself out. The road out of Ainhoa is lined with crosses, 14 of them, leading up to an oratory, Notre Dame d'Arantze, on the hill slope above. Scattered in the porch of the oratory, I can see a rucksack, an assortment of camping equipment, and a blue sleeping bag laid on the hard concrete. A face pokes out of the middle of the heap. Perhaps this is the young American woman that Paul met yesterday. She is walking the Pyrenean Way alone, camping. I leave her to sleep on.

Opposite the oratory is a row of three crosses stuck in the ground with life-size painted figures nailed to them. Their vividly pink torsos and legs and insecure loincloths seem indecent in the half-light, like Dylan's 'flesh-coloured Christs that glow in the dark'. Facing them, like the congregation in a church, is an altogether more sober spectacle: a score of gravestones, decorated, but without names. The graves themselves, if indeed these are graves, are completely flat and sealed by the same luscious turf which covers the surrounding hillside. Some of the stones are in the form of a cross, but the majority are decorated with incised geometric patterns. The patterns include crosses but most stones have little obvious Christian meaning.

There were a few of these *stèles discoïdales* in the churchyard in Ainhoa dotted amongst the more usual burial vaults. Worn by the elements, they seem to be making no attempt to defy time. Their friable stone and mysterious patterns speak to me of human fragility and incomprehension in the face of destiny, in sharp contrast with the visually arrogant, status-conscious polished-granite family tombs which dominate modern French cemeteries.

The Pyrenean Way now follows a cart track skirting around the hill, climbing imperceptibly. The *FFRP Guide* tells me that I can see the Atlantic port of St-Jean-de-Luz but I am cloaked in low cloud and can see only a few metres ahead. My map tells me that, after two days' walking, I have progressed a grand total of 16km from the coast.

There are no fields here, no walls, just rough pasture, bracken, and scrub. But the side of the track is newly planted with saplings, still in their protective plastic tubes, tied to stakes much stronger than they are. The line stretches for over a kilometre. In a future summer maybe these trees will provide welcome shade, but today the rain is dribbling down my face and glasses.

Further on, through the woolly atmosphere, I can hear the hum of engines and the grating sound of gravel against gravel as it is displaced by rubber tyres. The noise seems to get closer, passes in front of me, and then stops abruptly.

The cart track descends. I can smell diesel fumes and, coming out of the cloud, I see a collection of four-wheel drive vehicles. Half hidden behind them, a man shouts something unintelligible in Basque. Murmured replies, then silence. A rustling, a metallic squeak, and then the plaintive bleating of a sheep, taken up by innumerable other ovine voices. I am greeted by the lanolin smell of wet fleece, and the nauseous stench of trampled sheep dung.

There are four small wooden-fenced pens, partly hidden under the oak trees. Two are full to bursting point with a heaving mass of discontented sheep, one is completely empty, and one contains three trestle tables. Next to each of the makeshift operating tables stand two men, each holding a vicious looking instrument in one hand. In front of each man, on the table, is a sheep, its four feet tied together at the ankles, resigned, as yet uncomplaining. The apron of the man who seems to be in charge is still a pristine white.

I walk up to the enclosure and say '*bonjour*'. The foreman replies, also in French, thankfully. There are 200 sheep, he tells me, and the seven men will take all day to deal with them. Behind him the men start snipping, one hand holding a sheep by the ear, the other holding the shears, biting into the fleece. The first sheep has just been finished. As soon as its legs are untied it slips off the table and is shown to the awaiting empty pen. It shrugs its shoulders, waggles its rear quarters, and skips off like a lamb.

The foreman passes me the shears to look at: a strip of iron bent into a U-shape with opposing blades at the terminals. Squeeze the U and the blades cross and cut. Release the pressure and the blades spring apart. They are identical to shears that I have excavated on archaeological sites in Britain. They reached technical perfection in the Iron Age, over 2000 years ago, and have not evolved since.

The workers are systematic and quietly efficient but at fewer than 30 sheep a day each they will not go down in the history books. The world record holder, New Zealander Darin Forde, sheared 720 ewes in a single day – using electric shears, naturally.

'We also treat them for diseases and ticks,' says the foreman, showing me a freshly exposed backside where the ticks are feasting. He slaps a dollop of noxious, sticky, black tar on them and smears it around.

'It's now and in July that the ticks start to attack, so we have to treat them before it gets too bad.'

If the ticks are bad for sheep, they can be even worse for people. In 1989, my friend Gaby had a nasty bout of influenza. His temperature rose and he ached all over.

'One day I noticed that I didn't have any sensations in my left foot. It was like a lump of lead dangling off the end of my leg. I went to my GP and he asked me if I had been bitten, if I had any sore patches.'

Gaby had been walking. He remembered a bite and the subsequent rash.

'The ambulance came to fetch me straight away. The doctor at the hospital took some blood samples and came back a couple of hours later. I asked him "Is it bad?" and he replied "We'll try to save you." "What are my chances?" I said. "Better than 50%" he replied.'

The paralysis spread. At its worst, the only thing that Gaby could move was his head, but he did make a full recovery.

Ticks, as Gaby told me, are the temperate-climate equivalent of mosquitoes and can carry Lyme disease. It has a variety of symptoms ranging from a rash and fever through numbness, arthritis, and encephalitis to cardiac problems, so sufferers can find themselves branded as hypochondriacs. It has been around for millennia but the symptoms are so diffuse that it was not identified until the 1970s. In France, the Pasteur Institute estimates that there are 5000 cases every year, only the drier coast of the Mediterranean escaping.

'Do you have problems with Lyme disease?' I ask the sheep shearer.

'Not here. I've never heard of anybody round here catching it,' he replies blithely.

Skirting Mont Bizkayluze, I am below the clouds and above the mist in the valleys. Sometimes they meet. Sometimes rain falls. In the distance I spot an immense white residence, the Ferme Esteben, said to be a 'basic' hostel. I had imagined a tumbledown shepherd's cottage but this is a mansion on a grand scale. The only thing which seems to be lacking is a welcome. 'Private property', 'Keep out', say the signs hung on the pristine barbed wire fence. Has the hostel been bought by a rich businessman and turned into a private residence? Paul is due to stay here tonight. Perhaps it was a condition of planning permission in this unforgiving wilderness that the owners continue to take in bedraggled strangers. If I get to see Paul again, I will ask him.

A short stretch of road and half an hour walking across pasture closely followed by vultures brings me to the Col d'Espalzam. There, a collapsing dry-stone shed dug into the hillside overlooks the river valley. The roof is like a giant jigsaw puzzle which has been broken up and thrown into a heap, the thick slabs half falling into the gaps between the rafters. I clamber over the mossy wooden fence which bars the doorway, look warily at the roof, and search for a space between the piles of sheep dung to eat lunch.

From the hut, the path descends abruptly into the valley, 'a difficult section' according to the guide. I am unimpressed until I slip on the wet grass and fall forwards, overbalanced by my rucksack. On my knees, I look over the drop. My left hand finds a rock and I push backwards and restore my balance, collapsing in an unstable heap, my rucksack pressed against the slope behind me. My knees are still bent, my legs crushed underneath me, and I can't get up. One leg at a time, I ease my feet forwards until I am sitting down properly and can undo my rucksack. I shut my eyes and breathe deeply. I don't know how I'm going to manage when there are real precipices.

My walking stick has tumbled down the slope. Gingerly, I chase after it and then stuff it into my rucksack. If it gets stuck in a small crack it is more of danger than a help.

At Bidarray, an hour later, the hostel is already fully booked. This turns out to be a stroke of luck, as the owner also has an empty three-bedroom apartment, with bath, real leather sofas, and a fully equipped kitchen, all for me at the same price as a bed in a dormitory at the hostel.

In the early evening I watch a game of *pelote*. This time there are no bats. The boys – teenagers – are using their hands; their palms and wrists are protected by bandages. I am still unable to understand who has won a point. When the game finishes I ask one of the spectators to explain it to me, but get lost in the complexity of it all. There seem to be three basic games, with a bat, with bare hands, and with a *chistera*, whatever that might be, but lots of different ways of playing. Like tennis, it is descended from the *jeu de paume* which was played all over France in the 16th century, but unlike tennis it has never quite achieved Olympic status. Although exported by emigrants, with its impenetrable rules it has remained quintessentially Basque. If there really is an authentic Basque identity north of the Pyrenees, its heart must beat to the rhythm of a *pelote* ball against a *fronton*.

In Bidarray there are two *frontons* and, as if that isn't enough, the west wall of the church, in dirty pink sandstone, is the same shape.

Stone is also used in the houses here. At Ainhoa, Sare and towards the coast, the carpenter was the most important worker on the building site. At Bidarray, the foreman was a mason.

Bidarray to St-Etienne-de-Baïgorry

I leave at 8 o'clock, and head south-west through the pastures. For once the Pyrenean Way is making no compromises. There is a mountain nearby and even though it is in completely the wrong direction the path seeks it out.

'*Sente de crête très aérienne* – very exposed ridge path.' I've been looking at this description for some days. I'm not very good at heights and I definitely don't like exposed ridges. There is an alternative route but this seems rather wimpish. What is the point of walking in the mountains on your own if you don't confront the dangers? I decide... not to make a decision.

Some of the fields have already been mown. Pale greenish yellow stubble alternates with green dampness. The sky is a morose grey with a few fanciful wisps of cloud. The path climbs relentlessly and after an hour I reach a junction. The left-hand fork climbs steeply and then gets lost in a mess of rock. It seems to be heading for a cliff face. The right-hand fork climbs timidly and then follows the flank of the mountain through the heather to a grassy plateau.

The Pic d'Iparla is my first mountain. At 1044m above sea level it is only officially a mountain by 44m, but still it is higher than Scafell Pike in the Lake District, the highest peak in England. It would be a shame not to rise to the first challenge.

I take the easy option and the right fork, and half an hour later the deviation has brought me back to the main path which now runs along the top of the cliff. Looking back, the 'exposed ridge path' appears remarkably ordinary. I can even see a man skipping along it. Shortly afterwards he overtakes me. In tee-shirt and shorts, he is visibly well past 60, and running. He reaches the summit and turns round without stopping but by the time he has reached me again he has slowed down a little. He has come from Bidarray, he says. He set out at 9 o'clock.

'Excuse me,' he pants, 'but I must get back for breakfast.'

The Pic d'Iparla itself is an insignificant bump on the ridge, but walking along the cliff edge, picking my way between the rock slabs, is exhilarating. To the west the air is clearer and I persuade myself that I can see a silver reflection of the sun on the Atlantic. But to the south the clouds are black and menacing and soon the wind increases and the rain arrives. Peat squelches under my boots. Rain drips from my hat. My glasses are steamed up. I huddle in a cave. Wring out my socks. Force lunch down. Shiver. I just want to get off the mountain before the storm really arrives.

The path down into the valley becomes a slippery red scar. A gigantic black slug slithers by. For the last two days I have had ample opportunities to examine the local slugs. Without exception enormous, fat, and smugly unaware of their likely destiny, those on the road into Bidarray were black, just as they are here. But those on the Pic d'Iparla were a disgusting speckled yellowish brown.

In St-Etienne-de-Baïgorry in the valley there is a hostel outside the village but I want to be comfortable so I trudge from one hotel to another. They are either fully booked or ridiculously expensive and crawling with Americans. I take refuge in a bar where four old men are playing cards, speaking to each other in Basque. At the counter a group of people in their 20s and 30s are chatting, switching from Basque to French and back again every few words. The barman directs me to a hotel in Beherekokarrika. (Said out loud it sounds much nicer than it looks written down.) I had passed by the hotel earlier, thinking it was shut; it is merely decrepit.

The owner looks at me suspiciously. 40€ a night, paid in advance. I ask to see the room first.

'OK. No 4 on the first floor, with shower and toilet. The key is in the lock. I'll wait here for you.'

The key isn't in the lock but I push on the door and it opens. The electric light is already on and the curtains are drawn. The bed covers have been pulled down to the bottom and the pillows have been piled up in the middle but, aside from the residual perfume filling the room, there is no other sign of the occupant, nor of her profession.

I go down the stairs.

'It's fine but the bed hasn't been made.'

'Oh? Try no 7. No. That's taken. I've got one with a toilet and bath down the corridor, on the second floor, if that would do. 30€. Go and have a look at it. It's no 10,' he says, handing me the key.

Later, as I seem to be the only guest in the hotel and don't want to sit in the middle of the vast empty dining room, I go out in search of somewhere to eat and end up at the expensive hotel I had earlier rejected. The restaurant is plush and the food is superb, *foie gras* accompanied by a glass of Jurançon, *mignons de veau* with red Irouléguy wine from the Domaine Ametzia, but too rich for my stomach and I am too tired to really appreciate it.

St-Etienne-de-Baïgorry

I have decided to have a day's rest, so my fifth day on the Pyrenean Way begins with a visit to the bakery. In the shop, the baguettes are stacked up in wooden cases behind the counter with the regulation price, 70 centimes, clearly displayed. One of the baguettes has already been cut in half and I ask for the remainder.

'Seventy centimes,' says the baker, turning away to wipe some crumbs off the counter. I look at the price. I look at my half baguette. The baker looks up expecting me to pay, and I look at him. Several seconds pass in silence.

'Sorry, I should have said 35. I was thinking about something,' he mumbles.

Giving him the money I say, 'Yes, perhaps you were thinking that I was a foreigner.'

'Not at all. That's not the way I work.'

On the opposite side of the road, in the pharmacy, I buy plasters, sticky bandages, and some liquid skin. I left home with a first-aid kit capable of coping with minor battlefield disasters but the predicted tendonitis, diarrhoea, and blisters on my heel have not appeared. Instead a blister on my little toe has come back, deeper down.

I retreat to the hotel and hack off the dead crust with a blunt pair of scissors. The liquid skin and an impossibly large bandage complete the operation, but my feet no longer fit into my boots, so I hobble off to the supermarket to buy a pair of flip-flops.

I spend the day wandering aimlessly. In this village surrounded by mountains, the banana trees seem incongruous: but then St-Etienne-de-Baïgorry is only 160m above sea level.

In the evening when I come down from my room, Paul is already sitting at the solid wooden table in the back room of the hotel. The Ferme Esteben, he says, was fine, except that he had needed to ask for blankets. Two other walkers come in. I look discreetly at their legs. Strong muscles, skin somewhere between burnt red and tanned brown; weathered sober faces. Jean-Paul has a full beard but Richard is freshly shaved. They started at Hendaye on the same day as Paul and I. They have the easy familiarity of old friends who have been walking together since they were young, but as they talk I realise that they have only known each other for four days. They met by chance on the first section and have been keeping in step ever since.

The door opens again and another man walks in. He is conspicuously black: few black people are to be seen on the mountains, and he is wearing a black sleeveless tee-shirt and tight black shorts. He asks quietly if he can eat, though he is not staying at the hotel. I place his accent somewhere in rural northern France, but not in the Parisian suburbs or indeed in any large town: his French is too mellifluous. He has a few day's growth on his chin and a similar length on the top of his head; mostly black hair but with a few white strands. An angular face, without wrinkles though he must be about my age. He introduces himself and shakes hands with everybody. Big hands, like the rest of him.

'We are camping at the hostel but I wanted to eat a proper meal. Grégory is eating from a packet tonight,' says Aimé. 'We left Hendaye four days ago.' He is hoping to do the whole of the Pyrenean Way before the beginning of August. His friend will accompany him for the first two weeks.

We eat omelettes, duck *confit* and chips, *gâteau basque* and ice cream, far from the refined food of yesterday evening but more satisfying.

St-Etienne-de-Baïgorry to St-Jean-Pied-de-Port

In the cool of the new day, I cross the modern bridge over the *baïgorry*, the red river. It is not really red but the rocks over which it passes give it a reddish tinge and give the town a way of distinguishing itself from all the other St-Etiennes. Incidentally, the Revolutionaries of 1789 renamed Baïgorry: the 'red river' became the 'hot gates' – Thermopyles. Like their new names for the months of the year, the name didn't stick.

The valley is shrouded in mist but the path soon rises above the puffy clouds revealing harsh crumpled mountain ridges separated by shadowy valleys under a washed-out watercolour sky. On the hill slope I catch up with a walker. With his mop of untamed dark brown hair, sideburns, angular features, and long neck he looks like a character from *Astérix the Gaul*. He is wearing a shapeless turgid green hat, just like mine.

'Have you seen my friend?' he asks me.

'The tall black man?' I guess.

'That's him. He's not particularly tall though. People just think that he is.'

'He passed in front of the hotel when I was tying my laces. He must be about five minutes ahead of us.'

This must be Grégory. Gradually, I realise that he is the man who asked for water on the first evening. We spot a figure moving quickly along a road above us so he dashes off to catch up.

When I arrive at the first pass of the day, I see five identical white Renault mini-vans. Four of them speed off in different directions as I approach. 'We meet up here every morning for a chat after checking out the sheep,' explains the old man at the wheel. The dogs in the back confirm the story. 'We're bringing them closer to the road for shearing next week,' he continues.

Later, at the top of the Munhoa the wind is blowing hard and I have to put on all the layers of clothing I possess, but by lunch time in the valley just outside St-Jean-Pied-de-Port I can finally take off my tee-shirt and sunbathe.

I'm not the only one who needs to relax a little. At the hostel in town, when I open the door of the dormitory, I discover an Indian, in his 50s, lying on a bed, resting his bandaged feet. Married to a Dutch woman and living in Holland for 35 years, he started walking at Le Puy 36 days ago. He calculates that he is about halfway. It is not a pilgrimage: he is not even Christian. He is simply walking to allow himself time to think, and incidentally collecting sponsorship to educate Dhalit children in the village where he was born. He hopes that a walker he met a few days ago will catch up with him so that they can cross the Pyrenees to get to Roncevaux together. It is one of the longest and most arduous sections on the whole route.

St-Jean-Pied-de-Port is a major crossroads for walkers. Two paths – two cultures – intersect here and then go their separate ways. Profane meets Christian. Altitude meets distance. Clay meets tarmac. As well as being one of the few towns on the Pyrenean Way, St-Jean-Pied-de-Port is also the last resting place in France for pilgrims crossing the mountains on their way to Santiago de Compostela: *'pied de port'* translates as 'at the foot of the pass'.

Saint-Jean-Pied-de-Port

I go into town and cross the river Nive – the same river which passes through Bidarray. Here it is lined with houses, their overhanging wooden balconies reflected in the still water. The bridge and the balconies are festooned with baskets of flowers. A neatly laid cobbled road leads under the stone arch, through the town wall, and up the hill between an extraordinary array of ancient stone-built or half-timbered structures, mainly shops, restaurants, and hostels. The shop fronts are for the most part unobtrusive; some coordinating authority seems to have decreed that any exposed woodwork must be painted a uniform reddish-brown.

Heaped against the door of one of the hostels are a couple of tattered rucksacks, one red, one blue. They each have a pierced scallop shell – the emblem of pilgrims on the road to Santiago de Compostela – tied to them, and a pair of worn walking boots and a stick complete the pile. Kit left temporarily on the doorstep at the end of the day by hikers too tired to drag it upstairs? There is something wrong. They are exactly the right elements in exactly the right place. It is not a random collection of equipment but a carefully coordinated new-fashioned inn sign.

Half way up the main street of St-Jean-Pied-de-Port a stone arch leads into an attractively shady room. This is the home of the Friends of the Chemin de St-Jacques. Sitting behind one of the desks is Pierre, a Parisian. Newly retired, and with a girlfriend who lives on the coast, he likes to come down and help with the centre.

'I would say that the majority of walkers have some kind of spiritual motive, but not necessarily a Christian one.'

'Does this cause problems in Spain, in those hostels run by the church?'

'No, not as long as the walker keeps his *credencial* up to date.'

I look at the chart behind him. In 1996, just 1,264 visitors passed under the arch to get their *credencial*, pilgrim passport, stamped; in 2003 there were 18,196 of them. (In 2010 the figure reached 35,698.) The Pyrenean Way is much less popular. I reckon I have met just about everybody who set out from Hendaye at the same time as me: Paul, Aimé, Grégory, Richard, Jean-Paul, and the American woman. Allowing for a couple of campers who are keeping to themselves this makes nine people walking eastwards; I have seen no more than two a day walking in the other direction.

'Why are so many people doing the Chemin de St-Jacques? Obviously it isn't a sudden explosion in the number of faithful.' I say.

'Several reasons. The paths became a World Heritage site in 1998 and then 1999 and 2004 were holy years, when the saint day falls on a Sunday. Then there is the shorter working week and a snowball effect – with a lot more television time. But above all I think it is the increased number of hostels, which means that shorter walking days are possible.'

All the passes over the Pyrenees have been used by pilgrims at one time or another but of the four main routes, three, from Le Puy, Tours, and Vezelay converge just before St-Jean-Pied-de-Port. Pierre has done the route four times, once running the 2200 km from Basle in 45 days. He is thin – weighs 62kg, he says – and keeps his rucksack down to 6kg.

It is astonishing how St-Jean-Pied-de-Port has rediscovered its vocation as a staging post on the Chemin de St-Jacques de Compostelle in the last 20 years. It is a long story, going back centuries.

The area first entered into history books in AD 778 when Charlemagne returned defeated from one of the earliest attempts to kick the Moors out of Spain. His nephew Roland was ambushed at Roncevaux just over the border and killed by the Basques. But history has filtered this and removed some of the more unacceptable facts to give us the epic *Song of Roland*. In this version Roland was killed by the Moors; Charlemagne then returned to Spain and inflicted a crushing defeat on them. Neither is true, yet it is the *Song of Roland* which has captured the popular imagination over the centuries.

Half a century after the military failure, a saint was brought in to help. St Jacques – St James in English – was one of the disciples. He reappeared providentially around AD 825, when bishop Theodomirus 'identified' an ancient tomb as his last resting place. The first pilgrimages began. By the 12th century Santiago de Compostela was being actively promoted as a holiday destination for the politically aware Christian faithful. Through them, Spain would be wrested from the Moors and brought back into Christendom. The process took several centuries, but 1492 was a momentous year for Spain. In the same year that Columbus 'discovered' America, the catholic King Fernando and Queen Isabella finally took control of Granada, pushing the Moors back across the Straits of Gibraltar. For hundreds of years the Pyrenees had metaphorically divided Europe and Africa. Now Spain was set to become a truly European power. And the pilgrimages had played a key role.

Much history has been made on the Chemin de St-Jacques. Just as the past is distilled to become history, the paths over the Pyrenees are the funnels through which it is poured into the still.

St-Jean-Pied-de-Port to the Route de Phagalcette hostel

In the morning, I walk through the town, past the Vauban fortress, and head south. Here the Pyrenean Way and the Chemin de St-Jacques follow the same itinerary. They are waymarked from time to time by short painted stripes: a white stripe on top of a red one. When the FFRP was looking for a suitable sign to indicate the new long-distance paths, it borrowed the existing markings of pilgrim routes. The white stripe represents the sacred spirit which guides pilgrims as they walk with their head in the clouds. The red stripe represents the flesh: feet covered in blood. It is a nice tale but not true, as I discover some time later. Like the *Song of Roland*, it is just another reworking of history.

I catch up with Grégory and Aimé on the lower slopes of the first hill. They are looking alternately at a map and at a waymark painted on a gatepost.

'We continued straight on, following the fence, but it is a dead end,' explains Grégory.

I extract my GPS to check where we are.

'It was a good trick you played on me yesterday,' says Grégory grinning as we wait for the GPS to find the satellites and I explain how it works. 'After you said that Aimé was ahead of me, I ran up the hill trying to catch him up. It was only when I caught up with Richard on the top of the Munhoa that I realised that he must be behind me! He had gone for a cup of coffee.'

'Whilst you were chatting, I've been studying,' says Aimé. 'If you look carefully at the waymark, part of it has faded. We are supposed to turn left here.'

We walk together for a while, descending into the valley of Estérençuby where I leave Aimé and Grégory in the café, drinking beer. I climb again following the road in the direction of the hostel, the curiously named 'Route de Phagalcette'. Tiring of walking on tarmac, I just want to be able to take my boots off and sit down. I plod on, the road meandering through the forest, until I realise that I haven't seen any waymarks since the village. My map makes no sense. I can see only trees; the cartographers saw only fields. I extract my GPS but it tells me something improbable, so I stuff it back into my rucksack. In a kilometre or so I should be able to see where I am.

When finally I reach the plateau, I can indeed see where I am. The GPS was right: I really am off the map.

Much later, I open the gate into the yard outside the hostel. Aimé and Grégory are sitting at a wooden picnic table, complaining of the cold. The wind has blown in since this morning, crushing the clouds together to fill up the sky. Grégory has tendonitis. I give him one of my dwindling supply of tablets: for the moment my knees are holding out. The hostel owner appears at the door and offers me a beer. She has a perfect figure: we are going to eat well tonight.

This evening there are four of us around the table: Paul arrived two hours after me.

Route de Phagalcette hostel to Bagargrak

During the night the sky above has been torn in two, the ragged edge of the sailor's trousers flapping as the wind increases. Grey clouds are blowing in from the Atlantic to the west; the blue navy is scuttling away to the east.

Far below, down in the valley, the frothy white clouds are rucked up by the rising sun. They push up the valley, building up behind the hillocks, climbing up the mountain slope behind me, linked invisibly to the bank of clouds above. It is a stunningly beautiful scene.

I press on as quickly as possible to the top of the first hill, surfing in front of the breaking waves to be rewarded by a view of the mountain range stretching away into the distance. Over there, the low sun has coloured the sky a limpid blue. But each summit has its own wisp of cloud, a smoke signal announcing the changing weather. I fancy that I can identify the Pic du Midi d'Ossau, several days' walking away. A herd of cows is ruminating disconsolately. They have understood. One by one they lie down as the dreary dampness engulfs us.

An hour or so afterwards I stumble across a hand-painted sign saying '*ardi gasna*'. A few minutes later another sign explains: '*fromage de brebis*, sheep's cheese', adding 'sausages, water, wine' and – more enigmatically for I can see nothing through the mist – 'here!' A track leads down into a slight hollow where a low building emerges out of the whiteness. Flanked by a couple of forlorn trees, the rendered stone cottage is capped by a sparklingly new corrugated metal roof. The door is ajar. Through it I can hear two men speaking in Basque.

'*Bonjour*,' I say, pushing on the door. Inside it is dark, even with the door open. Hardly any light filters through the two small grimy windows. Opposite me is an old man sitting on a stool next to a large corrugated metal tub, like the one my grandmother used for her weekly wash. One arm is plunged into the tub, apparently stirring something.

'I'll be with you in five minutes,' he grumbles and I go round the back of the *cayolar* to wait for him to open up.

This is the first time I have seen the inside of a *cayolar*. They are shepherd's huts, and were an essential part of the traditional mountain economy. In the past, ownership of a *cayolar* included not only possession of the building and the adjacent land for a sheep fold but also the right to graze the sheep over a large area and to take wood for building and heating. *Cayolars* were the mountain outpost of the *etxe* down on the plain and a place for cheese-making and hospitality in an otherwise lonely environment.

The shop is a windowless room divided by a small counter, with sausages hanging from the wall behind it. Wooden shelves support rows of cheeses, about 60 in all. On the top shelf they are creamy white, those lower down are progressively more gnarled, gritty, and grey, like the man himself. He goes straight to one of the cheeses on the lowest shelf, cuts it in half and then places his knife on the rind to indicate a suitable portion. I nod in agreement.

'Three-and-a-half months old,' he explains, 'is the ideal age to eat it. Any younger and it is tasteless.'

He has 300 sheep. He will have them sheared in a couple of weeks. This reminds me of my recurring preoccupation. This morning Aimé found a tick in his navel. It had bitten him 'elsewhere' as well. Paul announced that he too had been bitten but claimed that it is alright as long as the tick doesn't make its home on you. I ask the farmer what he thinks.

'The little black ones, about 2mm long, will jump out of the ferns and bite you but they don't carry Lyme disease round here,' he reassures me. 'Then there are the little white ones on the sheep, which are not good for them... Excuse me. I must go. I'm in the middle of making the cheese.'

Outside, swimming in the cold white drizzle, I am disorientated, blindly following the direction indicated by my GPS, eyes on the ground. The dampness smothers all sound apart from the swishing of my waterproof leggings against each other. Suddenly, I hear a rustling and glimpse a streak of yellow moving jerkily through the long grass. I approach the place where it seems to have stopped and part the grass.

Staring up at me suspiciously are two tiny round black eyes under inflated yellow eyelids. The wee beastie's head is diamond-shaped, or rather would be, if its nose wasn't so flat. Wide, irregular, yellow-and-black stripes run along its body and tail. It is like a big lizard but it is too fat and the colouring and the head are all wrong. This must be a fire salamander and he must be lost. At 1050m above sea level, in daytime, in open countryside, and at least 100m from the nearest river, he shouldn't be here. These salamanders live mainly lower down, near watercourses through trees, and they only come out at night. He must have strayed from the forest which I can see on the map, but which is completely hidden from view. Salamanders are a protected species but their habitat is increasingly being eroded by human activities and I've never seen one before. It needed a misty day to make them visible.

Finally, I surface. My head pokes out of the wet and I can once again see where I am going. To the west, the mist covers the entire landscape, but to the east the sky and even the valleys are clear. Somehow, the mountains have managed to repel the humid onslaught.

I am just thinking that I haven't met any other walkers all day when a fat woman, a priest in a soutane, and a group of retired people come into view. I look at the map in disbelief to discover that there is a road only half an hour away. I am entering the Forest of Iraty, a popular holiday destination and the largest beech forest in western Europe. A large forest in an even larger forest. Trees cover one-third of the Pyrenees, more than a million hectares.

The hostel at Bagargrak is excellent value though rather anonymous. Clean, modern, individual rooms, lots of heating and even halogen rings on the stove, all for the same price as basic bunks elsewhere on the walk. There are two young women staying in the hostel. They are the first people I have met walking a significant section of the Pyrenean Way in the opposite direction and, apart from the elusive American, the first women on the route. They started from Gourette a week ago but had to hitch the first section because there was too much snow.

Bagargrak to Logibar

It rains 200 days a year here and in the night, the clouds seem to have finally won the battle: I spend several minutes finding the first waymark. Aimé and Grégory have camped on the only flat square of ground and are cooking breakfast in the shelter of a dry stone pen. We agree that it must be something to do with sheep, though we can't work out why there should be so many of them. It is only much later, when I am staying in the Spanish Basque country that I discover how these pens are used. Nothing to do with sheep. They are shooting hides, recycled each autumn for hunting migratory birds as they fly low over the Pyrenees on their way south.

As I am leaving Aimé and Grégory to continue on my way, Aimé says, 'Thanks for everything'. He does this at least once a day. I ask him why, but he can't explain.

I climb up the Pic des Escalliers and cross over to the northern side. The clouds are a little thinner here and I can see them being whisked past me up the cliff face and over the top. I can half imagine the vertiginous view which the map warns me is there.

Later, when I reach a road I meet a man with a white Renault van and dogs. He is herding sheep, taking them down to Larrau today and then up to the *estives*, the high pastures, for the summer. Although he is nearing retirement age, French still doesn't come naturally to him.

Barking dogs and tinkling sheep bells accompany me for much of the rest of the morning. Occasionally I hear the shepherd cry out 'Purr tchai,' but I don't see either him or the animals again. Crickets and skylarks are also invisibly present, tantalising me with their false promise of sun just a few steps away.

I walk into a herd of cows. *Blondes d'Aquitaine*, their heavy – but silent – bells hang from their necks on wide red ribbons, which complement their beige coats perfectly. Four of them are lying down, arranged like the spokes of a wheel, looking outwards over the cliff, their rumps together, protected from the cold by the clumps of bracken. Superb but stupid, indifferent to each other, indifferent to me, they look bored as only cows can look bored.

The *blondes* have taken over. The local girl was a petite country type, mousey, well used to life in the mountains. She sported a cute set of cheerfully upturned horns, reminiscent of the shape of a lyre, or so

Blondes d'Aquitaine

they say round here. '*Vive la vaca*, long live the cow', reads the inscription in the porch of one church. But the local girl lost out to her more flamboyant cousins brought up in the fertile meadows on the plains. There are now only a few hundred true Basque cows; in the 1960s there were 20,000.

Finally the path drops off the ridge down to the hostel in Logibar and I am below the clouds for the last twenty minutes. Aimé and Grégory took another route, descending directly to Larrau in the valley and then walking along the road to Logibar. They recount their day over a beer.

'Not easy in the fog, but Grégory used his GPH and we got through,' Aimé tells me.

'GPH?' I ask.

'Global Positioning Hooter,' clarifies Grégory, pointing to his nose, grinning.

'The walk wasn't much fun but it was worth it just for the café in Larrau,' continues Aimé. 'There was a tatty old sign on the street outside a house so we opened the door. Inside was a dark room with a long wooden table and an old couple at one end eating lunch. I said, "Sorry, we thought this was the café," and we were about to go out when the man said, "It *is* the café, please come in." The building used to be a *cayolar* and they want to maintain the tradition of informal hospitality rather than have an ordinary modern establishment.'

We compare wounds. My toes are now covered with blisters, despite wearing two pairs of socks and a pharmacy's entire stock of Compeed.

Aimé advises: 'I'll only give you one idea for your blisters. Two pairs of socks. I won't say any more, but think about it. You will thank me.'

Aimé and Grégory push on to find somewhere to camp. I eat with Paul again for the seventh time. Once we have reviewed the day's events we have little to say to each other. We have shared details of our families, our background, our work, and our holidays. Avoided politics and religion. But we always share a table. I do wish he didn't eat so slowly.

Logibar to Ste-Engrâce

I leave Logibar ridiculously late and regret it all day, the sun having recovered its powers. On the slopes above the hostel, gleaming white puffball mushrooms poke through the coarse grass. I break one in two and put it to my nose: hazelnuts. (In French they are called *vesse de loup* – wolf's fart – and if the mushroom is somewhat old and explodes in your hands you soon understand why.)

A worm – or is it a snake? – slithers by my feet. The suspiciously virulent yellow V on its forehead makes me think that I should have been more wary.

Recently cut trees are piled up at the side of the track, waiting to be dragged away. The aroma of broken bark and sawdust is complemented by the peppery smell of over-ripe *cèpes jaunes* mushrooms.

Coming out of the woods, I am overtaken by a large van, slipping along the still-wet track, thumping and bleating as it goes. It stops and the sheep tumble out, clashing corkscrew horns against the sides of the van, like tourists jumping out of a holiday coach, eager to be outside at last, but uncertain what to do next. They look around at each other, tossing their unshorn fleece out of their eyes, a little giddy from the journey, hoping for leadership or inspiration, until the shepherd and his dog chase them away onto the long grass. Unlike its bovine cousin, the Basco-béarnaise sheep is in no danger of extinction, thanks to its *appellation contrôlée* Ossau-Iraty cheese.

By lunchtime I am looking for somewhere to sit in the shade, so I try the door of the Cayolar d'Anhaou. It is open, but before crossing the threshold I go to look at the other two nearby buildings. The first is not much bigger than a large pig pen, constructed in dry stone, with the rafters tumbling dangerously into a mass of weeds. The door has disappeared. This must be the prehistoric-*cayolar*. Across the track is the 21st-century chalet-*cayolar*. All new wood and shutters, locked and unwelcoming. My *cayolar* must span the 200 years between them. Originally built of dry stone and tiled with wooden shingles, at some stage the walls have been concreted inside and out and the roof recovered with corrugated metal sheeting.

I can smell charcoal as I enter. Today the air seems full of smells: it must be the effect of the damp followed by the scorching sun. The one room contains an assortment of home-made furniture, constructed from tree trunks, empty oil cans, and irregular planks rescued from building sites. A gas oven and separate rings look as though they are in working order, though there are neither pots nor pans, nor indeed any gas. There are two double beds, one with a mattress: dusty and grey but still plausible. Basic but clean, so I settle in and munch my lunch contentedly.

I notice the smell of aniseed and looking round discover an empty bottle of Ricard *pastis*. Next to it is a bottle of Château la Roseraie St Emilion AOC 1996 with vinegary dregs still slopping about in the bottom. Ricard is not poor man's *pastis* and Château la Roseraie costs 13€ a bottle. Either shepherds are richer than they used to be or some visitors spent a well-oiled night here not long ago.

I finish eating and then leave the *cayolar* behind me, descending into the valley. I have run out of water. When will scientists find a way of compacting it, like dehydrated food? Will they ever invent *dehydrated* water? The stream looks tempting but I don't want to drink from it. Instead I fill my hat and upend it over my head. I trudge down the exposed slope in the mid-day fire, a walk only relieved by a short section sunk between two field walls, hidden under the trees. I cross the Pont d'Enfer, Hell's Bridge – the devil seems to be going in for quantity rather than quality – and look down at the water below. If the bridge belongs to hell, the river must flow from heaven. The still waters are translucent in the shade of the bridge; in the sunlight they are coloured with the vibrant blue and turquoise normally reserved for Polynesian lagoons. I contemplate jumping in like the sailors on Captain Bligh's *Bounty*, to re-hydrate myself by absorbing the water through my skin, but decide against it.

Instead, when I reach the top of the road leading to the Gorges de Kakouéta I attack the drinks stand. An Orangina and an ice cream, followed by a Perrier and another ice cream. In the bar at the entrance to the gorges I drink a beer, followed by another beer, and then make an unwise decision: to investigate further. I can leave my rucksack at the bar; the gorges are reputed to be cool, relatively speaking.

The gorge is indeed cool, and humid. Water cascades over improbable limestone formations between cliff faces hundreds of metres high. In places the heavens are reduced to a distant ribbon between the luxuriant vegetation clinging to the sides of the canyon. I am sandwiched between a large group of retired Spanish people, carefully picking their way over the slippery rocks, and a French family anxious to progress more quickly. Borne along at their rhythm, I am unable to go either faster or slower. Suddenly the man in front stops and turns to face me.

'*¡No pasa!*' he says, stretching his arms wide apart so that I couldn't possibly go round him without falling into the river. Beyond him I can see a woman squatting in the middle of the path. I look away.

The grotto at the end of the trail is full of stalactites but they are a bit of a disappointment. These are not glistening white daggers waiting to pierce you from shoulder to hip should they fall. They are more like petrified sumo wrestlers. You would still die if one fell on you. But crushed not perforated.

I ask one of the Spaniards to take a photograph. Looking at it later I can see that it captures my state perfectly: red tee-shirt, a redder face, and the reddest of lips; dilated pupils, eyebrows raised as if they were trying to catch up with my receding hair, and a completely inane smile.

By the time I get back to the road, I have added two hours to my walk and I am dead tired. The tarmac is melting and I am as well. I still have an hour to go. More worryingly, for the first time I am way behind the schedule for the day, even discounting the trip up the gorge.

At the hostel in Ste-Engrâce, Paul is waiting for me with a welcoming beer. The hostel owner asks him to show me to the dormitory but he can't find it any more. The sun must have gone to his head as much as it has gone to mine.

To be honest, these mountain houses are not simple affairs. If the *etxe* of the plains is a Renault Espace people-carrier with everything under one roof, the typical house here is an ageing saloon car with a roof rack. The sheep are in the car with the farmer sitting on top. Trundling along behind it is a trailer with the food; attached to the trailer is a motor bike, with its side-car stuffed with wood. The different elements of the house may be arranged in various ways but steep roofs and the use of stone are common features.

On the plain, the built-to-last *etxes* show a certain confidence in the future. Here, it is as if a new extension was added with the arrival of each extra child.

I go to visit the Romanesque church opposite the hostel. The capitals at the tops of the columns depict a range of scenes including Solomon and his queen enjoying themselves in an unreligious way, and the devil finishing off the mortal remains of a sinner. The legs and body have already disappeared into his stomach, but the arms and the head are still between his teeth.

When I return to the hostel Aimé and Grégory are slumped on the terrace drinking beer. Akerbeltz ambrée Gorrosta is an un-pasteurised amber ale made in a micro-brewery a little way down the valley. Unlike the big commercial mouthwashes, this beer has flavour. Malty without being syrupy, the black goat label has become something to seek out at the end of the day.

'Since Paul is only going a short way tomorrow, this is the last time we will see him. How about eating together?' suggests Aimé. We accept.

We climb the stairs to the dining room. The hostel is full for the first holiday weekend of the summer and the tables are crammed together. The food is both tasty and plentiful.

I say – with the kind of stunning originality brought on by dehydration followed by alcohol – 'What I like about walking is the contrast with being at work, sitting in front of a computer all day. I like being "elsewhere". And it gives me the opportunity to think about things, to put them in perspective.' Even though it's true, I'm not sure that it goes very far to explain my reasons for walking the GR10.

'*Moi, je pense que la marche rend con* – I think that walking makes you pig stupid,' comments Aimé, continuing: 'At first you think about your life, your relationships. Then when you have exhausted the possibilities of that you look at the scenery. You think about where you are going, how long it will take to get there and what you will eat. But after three or four days all you think about is walking, putting one foot in front of the other. Then the mind goes completely blank and you think about nothing at all. *Ça rend con.* Mind you, yesterday evening I managed to learn a page of script in half the time it would normally take me.'

Aimé and Grégory are actors, and have been playing together in a Parisian production. Grégory is an actor by training; Aimé 'just started doing it'. A bit like their approach to the Pyrenean Way. Grégory spent a fortnight walking every day to practice. Aimé, whose idea it was, simply got up last Thursday morning and started.

They ask Paul what he does for a living. It is noisy and difficult to follow the conversation. In any case I have heard it all already. My attention starts to wander.

Behind us is a group of young potholers, off to explore a new gallery tomorrow. To my left is a French family who seem to know the hostel owner. And to my right there are four men all substantially the same age and build, talking in a mixture of Basque and French. I think about how improbable we must look to them. The Englishman, the hunchback, the black, and the Gaul.

'You're not listening, are you?' exclaims Aimé, indignantly, looking at me. 'You've already switched off. You know you're not going to see us after this evening. You don't give a damn. You're already in another world.'

'No, I was listening,' I lie, unconvincingly, and then revise myself. 'I can't hear for all the noise,' I splutter. I am just too tired.

Outside before splitting up to go to bed, Grégory suggests we swap addresses. And surnames, for we only know each other's first names. Aimé M . . . writes Aimé on the back of a cigarette packet.

'That's an Arab name, isn't it?' remarks Paul.

'And . . . What about it?' snaps Aimé, stiffening.

'Nothing. Nothing at all,' says Paul meekly.

We are all exhausted and irritable.

Ste-Engrâce to Lescun

The Pyrenean Way follows a narrow valley out of the village. The tumbling ivy and swishing ferns, the exaggerated shadows cast by my lamp in the darkness and the early morning fog throw me back into the primeval soup. At the head of the valley the path winds through the forest and just before emerging into daylight deposits me in front of a row of lichen-covered stone water troughs. Next to them, carved in the native rock, is a larger-than-life head, ostensibly human but sinisterly distorted. Its mouth is wide open, and painted red as if blood were dripping out. This is the spirit of the spring: beware he who tampers with nature's gift! I smile instinctively at the artist's naivety, and then change my mind, remembering what Pierre Minvielle wrote:

> Instead of smiling at these superstitions, let's stop for a instant considering the Pyrenees as zones to be developed, ski slopes, or even picturesque landscapes... and imagine each summit, each slope, each forest, each spring, sheltering a god, a fairy, a witch. Suddenly, the countryside comes to life, is metamorphosed. Pressing an ear to the rock, one can hear the oracles of the Pic des Encantats [fairies], that petrified giant who may get up and walk at any time... Trees pursue their objectives. Above our heads, crows go about their business, on which our fate depends... reality is just the surface. Behind the immobility of the landscape the secret mechanism of the world is set into motion, the exclusive domain of the divine...
> ...today, all has changed. Because in the 18th century, there came forth men from the plains, animated by another faith, that of Science... And, immediately, the Pyrenees of weeds and nasty smells are transformed into the abstract Pyrenees of books.

I leave the forest for the short-cropped moorland grass, and brilliant sunshine. With the bank of clouds below me, I climb, avoiding the unprotected *gouffres*, natural pits, which dot the slope. Another flock of sheep stumbles out of a trailer.

When I reach the ridge and look across into Spain, the contrast with the French side of the frontier is horrifying. In Spain there is the joyful azure sky above and fluffy clouds below in the valleys, just as in

France. But over the border, the mountains are injured, badly burned, irredeemably scarred. Everything is grey, that numbing neutral grey, halfway between black and white. The rocks are fissured and irregular. Some grass has regenerated but not much. The pine trees are woefully rare. As I approach the pass I can see that the damage is not restricted to Spain. Whole swathes of the mountain have been devastated. But then, when I finally reach frontier post no. 262 and walk between the lonesome pines, I can see that they have not been burned at all: the rock is *naturally* ugly. I have entered the commune of Arette-La-Pierre-St-Martin.

If there is one commune in the Pyrenees which has been moulded by its geology it is Arette-La-Pierre-St-Martin. Here at the Col de la Pierre the limestone karst is like a giant drain grid, with crazy fissures to be avoided every other step. No sooner has rain fallen than it is swallowed and then digested in the bowels of the earth. The consequent scarcity of pasture and drinking water for sheep necessarily created tensions between shepherd neighbours on either side of the frontier.

It is a story of low murder and high farce. According to one version of the events, two shepherds have an argument about the right to water their sheep at a spring near here. The Frenchman, Pierre Sansoler, from the Barétous valley to the north is killed. His relatives take up arms, traverse the mountain and descend into the Roncal valley in Spain. Finding only the pregnant wife of the murderer, they kill her and cut her open, hanging the unborn boy from the branch of a beech tree along with the entrails of his mother. A series of retributive attacks follows. So much for the low murder. The high farce is contained in another version, which relates that the whole series of attacks and counter-attacks is brought to a halt by a young woman, acting alone. Hearing of the feud she takes off her clothes and covers her body with honey and then feathers. On seeing her, the belligerents are so frightened that they return meekly home.

There must be a kernel of truth somewhere in these tales because in October 1375 a meeting was called between the inhabitants of the two valleys to establish a lasting peace. The arbitrators decided that both sides had suffered equally. The Barétounais were to give the Roncalais three heifers each year, as they had done in the past. In a masterpiece of diplomacy this is described in the pact as 'for the use of the springs or to atone for the murders' – reflecting the different views of the two sides.

Conflicts over grazing rights were common in the Pyrenees and there are several examples of these *lies et passeries* agreements, one even declaring that the two communities involved would never take up arms against each other, even if their respective governments ordered them to do so.

Nowadays, in a ceremony which has more meaning for tourists than local residents, the cows are led to the boundary stone – hence the name La-Pierre – and given to the Spanish mayor (he gives them back later and takes the money instead). In return the Spaniards lay on a feast.

I walk down the road to La-Pierre-St-Martin, one of the two nuclei of the commune, and enter the village. Anything that nature can do, man can do better: the tower blocks would disgrace a Parisian suburb, never mind a Pyrenean hillside. They are facelessly monolithic; grey, greyer, and greyest. There are some zones of white, but the only colour visible is a kind of muddy beige. Between the buildings there are wide roads and car parks. Which blend in extremely well with the tower blocks. The village is even uglier than its surroundings.

I need to buy some food. Looking at the map last night, the village appeared big enough to have a couple of shops. But I can see nobody to ask. I try in one of the blocks, but it seems to be entirely residential – though singularly lacking in residents. The next block looks more promising. There is even a sign pointing to a bar.

I am walking up the steps into it when I meet a little girl and her mother.

'Hello,' says the girl.

'Hello,' I reply.

'Are you on holiday?'

'Yes.'

'What are you doing?'

'Walking.'

'Me, I want to go sledging.'

Even a three-year-old can recognise the essential. La-Pierre-St-Martin is dedicated to winter sports. It is of no interest whatsoever in the summer.

I walk along bleak corridors, up and down stairs (the lifts are not working) and finally discover the bar. I sit on the terrace, holding down my papers to prevent them being blown away in the wind, and sip a mineral water. According to the barmaid there are only 30–40 inhabitants at this time of year. There will be 300–400 at the height of summer and 3,000–4,000 in winter. No, there are no shops open. Actually the bar is the only place open in the whole village. But she searches around and manages to find me a couple of low-calorie granary bars.

Not everybody shares my view of the village and its geology. It is an internationally renowned centre for caving. A vertical 330m *gouffre* drops down to the galleries, over 50km of them. The system contains some of the deepest and biggest caves in the world, stretching as far as the lake at the bottom of the Gorges de Kakouéta, where an underground river emerges. There may be no water on the surface but there are real rivers below it, where the permeable karst meets the impermeable rocks below. At one time the French Electricity Board even considered using the water for hydroelectric power, boring tunnels into the massif and financing exploratory expeditions. Evidently La-Pierre-St-Martin has hidden depths.

The commune is also known for a different geological phenomenon. Arette, its other nucleus, was the epicentre of the last significant earthquake to shake the French Pyrenees, on 13 August 1967: 5.3 on the Richter scale. One person was killed and 80% of the houses in the village were uninhabitable as a result.

The name Arette is derived from the Basque *ar*, stone. *Pierre* is French for stone. Arette-La Pierre-St-Martin: even its name is made of rock and fissured like the landscape.

I leave the village, walking with my eyes on the ground, picking my way between ankle-twisting cracks and neck-breaking pits. There is a small patch of residual snow in a crevasse. I tread warily, remembering the warning sign: 'On 17 February 2001 Élodie and Loriane fell into a *gouffre* 35m deep whilst sledging. Now, they beg you not to stray beyond the safety barriers.'

Ahead of me is an unforgiving vertical rock face. I can't see a way through but the map is quite clear. I will have to scale it. When I arrive at the Pas de l'Osque there are only four metres to climb but it frightens me silly. If I fall off I will inevitably tumble heels-over-head down the steep incline behind me. If I am lucky I will come to rest 50m below. But there is no alternative and in a few seconds I am at the top, quivering.

Down below in the next valley I hear a whistling. A *marmotte* – groundhog – its sunbathing disturbed, is warning its neighbours. Way in front of me, there are two larger specks gambolling down the scree. I make a big effort and catch up to them.

'You're doing well today,' says Aimé.

'You're doing better. You were still sleeping when I left. I didn't even notice you overtaking me.' I reply.

'It was foggy so we decided to follow the road to La-Pierre-St-Martin. And then a milk lorry came along so we hitched a lift,' explains Grégory.

They feed me and we walk together as far as the Cabane du Cap de la Baitch. The scree is replaced by pasture. At an hour's walk from the nearest road, it must be a hard life for the couple who live there all summer, milking sheep, making cheese, and rearing pigs. No electricity, of course, but abundant clear spring water and an idyllic location.

I had set my heart on the hostel at Labérouat where the path meets the road, but when I push on the door it is locked so I continue disconsolately on to Lescun. I have been walking ten and a half hours. When I stumble into the village square Aimé and Grégory are already sitting on the terrace of a bar. Inevitably, they are downing beers.

'It's a dangerous drug,' I say.

They look at me surprised, wrongly thinking I'm talking about the beer.

'You start with a milk lorry in the morning,' I continue, 'and by the evening you're already hooked on hitch-hiking. You'll be climbing into 40 tonne artics soon, dreaming of the poppy fields in Afghanistan.'

'No, we didn't hitch,' corrects Grégory, 'we walked.'

We compare notes. They took the old path, which still has the waymarks intact, whilst I followed the official route.

Jean-Paul and Richard are also in the village. Thanks to the long haul today, we have caught up with them.

Lescun to Etsaut

In the timid dawn light, Lescun resembles a Yorkshire mining village in the depths of winter seen through a hangover. It isn't raining but the roads are running with water and the roofs are dripping methodically. Yesterday evening's honey-coloured stone has been reduced to shades of grey. Everything is out of focus. Not a breath of wind. The clouds have come down from the *estives* for breakfast.

Later on, in the next valley, I discover the base of the clouds. It is like being in the audience at the start of a play. The lights have been dimmed and we have all settled down. We are looking in the direction of the stage, waiting. The curtain shivers and then starts to rise slowly. At first all we can see is a line of bright light, then the scenery – an enchanting Pyrenean valley criss-crossed with hedges, sprinkled with farmsteads, and dotted with sheep. But the curtain gets stuck at shoulder height and the actors stay in the wings. The high pastures and the sky remain hidden. Frustrated, we are all willing the curtain to rise, but to no avail. It falls again and the theatre reverts to its grey obscurity.

The rest of the day is spent in the drizzle. Eyes on the ground, I catch sight of a slow-worm slithering across the path. Finally the clouds disappear and I can see below me the twin villages of Borce and Etsaut, separated by the river Aspe. The path leads down to a new wire grid fence and then runs along the side of it for some distance. The thickness of the wire, the height of the fence, and the strength of the supporting posts all make for an impenetrable enclosure. Something is being kept in, or out. At the other end of the fence there is a notice: Espace animalier de Borce. This is a new extension to a wildlife park, the latest manifestation of the love–hate relationship between the Pyrenees and the brown bear.

It has to be said that bears are *the* big issue in the Pyrenees. In recent years, demonstrations for and against their presence have attracted thousands. Yet they have always been a feature of the mountains.

To some extent bears were respected. *Lo Moussu*, the gentleman, was one nickname. But mostly they were killed and exploited. The damage they did to crops and animals led to hunting by upland farmers struggling to survive. And cubs were taken from their mothers by bear tamers to be shown at country fairs.

By the 1970s however, when there were only about 40 bears left and they were no longer considered a threat, the relationship began to change. The change was subtle at first and has not been universal, but if I were to choose one date to mark it, that would be 17 May 1971. On that day, some children were walking in the Belonce valley above Borce. Passing through a thicket they heard a cry and discovered a baby bear. There was no sign of its mother so they took their find back to the village. Baptised Jojo, he became something of a mascot, and lived for 20 years – a reasonable age for a bear. He then passed through the hands of a taxidermist and has since been on public display. So his fate was little different to that of a cub stolen from its mother by a 19th-century tamer. But the interest he evoked had shown that bears were a powerful symbol.

Despite this interest, during the 1970s and 1980s the population had dwindled even further. Although hunting had been outlawed in 1970, poachers continued to operate. But even their activities cannot account for the long-term decline of the Pyrenean bears. One estimate puts the number of bears killed – legally and illegally – over the last four centuries at 3000, or less than 10 per year, a small figure in comparison with the medieval bear population.

So, if they weren't over-hunted, why have they disappeared? In fact the inhabitants *were* responsible, but only indirectly. Before the exodus of the 19th century, agriculture was practised much higher up the valleys and the bears took their tithe of the corn and other foodstuffs. When the mountains became poorer, the bears became scarcer. Those bears who survived gravitated towards the zones where agriculture and pastoralism remained relatively active – as here in the Aspe valley.

A second environmental change is the recent return of people to the heights, with 5000km of paths created in the high Pyrenees between 1950 and 2000. Walkers like me are a nuisance to bears and don't provide any compensatory benefits. We don't even get eaten!

So, little by little, the bears disappeared. By 1995 there were only six brown bears left in the whole of the French Pyrenees.

The government's response was pragmatic. In its eyes, the only option left was reintroduction. However, local hostility had to be taken into account. Finally, in 1996–1997 a mere three bears were kidnapped from Slovenia and released in the mountains.

The immigrants quickly learned the new language and adapted themselves to local customs, but their presence has been hugely controversial. Having spent centuries eradicating them, mountain communities are far from united in welcoming them back. After all the brown bear isn't in danger of extinction. It is only its presence in the

Pyrenees which is in question. The debate is wide-ranging. If there are no bears in the high mountains can we really claim that this is a natural wilderness? Do humans have the right to manage the environment for their own purposes? Do bears have the right to eat sheep, or do sheep have the right to graze in peace?

A postscript to the life and death of Jojo. Now, when bear cubs are orphaned they are helped to stay in the wild. In November 2004 when Cannelle – the last pure-bred Pyrenean female – was killed at Urdos near here, her young son was provided with dumps of food to supplement his rations before winter set in. He survived. Less encouragingly, some voices are suggesting that any new introductions who 'misbehave' should be imprisoned in the wildlife park.

By the time I arrive at Borce the sun is shining, but the stone walls are still cold. The main street is dark, hidden from the sun by the high ski-jump roofs designed more for winter than for summer: the top part of the roofs is steep so that the snow doesn't stick, while the lower part is flatter so that the avalanche is projected onto the other side of the road or, frequently, onto poorer neighbours with smaller houses.

Aimé and Grégory are sitting on the terrace of a bar. I join them for a while and then slip over the river to Etsaut. Beyond the footbridge, a disproportionately wide road embellished with new street furniture cuts a wide swathe along the valley floor. Parallel to it, a disused railway track comes to an ignominious halt in a tuft of grass.

The railway track in front of me is the relic of one of the attempts to link France and Spain through the central Pyrenees. Most of the projects have consumed more paper than concrete and the idea is still divisive. For Parisian diplomats more concerned with international relations than with environmental conservation the Pyrenees are simply a nuisance. As the French foreign minister said in 2001: 'The Pyrenees are not our fault…'

The Aspe valley here leads to the Col de Somport. At a mere 1632m, it inevitably attracted pilgrims on the way to Santiago de Compostela.

The emperor Napoleon III built the first road in 1859, but it was 1928 before the first train crossed the border. One of the problems was the steep gradient. The engineers came up with an ingenious solution: a tunnel in the form of a helix, the sole purpose of which is to gain height – 60m of climbing for a tunnel 1800m long. Even so, the line never attracted much traffic and was closed down after an accident in 1970.

Instead, a new road tunnel was projected. There was some support for the idea but it was the opponents of the project who captured the media's attention. Why not revive the railway, they asked. What about the bears? The worst of it is that, although the road tunnel was opened in 2003, the road access is still sub-standard. So another crossing is being planned: a rail tunnel under the Vignemale mountain, in the centre of the National Park, perhaps.

At the hostel in Etsaut, I rediscover Richard and Jean-Paul and we eat a convivial evening meal with a large group of walkers, including some Canadians. The hostels are filling up.

Etsaut to Gabas

In the dreary morning mist – I'm beginning to get used to it – I walk towards the Col de Somport. On the road there is a snake, a yellow-and-black monkey ladder pattern running along its spine. Yellow and black shivers run along mine, but then I see that it is dead. It is probably a Seoane's viper; recently eight live ones were seen near here in a single day.

The Pyrenean Way turns its back on the road and I find myself approaching the Chemin de la Mâture. I don't relish the prospect. The path is cut out of the vertical limestone cliff, says the *FFRP Guide*, creating a ledge just wide enough for two oxen to walk side-by-side. I will see a frightening drop to my right. But I have chosen the right day – I can see nothing. I am air-bagged by the mist.

If I'm shivering with fear although I can't even see anything, what would it have been like for the workers who built the path? How many men died during the construction? The account of the works, written by an engineer more concerned with his place in history, omits to mention the negative side of his exploit.

Originally, the Chemin de la Mâture gave access to the forests higher up the valley, where the centuries-old trees were felled to provide masts for the French navy. In the 18th century, the demand for wood was phenomenal – 800 log rafts were arriving in Toulouse from the Pyrenees each year. And for a short while the trees of the Aspe valley were an important natural resource.

I can imagine the difficulty of hauling the massive trunks – up to 30m long – along this narrow shelf. How many trunks fell into the void, dragging the oxen with them, the workers trying desperately to control the situation?

The path was finished in 1772 and in six years the forest was razed. Now, except for the Chemin de la Mâture, the passing of the French navy has been obliterated.

Further up the valley, I hear a rustling. Grégory is standing in a small clearing, stretching his arms, yawning. Aimé pokes his head out of his tent. Trying to find a patch of flat ground yesterday outside Etsaut, they had followed the Pyrenean Way and walked the Chemin de la Mâture in dangerous sunshine.

I leave them to pack up and shortly emerge from the mist. At the end of the long valley ahead of me I glimpse patches of glistening snow, but for the moment I am strolling through the luxuriant pasture which marks the beginning of the National Park. When I arrive at the Cabane de la Baigt de St-Cours, the door is shut but I push it and it swings open. Graffiti everywhere, rubbish littering the floor, furniture destroyed, the ladder which should have given access to the mezzanine missing. This hut is two and a half hours' walking from the nearest road but it has suffered the same fate as many an urban bus shelter.

I meet a man striding down the valley. He has recently brought his cows here for the summer. Cows don't have a herding instinct, he tells me, so for the next week he will be coming to see them every other day and bringing the more adventurous ones back until they get the idea.

At the head of the valley, just before the zigzag assault on the pass, I sit down quietly to watch a group of eleven *isards* grazing. Called *chamois* in the Alps, with the body of a goat but the grace of an antelope, at the slightest sound of humans they will bound up the hillside, leaping from rock to rock. Piew . . . piew . . . piew. A *marmotte* whistles, and I manage to identify its brown-ochre fur against the mottled grey rock on which it is squatting before it disappears into its burrow.

The two species ignore each other royally. They are only suspicious of humans, and with good reason. It is we who have dictated their past, present, and future, although the declinations have been different.

Marmottes and *isards* are both now thriving in the Pyrenees and indeed *isards* have always been present. But by the middle of the 20th century their numbers were declining seriously, principally as a result of hunting. They were saved by the creation of reserves and there are an estimated 40,000 today. *Marmottes*, on the other hand, were only reintroduced sixty years ago. They had died out with the retreating glaciers, when the advancing forests encroached on their habitat, 10,000 years ago. Then, in 1948, a certain Dr Couturier introduced six one-year-olds, without any study of the impact they might have. These youngsters and a few others released later have between them managed to populate much of the mountain range.

I get up carefully, but it is a waste of time. The *isards* disappear immediately. Arriving at the top of the pass shortly afterwards, I can see the Pic du Midi d'Ossau again for the first time since the Route de Phagalcette, with behind it the peaks stretching into the distance. In front of it the high pastures drop dramatically into the forest, slumping

The refuge d'Ayous with the Pic du Midi d'Ossau in the background

into the valleys. The mountain itself is conical, fissured down one side, the shady crevasse still filled with snow. It looks like a volcano, and indeed that is what it is, or rather was, 280 million years ago.

A quick ice tea at the Refuge d'Ayous, a downhill yomp accompanied by dozens of other walkers, tick bites at the Lac de Bious-Artigues, and the Pyrenean Way is finished for this year.

I've decided to stop here. I tell myself that I am tired, that I will need a tent for the stage between Gabas and Gourette, that the pass at the Hourquette d'Arre will be snowed up. But the real reason is that I have read and reread the FFRP guide, and I don't like what is in store

II

The High Pyrenees:
Gabas–Luchon

Gabas

It is a year later and I can't wait to return to Gabas, although this time my excitement is tinged with foreboding. I repack my rucksack, adding a tent, a sleeping bag, a stove, and two days' food and water. It weighs 5kg more than last year but the only unnecessary item is the half-empty phial of seawater from Hendaye. The top was screwed on tightly but somehow the water has escaped. I wrap some sticking plaster around to seal it better. Then I check the email which has arrived overnight – nothing important – turn off my computer, shut the office door, and catch a train back to the Pyrenees.

On the train, the luggage racks are partly taped off and clearly not for use: following a terrorist bombing, the authorities are wary. Thankfully, with remarkable insight into the warped minds of international terrorists the SNCF has come up with a solution: sticky tape. Presumably if this doesn't work they will use string.

The town of Pau, where I get off, is bustling with tourists. I take a taxi up the *gave*, the valley, back to Gabas and pay the 78€ on the meter. The taxi driver gives me my change and, with a wink, a receipt for 100€. He suggests that I can use my tip from him for lunch in a nearby café.

Today's special is *garbure*: a chunky heart-warming soup made of cabbage, lots of vegetables, haricot beans, and a few scraps of meat. At the next table, talk centres around the problems of transhumance.

'I'm transporting my horses up in a lorry this year,' says one woman. 'It's just too much trouble to do it on foot. Most of the car drivers are careful but you only need one idiot to ruin everything.'

Afterwards, walking towards the hostel along the empty main street, I pass under a road safety campaign banner inciting vigilance. Below it, the bitumen is stratified under a pale brown coating; the hot sun is extracting the last volatile molecules from the squashed cow pats. My transition from urban concerns to rural life has been remarkably quick.

I dump my rucksack at the hostel, and then continue up the valley for an afternoon stroll to the reservoir at Fabrèges. At first all I can see of the dam is the top of the concrete peeking out above the trees with a monstrous white letter R painted on its vertical face. As I get nearer, an E appears below it and then the painted paw print of an animal to one side. The rest is hidden behind the trees. As I advance more letters become visible until finally I can read the word REINTRODUCTIONS stretching vertically down the concrete. A series of paw prints, in red, clamber up from the valley floor. This graffiti is no small achievement. The dam is 30m high and rock-climbing skills would have been essential.

The paw prints identify the species: bears. Following the death of Cannelle, the only surviving female bear to be born in the Pyrenees, the environment minister Serge Lepeltier wants to reintroduce fifteen pregnant females to create a viable population. The controversy surrounding the idea is as big as the graffiti.

When I get to the village of Fabrèges at the other end of the reservoir, I ask a woman if they know who was behind the graffiti.

'*Non. Sinon il aurait passé un sale quart d'heure* – No. Otherwise he would have had a really bad time.'

She directs me to the ski-lift which takes me up the mountain to the ski resort of Sagette the terminus of the Petit Train d'Artouste. At the top, it is cold, much colder than I would have expected given the small difference in altitude. A train is just coming in, balancing precariously on narrow-gauge rails only 0.5m apart. The engine looks like a child's toy which has been scaled up, its corners rounded to avoid cutting tiny hands. The open carriages behind it could be a string of shopping trolleys being dragged, rattling, across a windswept supermarket car park. It might be fun when it is warm, but today the few passengers are wrapped up in parkas with hoods pulled tightly around their heads. Shivering, they descend quickly and run into the café. I walk for a few minutes to the top of a nearby hill and look down at the railway track.

It doesn't seem right. There shouldn't really be a railway here; it ought to be down in the valley, connected to something or other. But here it is, defiantly clinging to the side of the hill, following the 1910m contour in sumptuous curves to the other terminus, an isolated reservoir at the Lac d'Artouste 8km away. And that's all there is to it: quite simply, it runs from nowhere to nowhere.

Originally, of course, it had a genuine purpose. It was built in 1920 for the construction of the dam at Artouste by the Compagnie des Chemins de Fer du Midi. Their project was to supply hydroelectricity to their railway network, which spread over much of the south of France. Once the dam was built, the train was always destined to become the tourist attraction it is today. Publicised by the company, it has helped fill the carriages of trains coming from Paris, thus paying for itself a second time. It is claimed to be the highest railway in Europe.

I walk for a few minutes more before joining the railway passengers for a hot chocolate in the steamy café. I rub my ears to warm them up. I am tense, anxious. Do I really want to do this? Do I want to walk in these conditions for days on end? Suddenly, it all seems too difficult. It is a silly idea, an arbitrary challenge, to walk the length of the Pyrenees. What am I searching for? It took me years to learn how to relax on a beach all day without getting bored. What a waste of a summer not to use this skill earned by the sweat of my brow.

The first problem is tomorrow. I need to practise, again. So on the way back to the hostel I scramble onto the wall which holds the road in place. Standing up on the wall, the river on the other side seems a long way below, though the drop is insignificant in comparison with any respectable cliff. Normally, I wouldn't look down for more than a few seconds but I force myself to stare into the emptiness below. Am I a little off balance? I move my left foot backwards. I have overdone it. I correct myself. I shift my weight onto the other foot. No better. Only when I turn away from the drop does stability return. Not a good omen.

My father had the same problem. When we went walking together he would often warn me: 'Don't go so near the edge.' At the age of 18, with his best friend Ken, he had climbed up a ladder to the top of a gasometer for a better view over the sooty roofs of industrial Leeds. Going up was no problem, but when it came to climbing down again he needed to put a foot over the edge of the tank, out into the void to feel blindly for the top rung of the ladder. He couldn't do it. Somehow Ken coaxed him down. He realised for the first time that he had vertigo.

Ken, on the other hand, realised that he didn't have a problem with heights, and went on to frighten his family for many years, climbing and occasionally falling off cliffs in the Lake District and the Alps. 'I could always tell when I was going to fall off. I knew I was doing something silly, something which was too much for me,' he claimed.

And me? Am I going to do something silly?

Back in Gabas, I stroll around to pass the time before dinner. The village has been transformed. A stream of lorries fills the main street. One of them, a double-decker, shudders to a halt and disgorges its cargo, first the cows from the lower deck and then the sheep from above. Fresh cow pats sizzle on the hot tarmac. The man in charge explains to me that the lorries have come up from the plain. This afternoon he will walk the animals up to the lake at Bious-Artigues.

Doing the whole journey on foot tires the sheep out so he has been using a lorry for the last five years.

Later, at the hostel, dinner starts with *garbure*, continues with a beef stew, and has just finished with a pear tart when the door bursts open and a man falls through it. He is wearing green-and-beige camouflage and dripping sweat. He picks himself up, stumbles unsteadily over to the kitchen counter and mutters something unintelligible to the cook who shakes her head. She calls me over to translate: although the walker is from Munich he speaks some English. The cook says that there is still room in the dormitory and food for the table, but he must eat now and tidy himself up when he has eaten. The walker smiles weakly, waiting for me to interpret, and then sits down opposite me.

'I stayed at the hostel in Gourette last night,' he tells me. 'I didn't realise that Gabas was so far away. It took me a long while to get to the pass but then I thought the downhill would be easy. It wasn't. It just kept going on and on.'

'I'm glad I've got two days to do it, in the other direction,' I reply.

'Is there another hostel then? Did I miss it?' His mouth drops open.

'No, but I've got a tent,' I explain. 'Where did you start from?'

'Lourdes. I'm going to Santiago de Compostela. I didn't want to follow the crowds on one of the standard Chemins de St-Jacques so I bought all the maps and have worked out my own route.'

'How much does your rucksack weigh?'

'I don't know.'

I pick it up: 'I'd say 20 kilos, perhaps more.'

'And you?' he asks me.

'Seventeen.'

I introduce him to a clean-cut American trainee priest from Denver, Colorado, who is also walking from Lourdes to Santiago de Compostela. Thankfully, they agree to team up for tomorrow. At least the German has a map – the American seems to be relying on divine inspiration. The map he has been using consists of a single wiggly black line with half a dozen place names dotted along it. On the other half of the page is an explanation, in French, of the itinerary. I realise how little French he understands when he asks me the meaning of the word *chemin* in the description.

After dinner I go outside into the twilight. Lorries are still arriving but now a combination of young undisciplined cows and young inexperienced cowgirls is creating havoc. The cows first wander into a hotel car park and have to be rounded up. Then one of them sees a track leading up to a grassy field and sets off running skittishly. Her sisters follow her in a cacophony of jingling bells and clattering hooves, splattering the fresh cow pats as they pass. The cowgirls run after the escapees shouting and waving their arms, but only succeed in driving them further into the field. It is ten o'clock; the cowgirls are also going to Bious-Artigues. It will take them about three hours, they claim.

I sleep badly. I've never climbed to the top of a gasometer, but I can just imagine it.

Gabas to the Mines d'Arre

The next day I start *my* transhumance. Leaving the road behind I walk up the flank of the mountain under the fir, beech, and birch trees, through clearings prettily decorated with flowers: wild chicory, St John's Wort, martagon lily, and Pyrenean iris.

Then I stumble over them. In the middle of the path indulging in messy sex, completely unconcerned about possible passers-by, and producing a disproportionately large quantity of white gunk, are two very black slugs. The mess isn't really their fault, I suppose: sex is not a simple affair for slugs.

The most conventional thing about it is that slugs have male and female sexual organs. Slightly less conventionally, slugs have *both* male and female organs: they are hermaphrodites. So that if you are a particularly ugly slug and self-conscious about it, or you simply don't like going to parties, you can have babies without all that fuss of having to find a partner. If, conversely, you happen to meet a particularly attractive slug and after a bit of preliminary cuddling you jump into the nearest flower bed: beware. The problem isn't so much deciding who should do what, and to whom, but what to do afterwards. No question of lighting up a cigarette. Slug penises often get entangled. There are two solutions. You gnaw off your partner's penis. Or you gnaw off your own. If the worst comes to the worst you can still be a happy fulfilled female slug, after all. And then there are some kinky slugs who go in for acrobatic sex, entwined around each other, suspended from a long filament, swinging wildly in mid-air. But these two don't look as though they have ever tried anything so demanding.

I leave the slugs to experiment, and shortly afterwards reach a bifurcation in the path. A wooden signpost indicates: 'Corniche des Alhas. *Passage vertigineux*'. I have already read the *FFRP Guide*: 'The Corniche des Alhas is crossed by a path carved in a granite cliff which overhangs the Soussouéou gorge. Narrow, in places damaged by avalanches, this path can be considered vertiginous, even dangerous, although equipped with a handrail.'

This is what I was practising for yesterday. This is why I stopped walking at Gabas last year. I still don't like the sound of it. Clinging onto the handrail nailed into the cliff with my right hand, looking over the drop by my left foot. One foot in front of the other on a narrow ledge. No room to pass if I meet somebody coming the other way. One slip, and even with a hand on the rail I will be left dangling over the void. With a heavy rucksack on my back, will I be able to pull myself up again? There is an alternative route, but this is my first day. I really must...

By the time I arrive at the start of the corniche, my back is locked solid, as if my pelvis, spine, and skull were a single bone. My hands are tingling. My arms and legs trembling. My stomach is churning over.

This is stupid, I don't *need* to do this. Even now I can retrace my steps and bypass the problem.

I see the start of the ledge. I tell myself it will only take ten minutes. Like going to the dentist, in a few minutes it will all be over. One way or another. At first it doesn't seem too bad. The path is a bit narrow and the edge a bit crumbly. I take care not to bang my head on the overhanging rocks. Then there is a passage through the trees. Fine so far. I don't know how the trees manage to hang onto the slope, but they look comfortingly secure. And then… and then… that's it, I am at the end of the corniche. All the tension flows out of me, from my neck, down my arms, down my back, down my legs. I burst out laughing, uncontrollably. I have to sit down. That was vertiginous? I regret not having tackled the 'very exposed ridge path' on the Pic d'Iparla.

Four more hours' walking brings me to the Cabanes de Cézy where crickets are chirping in the late morning warmth. Four stone huts and even a house for the shepherd. Roofs, walls, and doors are intact, all that is needed for a night on the mountains. I could have comfortably squatted in any one of the huts overnight and carried much less kit. The *FFRP Guide* is annoyingly badly informed on this point.

I eat lunch outside one of the huts and then look around the other side to discover a *Mary-Celeste* meal. A tin with a good chunk of pâté remaining, a wheel of camembert with one portion untouched, and half a slice of Emmental cheese, still in its plastic wrapper, garnish an improvised hearth. It is as if the meal has been hastily abandoned, but there is no sign of the diner. I bury the detritus under a stone.

Across the valley, the Petit Train d'Artouste emerges from the tunnel and tootles happily to itself in the sunshine.

My path – a former mule track – climbs slowly through the ferns leaving the limestone behind. The rock under my feet is now friable, reddish-brown, and mineral-rich. I climb up an enclosed valley which opens out into a small grassy plateau cradled by a string of high, angular peaks. On the tops, the clouds are forming, dissolving, and re-forming, decoratively. The only sound, now that the wind has dropped, is the piew-piew of *marmottes* as they scuttle away. The hillside here is pockmarked with their burrows, each one with a little mound of earth at its entrance. Higher still there are some larger holes, also with spoil tips: the mines of the Société des Mines d'Arre et d'Anglas which operated for a few decades around the end of the 19th century. With the passage of time, even these spoil tips have blended into the rocky landscape.

On the plateau there are a couple of low stone walls outlining the foundations of long-abandoned buildings. I pitch my tent on the flat ground near to one of them and sit with my back against a rock, cushioned comfortably by the short-cropped grass, reading about the history of the site. Initially the ore – blende – could only be extracted during the summer months but, in an attempt to improve productivity, at the end of 1882 the company decided to lodge the workers here throughout the winter. Mining continued comfortably underground as the snow fell outside. The accommodation was well constructed and there was food for many months. Then, unexpectedly, on 18 November in the middle of the night, an avalanche roared down the mountain pulling out the rocks in its path and tumbling onto the sleeping quarters. Sixteen workers were killed and four badly wounded. The few survivors descended the valley with great difficulty but the bodies had to be left until the following spring. Was this where they died? I ask myself, suddenly uncomfortable.

Winters here must be awesome. Although it is already summer, a little distance away I can see a small pond still surrounded by snow. Icy cornices drip into it, chunks falling off to become miniature summer icebergs.

I go in search of the spring marked on my map. I don't find it, but down in the valley there is a collection of huts by a stream. One of the huts is in ruins, another intact but dilapidated, and the third pristine, with a solar panel and an aerial on the roof. It reminds me of the Cayolar d'Anhaou, which I came across last year between Logibar and Ste-Engrâce, except that here the newest hut is occupied. There is washing hanging on a line outside. Nearby, a couple of donkeys are munching their way across a rectangular enclosure. There is also a ramshackle construction built on metal poles, with cages and chairs, roofed with plastic sheeting.

As I approach the huts, two collie dogs appear, barking. The top half of a door opens with a metallic squeak and a man sticks his head out. From his greying hair and the exuberance of his moustache, I put him in his 50s. Through the door I can see that the walls are decorated with children's drawings.

'I hope I haven't disturbed your siesta,' I apologise.

'No, I was just sorting letters ready for the post,' he replies.

'Could you tell me what that is for?' I ask, pointing to the raised metal structure.

'For milking sheep. I'll be going to fetch them back shortly.'

He takes his sheep out to pasture each morning and brings them back at night for safety, as he has been doing in the summer for the last forty years. He doesn't seem particularly inclined to chat – he has only been here for a week – so I leave him in peace. As I am climbing back up the hill to my tent I notice three walkers – two adults and a child – and a donkey making their way up the valley to the hut: the postal service.

The clouds are no longer disappearing as quickly as they are forming. They hug the cliffs for a little while and then lose their grip and slide down the slope towards me. It is getting cold so I eat and then slip into my sleeping bag. Starting to doze off, in the half-world between consciousness and sleep, a dim memory comes back to me.

One moonless night, aged thirteen, I was camping in safe rural England when I was woken by a noise outside. Heavy breathing. Something scraping against the canvas. A large shape, bigger than the tent. The canvas being ripped apart. Then there was a crunching, crackling, slobbering noise. Inside the tent. Squeezing to the other side, I felt around for my torch and turned it on. But there was nothing to see, except for a mangled packet of digestive biscuits and a hole. Then I heard a whinny from outside and remembered that there were horses in the field. One of them had managed to detect the biscuits through both their cellophane wrapping and the canvas. The worst of it was that, when I got home, my parents blamed *me* for the hole.

I get out of my sleeping bag, unzip the flap, and hide the remaining food under a stone, well away from the tent. Even if that doesn't work, surely a hungry bear will be more interested in a herd of sheep than a lonely walker?

Mines d'Arre to Gourette

By dawn, the wind has returned and blown the clouds away. The valley of the Soussouéou is still in deep shadow but the sun is already warming the Pic du Midi d'Ossau, starting at the top and working its way down, colouring the cliffs a Barbara Cartland pink.

Crossing a slippery snow field on the way, I climb up to the pass at the Hourquette d'Arre. As the name indicates, I have left the Basque country behind and entered Gascony. This is one of those names which looks impenetrable at first. Translated into French it becomes even more baffling. Hourquette becomes *fourchette* and Arre becomes *rocher*. The rocky fork doesn't seem to make any more sense, unless you make a leap of imagination. This is not a fork lying on a dinner table, but a fork in the rock – a narrow passage, somewhat narrower than a pass, somewhat wider than a crevasse. The *rocky fork* is the highest point on the Pyrenean Way so far. Behind me, on the west side of the pass the wind is blowing furiously; on the east side it is calm.

I twist down the path to the Lac d'Anglas, an extravagant, vivid blue jewel in a lurid mossy emerald setting. In the distance, there is a colony of perhaps 30 *marmottes* gambolling in a hollow, bounding up and down amongst the flowering rhododendrons, running away and then returning to the fray. I approach cautiously, but one of them flies away! They are not *marmottes* but vultures. More exactly *vautours fauves*, griffon vultures, and much bigger than I thought – two or more metres across from wingtip to wingtip. Looking up, I see that more are arriving, circling high above, scrutinising the scene. On the ground, one runs up the hill flapping its wings ineffectively, more to keep the other vultures at bay, than to take off. It has a lump of something red in its beak and blood splashed down its long, fine, white neck. A white and inappropriately fluffy collar protects its mottled brown plumage from the dribbles.

The others set up a kind of hoarse jabbering which becomes more intense as I approach, and then, in a dramatic whoosh, a menacing dark shadow rises into the sky. They have left behind them a corpse. The leg bones have been stripped clean but the ribs are still splashed with drying blood. Little remains of the innards, except for a large brown, fleshy, oozing bag. The wool has been stripped back from the neck to reveal a pink and as yet undamaged throat. The head, except for the eyes, is intact. The stink keeps me from examining the carcass more closely.

As I have just witnessed, vultures like to dine in company. Leaving the colony at dawn, they may travel up to 100km in search of food, spreading out over a large area but keeping visual contact with each other. They can spot a dead *marmotte* 3km away. (I can't even distinguish a *marmotte* from a vulture at 30 metres.) Once they have identified their objective, their cry and sudden descent invites the other guests, and the feast can begin. In principle, vultures only eat dead animals – sheep, lambs, calves, and wildlife. But recently, livestock farmers have started saying that they also attack weak new-born lambs and calves, and even their mothers, exhausted by giving birth. There are only a handful of reports each year, which may seem trivial when compared with a livestock population measured in hundreds of thousands. But the whole question has given rise to a heated debate, second only in acrimony to the dispute surrounding the reintroduction of bears.

Has the number of attacks increased following a population

explosion which has left the vultures short of food? Should shepherds once again be allowed to leave the corpses of dead animals to the capable claws of nature's avian undertakers? Or are the attacks reported more often because farmers can now claim compensation? Or perhaps because they are lumped together with bears on the list of undesirable wild animals which naïve townies wish to foist on hard-working country folk?

There is also the big question of nature versus nurture. Vultures are naturally carrion eaters. Their in-curved claws are useless for attacking living animals. And as I have seen, once on the ground they are ungainly lumbering monsters, incapable of mounting a serious attack. Could they really have *learned* to kill weak animals? Can we expect them to distinguish between a stone dead animal – which is theirs by right – and one which is merely 'resting'?

Humans and vultures have coexisted in the Pyrenees for a very long time. Twenty-five thousand years ago, a Palaeolithic musician carved a flute from a vulture's wing bone, leaving it for archaeologists to discover in a cave near here. This was well before the first pastoralists took possession of the mountains. So, initially at least, vultures must have been feeding on dead bison, *isards*, deer, and so on. But over the years, the combined efforts of hunters and livestock farmers have reduced the number of wild animals, whilst at the same time increasing the number of domestic ones. In the process, the farmers also cleared the forests creating wide open spaces which can easily be inspected from the air, one of the prerequisites for vulture survival.

In the 19th century, vultures were still to be seen in many areas in the south of France but by the 1970s there were only a few score left. Years of deliberate and accidental poisoning had nearly exterminated the last colonies in France. There were also fewer undisturbed cliff habitats available for nesting. And then there was the impact of the hygiene regulations insisting that dead sheep and cattle must not be left to rot where they died. Having first eliminated vultures' wild food resources, shepherds were now obliged to remove the substitute which they had unwillingly provided over the millennia.

So by the 1970s, despite their decreasing numbers, vultures on the French side of the Pyrenees were suffering from malnutrition. The Pyrenees were at the northern limit of their distribution: it wouldn't have taken much to push them back over the frontier. Yet it didn't take much to encourage them to stay.

Hunting was outlawed and a winter feeding site was regularly supplied with the carcasses of dead animals. The measures to protect *isards* and the reintroduction of *marmottes* may also have had an influence on the vulture population. But most important of all was the creation in 1974 of the Réserve naturelle de nidification des vautours fauves in the Ossau valley, specifically set up to protect the nesting sites. By 1997 vultures were becoming so common that they were competing with other birds for nesting sites, so the ONF (French Forestry Commission) stopped feeding them. There are now around 500 in the Pyrenees.

Like bears, they have been harnessed to promote the mountains, particularly the Ossau valley where visitors can watch the nesting sites through the intermediary of a remote controlled camera.

Initially independent, vultures have gone through a phase of dependence on humans. Are we now working our way – vultures and humans – to a kind of uneasy symbiosis?

My feet are already playing up and my knees are giving out warning twinges, so I slow down and rest frequently until I reach the next village, Gourette.

The outskirts of the ski resort of Gourette are as degraded as those of Arette-La-Pierre-St-Martin. The combined blades of thousands of skis have cut ugly gashes through the pine forest. A few stalks of grass are starting to knit together the rocky grey scars but the wounds will never heal before next winter's massacre. In the village itself, the buildings are unimaginative Stalinist blocks designed to accommodate a maximum of holidaymakers at a minimum of cost.

Unlike its cousin Arette-La-Pierre-St-Martin, however, Gourette has an impeccable pedigree. Not only was it a scion of the bourgeois spa town Eaux-Bonnes where Eugénie took the waters before she married the emperor Napoleon III, but it was also here that a group of Pyrenean alchemists set up their laboratory and first discovered how to turn snow into gold. In 1903 Henri Sallenave carried out one of the first Pyrenean experiments in downhill skiing on the slopes above Gourette. By 1909, the Concours International, held here, was a focus for the best European skiers, but it was the presence of the Spanish king Alfonso XIII which really attracted attention. Snow had acquired a new importance, becoming known as *or blanc,* reflecting the eternal values of the mountains and their mines.

Although the outskirts of the town were deserted, the centre is bustling with clapping crowds pushing against the crash barriers which line the road as it winds its way through. I can see literally hundreds of cyclists climbing the hill. They each have a number stuck on the back of their tee-shirt, and a Velcro bracelet wrapped around their right ankle. Nearly all the competitors seem to be in their 40s; there are very few women. Nos 2053, 596, and 4575 pass by, teeth clenched.

I talk to the wife of one of the competitors, who is there to support her husband and his cycling club. They have come down from Angoulême for the event, l'Étape du Tour. Organised by the cycling magazine *Vélo* every year, it follows the route which will be taken a week later by the professional Tour de France. At 7 o'clock this morning, she tells me, there were 7885 cyclists on the starting line at Mourenx, 108km away. She points out the new white lines on the road, and the spotless state of the tarmac.

'It wasn't like that two weeks ago, when we came to do a reconnaissance,' she tells me.

'What are the ankle bands for?' I ask.

'Timing. It takes half an hour for the racers to set off so they each have a chip which means they can be timed individually.'

It is now 12:20 and the radio playing in the bar behind us announces that Laurent Marcon has just crossed the finishing line. He passed through Gourette nearly two hours ago. Those who are labouring through the village now still have 70km to do and the *voiture balai* is brushing at their heels. Though the highest point, the Col d'Aubisque, is only 5km away, there is still 400m of climbing. And after the pass the finishing line is still a long way off.

They say that professional cyclists dance on their pedals as they climb up hills but those who are passing in front of us are sitting firmly on their saddles. As we watch, two competitors look at each other, nod silently, and put their feet on the ground. They throw their cycles against the barrier, walk to the terrace of a café, and order beers.

The town centre looks quite prosperous, at least today, with several cafés and restaurants, sports shops, and a supermarket doing a brisk trade. But it is the names of the hotels which give the game away: the Boule de neige, the Face nord, and the Glacier are not principally aimed at the summer market.

I go to the tourist information office. Behind the counter there are three young women. I am the only tourist.

'Is there a launderette here?' I ask. I haven't many spare clothes, and I want to keep on top of the problem.

'No. There is one in Laruns.'

I also want to send my tent and sleeping bag back home. I won't need them any more.

'Can you tell me how to get to the post office? I thought I saw a sign on the way in.'

'No. It's only open in winter. There is one in Laruns.'

The card in my digital camera is rapidly filling up.

'Is there anywhere I can transfer photos to a CD?'

'No. You could try Laruns.'

'A bank? A pharmacy?'

'No. They're only open in winter. There are some in Laruns, though.'

This is beginning to sound like one of those language learning CDs where you have to ask a series of standard questions and then try to understand the reply. Except that in this case the reply is always 'no'.

'Are there any buses to Laruns? Taxis?' I try, and instantly regret it.

'No. You'll have to hitch.' I am almost pleased that there are no taxis in Gourette. At least I get to learn a new word, *autostop*.

'There's nothing here, is there?' I suggest, hoping to elicit a different reaction.

'That's right,' is the reply.

However, I have no difficulty in thumbing a lift to Laruns and back again. Hitching is the one thing which does work in Gourette in summer, presumably because the inhabitants know that very little else does.

Gourette to Arrens-Marsous

In the morning, within ten minutes I have lost the path, so I decide to take a compass bearing up a small but increasingly steep valley. Initially the ferns are knee high but they soon reach up to my waist. When finally I reach the plateau, the surface is dissected by huge crevasses filled with thorns and small birch trees. After a few minutes of clumsy hopscotch, I finally locate the footpath, coming from a completely different direction. Evidently the route has been changed.

My path descends to a road. I have the possibility of walking along the liquefying asphalt following a contour or the more interesting alternative of dropping down further into the valley and then climbing out of it again. The point of departure is clearly identifiable on the map, but I can't find it, so I go to a nearby hut. Outside it, under the porch, a tall, handsome young man is sitting on a small stool, leaning against the wall, sunning himself. He is wearing a large white apron which covers him from chin to ankles, looking like an illustration from a women's cookery magazine, designed to show that cheese can be both tasty and sexy. A slightly acrid smell of cheese-making wafts out of the door.

'Yes, it is difficult to see, but it *is* right by the bridge,' he tells me. Back at the bridge, I part the undergrowth, discover the path, and walk down to the river, through a colourful patch of flowers: delicately frayed pink wild carnations intertwined with the vicious blue spiky flowers of the Pyrenean thistle.

The path lunges headlong into the woods but I follow it suspiciously; soon it has vanished in a mess of cow pats. I struggle through to the other side, back into the shimmering mid-day furnace, and walk over a patch of bare soil and dead vegetation. Then I slip. Underneath the soil there is a thin layer of snow. Underneath the thin layer of snow, I now realise, there is a very big void spanning a nearly dry stream bed, creating a bridge high enough to ride a horse through. The earth and bracken which protect the snow from the sun must have been clawed out of the hillside last winter as the avalanche gathered momentum. I should have known. This is the Cirque du Litor. *Lit tort* in Occitan means tormented avalanche, giving the image of snow and ice thundering down the slopes from all directions.

A shepherdess later tells me: 'Avoid snow bridges. Gilbert, a shepherd friend of mine, fell through one and broke his back. If I hadn't being going to visit him that day, he would have died.'

The path starts to climb again and I start to overheat; my hat is nowhere to be found. Wiping my forehead with my handkerchief, I decide I must do something. I look at my handkerchief and spread it over my head, but it falls off so I tie it to my glasses, knotting it above my ears, and set off again.

In the next valley, an easy stroll takes me to an extraordinary building balancing on a very small knoll, like a snail on a marble. The architecture – all rounded corners, gangways, and balustrades, painted cream, evoking the bridge of a cruise liner – signals an origin between the wars. Six storeys high, the building curls round the hillock, a recently mown lawn curls round the building, and a road encircles both of them. The sliding glass doors of the reception area open automatically as I approach but nobody comes out to greet me. I open another door, mount the stairs and clump along a curved corridor but there is nobody around. The snail has left home. After some searching I find a plaque which explains that this was a hospice for wounded soldiers, and has become a centre for handicapped adults. But where have they all gone?

On the top of the knoll, protected by the hospice on three sides, is the 'famously beautiful' golden chapel of Our Lady, a baroque monument to decadence. Even though the Protestants were going in for simplicity, this was no reason for the Catholics to follow suit. The result is a chapel bedecked with gold leaf. There are some touching details, like the quarrelling disciples. But the overall effect is grotesque, particularly when juxtaposed with the hospice, where for decades men and women have been struggling merely to exist. There, in the hospice, decadence is not an option.

My destination for today is Arrens, only ten minutes' walk away. In the village, everything is in its place. The newly painted, recently re-roofed cottage has a freshly mown lawn and a professionally trimmed privet hedge. The mill leet is constrained in a concrete channel. The paving stones on the medieval hump-back bridge have been re-laid and carefully concreted to avoid tripping. The mulberry trees are evenly spaced. There is no rubbish. It is pretty; but also artificial, unnatural. It is difficult to believe that people really *live* here. There is none of the shit of Gabas, nor the ice cream wrappers of Gourette. Even the topography has been tamed. The flat valley floor is an astonishing 500m wide.

The only hat remaining in the newsagent's looks as though it might have been worn in colonial Sudan, and it is too big for me. The shop assistant says that they sell lots of them, and insists that it suits me. I tell him that I would look less ridiculous wearing a knotted handkerchief tied to my glasses. But at least it will shade my neck, so I buy it anyway.

The hostels in the village are full so I go to a hotel and ring the bell on the desk in the gloomy reception area. An old woman, her white hair pulled back from her forehead and tied into a top-knot, shuffles out from one of the rooms at the back, bent over her Zimmer frame. She is wearing a long black dress with a high neck. She doesn't seem to notice me but the woman who is following her says hello in passing and then helps her charge to sit down on a stiff-backed chair in an even darker corner. Yes, they have a room. Yes, there will be *garbure* for supper. No, there is no alternative.

Arrens-Marsous to the Lac d'Ilhéou

Walking out of the town next day, I discover a ramshackle house, with a derelict car in the garden, teeming with cats, startling evidence of rebellious individualism. Yes! But it is too early to wake up the inhabitants to congratulate them, so I follow the path over a small rise into the long, pleasant valley-garden of Estaing and head back for the hills.

Just before the Lac d'Estaing there are two curious beehive-shaped stone structures, side by side, next to the path. Each of them has a small rectangular opening in one wall, just over a metre high and, inside, a stone seat with a circular hole. There is no door. Looking through the hole I can see running water: part of the flow of a stream has been diverted to flush out these primitive toilets – in the middle of the countryside. I try sitting on the seat but the opening is so small that I have to bend double in order to fit in. It doesn't seem very practical.

Later I learn the real explanation, from the writings of the botanist Augustin Pyramus de Candolle, who was probably the first person to cross the Pyrenees from end to end, in 1807.

We supped from the milk which we found in a cavity covered with stones and cooled by the water of a stream. It is the custom of the farmers here to hide their milk from the sun in this way to keep it fresh. Travellers may drink without asking permission of the owner as long as they leave money in the basin.

So these are not toilets but another kind of household appliance: refrigerators.

The Lac d'Estaing itself is completely unruffled. *Estaing*, I should explain, means lake in the Gascon dialect. I turn the idea around in my head:

Sometime in the 19th century, two cartographers are surveying the valley. They approach a fisherman at the waterside and ask him its name.

Fisherman: 'Estaing.'

Cartographer 1: 'But surely it has another name to distinguish it from all the other lakes around here.'

Fisherman: 'No. We just call it the lake. It is the only one in the valley. There isn't any other name.'

Cartographer 2: 'Just put down "Estaing"'.

Cartographer 1: 'I can't do that. When we get back to Paris they will ask us what it means. When we tell them that it means 'lake', they won't believe us. Worse still, they will send us back here again. I've had enough of these mountains and the fishermen who are too stupid to invent real names.'

Fisherman: 'You're frightening the fish with your philosophical discussions. Bugger off!'

Cartographer 2: 'Just put down the Lac d'Estaing. In Paris they won't know that it means Lake Lake. They will think that Estaing is a village or something. They won't know that it doesn't make sense.'

So they put down Lac d'Estaing. Now that the technique was well honed they had no problem further along the Pyrenean Way with Ilhéou, Gaube, and Aumar. So there were now four Lake Lakes within a short distance of each other. But Paris got wise to them. They were banished just over the border into Spain; but they took their revenge, secretly insinuating the Valley Valley (Val d'Aran) onto their maps.

I am brought back to reality by the heat. By the time I reach the top of the pass into the next valley, I am flaking so I sit down near to a herd of cows. They are behaving strangely. It is a perfect summer's day. Clearly, it is not going to rain. The grass looks juicy and the cows should be dispersed across the hillside ruminating contentedly. Instead, they are gathered together in a compact group, heads up, looking across a ravine. I follow their look. On the other side of the ravine I can see something jumping about, flying in and out of the abyss: a flock of vultures, feasting. The cows look on, powerlessly.

Further down in the valley, on the shores of another lake, the tables outside the hostel where I am going to spend the night are full, so I buy a glass of beer and slump against the wall of the terrace. A gust of wind caresses the silky turquoise shallows, brushing them with ephemeral fingerprints. Above the lake, the peaks are grey, smooth except for their geological wrinkles. The snow-flecked upper slopes are half hidden by rivers of scree – rocky torrents in perpetual movement, needing only the heat of a sunbeam to unhinge their precarious equilibrium and send them crashing down the incline. It is only lower down, by the shore, that grass and heather have installed a relative stability. The pink wild roses bloom gaily; the few sombre pine trees struggle along wearily. It is a quiet, unassuming beauty. This is not the ostentatious spectacle of the Pic du Midi d'Ossau. This is nature being modest, hinting at her powers. Look, she says, in winter, those ripples become waves, those patches of snow become avalanches. Given time, those mountains will disappear. For now, I am taking it easy.

The hostel is perched on the rocky plug which dams the lake, the Lac d'Ilhéou. Like a traditional A-frame tent, the roof nearly reaches the ground and the gables are vertical. Visually, the hostel is all roof.

Refuge d'Ilhéou

Clearly, snow will not stick, and the sun's rays will quickly heat the dark slates. The ground floor consists of the kitchen and dining room, the first floor is the dormitory, and the manager's quarters are crammed into the attic. The *garbure* is excellent.

Ilhéou? The lake was renamed the Lac Bleu in the 19th century. The hostel, built in 1970, is officially called the Refuge Ritter. But these names have slipped into oblivion like the snow off the roof. The Refuge Ilhéou stands defiantly on the shores of the Lac d'Ilhéou.

Lac d'Ilhéou to Cauterets

I wake up feeling off-colour, and not for the first time. A churning stomach ache is the least dramatic of the symptoms. But it is sunny and I don't have far to go, so I quickly forget about my defective digestion. I follow the path as it curves gently down the valley, intersecting from time to time with the dirt track used to supply the hostel. Grey patches of paint signal the way. Painted on the equally grey rocks, they blend into the natural surroundings much better than the usual red and white waymarks. Of course, they are not *supposed* to be waymarks; they are supposed to hide the oversized splodges which were painted before the FFRP imposed its standards, but they function just as well as the normal ones.

I see a group of walkers some distance below me on the track.

'The path is over here,' I call out to them, pointing at my feet.

'*Il est où* – where is it…?' The rest of their reply is lost in the breeze. One of them points up the valley towards the hostel.

'It's here,' I insist indicating the path with a broad sweep of my arm.

They continue pointing along the track, so I dump my rucksack and scramble across to meet them.

'You must have missed the turning a little while back,' I explain.

'No. We wanted to take the easy route. The GR10 is too steep, too uneven,' they reply.

Disgusted, I stump off back to my rucksack. When I get to the turning, I tear up the fern which is half hiding the waymark at the bifurcation. Do people really prefer walking along roads to paths? Perhaps we need a Campaign for Real Paths.

Below, in the woods just before the town of Cauterets, with the sun filtering through the leaves, my footsteps are accompanied by strange sounds: regular dull thuds, a series of burps varying in intensity and pitch, and occasional metallic crashes. Today is 14 July. A brass band is celebrating the national holiday.

Cauterets is full of bunting and the streets full of holidaymakers. All the shops are open, but the one which interests me most is the pharmacy. I am looking for cures, appropriately enough in a town which has been dedicated to medicine from its earliest days. The thermometer outside the pharmacy reads 32°C. Inside, I ask for plasters, sun cream, Imodium, toilet paper, and the address of the nearest doctor.

Cauterets

'No, it's not the *garbure*,' the doctor reassures me. 'You've suddenly started using a lot of energy and replacing it with large quantities of food. Your metabolism will take a while to get used to the idea. I'll prescribe you something to settle you down.' I tell him that it will be four days before I get to the next village so he adds some anti-inflammatory cream 'in case your knees start playing up again'.

My next stop is the Bureau des Guides to ask about walking conditions on the next section. In a few days I will reach the highest point on the Pyrenean Way, in the shadow of Vignemale mountain, and I have heard that there was a lot of snow last winter. If there is too much I will take a short cut.

'Yes, there's still lots of snow on Vignemale, but the pass is not a problem,' says the girl behind the counter. 'Just in case you are interested, the snow makes climbing Vignemale easier. If you want to do it there's a guide going on Sunday,' she adds hopefully. 'Since you'll be staying at the Refuge de Bayssellance you'll be half way there.'

'But I've never used crampons, and in any case I haven't got any.' Vignemale is the highest peak on the French side of the Pyrenees. Climbing it involves crossing the Glacier d'Ossoue.

'The guide will bring some with him and show you how to use them.'

I look at her suspiciously. 'What about an ice axe? You need an ice axe, don't you?'

'Absolutely. Jean will bring one with him as well.'

So the rendezvous is fixed for 8 o'clock, in three days' time, at the Grottes Bellevue. I was intending to be there tomorrow; I will have to slow down. Sitting in a café afterwards, I wonder how I have managed to sign myself up for this – the final assault on the summit involves hands-on rock climbing. It must be something to do with the unadventurous group of walkers sticking obstinately to the track this morning. Perhaps also something to do with the atmosphere which reigns in the Bureau des Guides.

The Bureau des Guides caters for all kinds of tourists, from happy-go-lucky day-trippers to very hard men, but whatever category you might fit into, it takes itself seriously. I left the office with no doubt that the guides know what they are doing. *You* may not think you are capable of climbing Vignemale. But *they* have been taking tourists there for 150 years. So *yes we can*. The Bureau des Guides has been saying this since its creation in 1862 when the major Pyrenean health spas – Eaux Bonnes, Cauterets, Luz-St-Sauveur, Barèges, Luchon – were starting to organise tourism on a more professional basis.

Before 1862 guides and clients were left to negotiate their prices and itineraries and sort out their own disputes. Sometimes the guides learned as much from their clients as the other way round. As *Les Grands Guides des Pyrénées* puts it: 'In 1787 a certain Ramond stuck his nose in … His ascents, numerous scientific observations, and detailed reports started a Pyrenean revolution in its own right … A revolution born elsewhere, launched by strangers, but surviving thanks to mountain people: guides and porters.' Curiously, the new way of looking at the mountains had coincided with the Revolution.

The conquest of Vignemale well illustrates the status of the local guides at that time: low. In 1792 a group of shepherds under the direction of Louis-Philippe Reinhard Junker climbed to the top as part of a military survey to map the frontier between France and Spain. The shepherds' names are unknown. It was another 45 years before the next recorded visit to the summit, by Henri Cazaux, a guide from Luz-St-Sauveur, and his brother-in-law Bernard Guillembet on 8 October 1837. But the names which count are not those of the guides but those of Ann Lister and the Prince de la Moskowa who disputed the summit in August 1838. Miss Lister, from Halifax in Yorkshire, engaged Cazaux and three other guides, and reached the summit on 7 August, leaving a bottle with their names written on a piece of paper as proof. Four days later the Prince de la Moskowa climbed to the top, again accompanied by Cazaux, who had told him that Miss Lister had been taken ill and had not arrived at the summit. The Prince, he said, would be the first to climb the peak (and Cazaux would be better paid in consequence). When they approached the top, one of the guides rushed ahead and destroyed the incriminating bottle so that the Prince came back thinking that he was the first 'outsider' to conquer the mountain. Although he was told soon after his return that Miss Lister had beaten him, he pretended not to believe it and published accounts of his exploit on 21 August in the *Messenger* and on 15 September in *Deux Mondes*. (Later, Ann Lister extracted a confession from Cazaux, though it was many years before the truth was universally accepted.)

So, the conquest of Vignemale is usually presented as a story of rivalry between the two tourists. As usual, the guides are relegated to the shadows; the shepherds are completely invisible. It was all very well to be the first to climb a mountain, but an illiterate shepherd could never rival the status of an English 'lady' or a prince. As one Pyrenean author (Beraldi) wrote: *le bâton ferré ne vaut que par la plume*, roughly – the pen is mightier than the walking stick. Guiding was a part-time occupation, a useful supplementary income in hard times, but insecure and without glory, and bedevilled by quarrels with clients. This, then, was the reason for the creation of the Compagnie des Guides – which subsequently became the Bureau des Guides – which set standards, determined fees and uniforms, organised insurance on the lines of a mutual society, and regulated disputes.

Later in the afternoon I sit down on a bench in the park opposite the Bureau des Guides. From my viewpoint, Cauterets appears small: crushed by the enclosing hills. Their wooded slopes nibble at the outer layer of long terraced streets embellished by delicate wrought iron balconies. This fragile shell protects the inner core of wedding-cake hotels built in the second half of the 19th century. Then there is a gaudy commercial bubble but the real centre of the town is the casino, its park, and the arcade which lines the river. For the national holiday, the park has been invaded by roundabouts and souvenir kiosks but most of the attention centres on an artificial climbing wall, the *Challenge*. Painted in primary blues, reds, greens, and yellows, the shiny plastic blocks remind me of a deformed bouncy castle, an impression accentuated by the piles of soft orange mats on the ground. Of course the blocks are more solid than the walls of a bouncy castle, though the giant gecko logos are the only things to stick to them for any length of time. One after another, hopeful youngsters fall onto the mats to the applause of onlookers. It looks like some kind of a cruel joke. The handholds are either tiny plastic oysters bolted onto improbable overhangs or voluptuous bulges too big to caress and too smooth to grip.

Later the real competition starts and it is now that I realise quite how serious it is. One young man stretches across the vertical block face, leaning over at an improbable angle to reach a slight bulge in the surface to the side of him. The handhold is only big enough for a couple of fingers but he manages to use it to support himself while flinging his other arm around the opposite side of the bulge. In the same movement he swings across the block so that one foot lands on a ledge and he can haul himself up to the top. Even these competitors find the challenge difficult. Their displays of grace and power are punctuated by ungainly falls. Here it doesn't matter, but on 20 November 2004 Régis Barraque, an experienced climber, was found dead at the foot of the natural stone blocks called *la Russe*, just outside Cauterets. This year, the *Challenge* has been renamed in his honour.

In the evening, I go back to the gardens of the casino for the continuing festivities. According to the publicity, today marks the start of the 'Festival Latino-Roc ... three days of Brazilian madness in a Latin-American ambiance'. Concerts, encounters, exhibitions, films, and shows with, this evening, the band Via Brasil on an outdoor stage of glittering aluminium and billowing smoke. With a bewitching *joie de vivre* which sweeps all incongruity before it, the group captures the attention of the spectators and sets them bopping. Or more accurately hopping – from foot to foot. With remarkable lack of forethought the organisers have failed to cordon off an area for dancing, but it doesn't really matter. The whole park sways rhythmically.

I am soon thirsty so I grab a beer at one of the tents and go to sit down at a long table. Opposite me, finishing their desserts, are two women with festival committee name badges.

'This is the second year. Before that, there were just the usual events – local bands, outdoor meals, stalls – just like all the other towns in the area. Nobody came from outside,' says Nathalie, the older of the two.

'Why Latino, then?'

'I don't know. Do you?' she asks her friend, Aurélie.

'No. I don't think there was any particular reason. Perhaps it was inspired by the festival at Vic-Fezensac.'

'Has it brought more people into the town?'

'Last year there were loads more. There are not many today because there are things going on everywhere. But I expect the town will be overflowing tomorrow and Saturday.'

Even today the park is full, though many must also be attracted by the fireworks which are about to start.

Nathalie continues: 'It's the young people who have organised it and I think it is a good thing. It's different from the usual local events. *It isn't Gascon.* Don't get me wrong. I was born here. I'm proud to be Gascon and I think preserving our culture is important. But we don't have to be Gascon *all* the time.'

She's right. There is no reason Cauterésiens should conform to visitors' expectations. Visitors don't even conform to their expectations of each other. They never have. As George Sand complained as long ago as 1825:

> They want me to sing *Ebbene, per mia memoria* this evening... Did I come to Cauterets to go to *soirées* and rediscover Paris in this country of eagles and *chamois*? No. I am going out to see the snows, the torrents and, God willing, the bears. There was one the other day a league from here at a hundred paces from the path. He watched mockingly as we passed by.

Eight years later the young architect Eugène Viollet-le-Duc, also staying in Cauterets, is even more violently disgusted by some of the visitors to the Pyrenees. The worst ones, he says are the rich old men who have come to take the waters.

> They go to pick up girls at Pierrefitte to take them to Barèges. They count on the evening shower to cleanse themselves of the day's debauches. They know that a summer by the waters compensates

for a winter of dissolution. They are masters of debauchery; they keep themselves going with good wines, sulphur baths, and pure air. Take that away from them and their legs will refuse to work, their emaciated features will turn pale, all their limbs will lose their strength and rot. Yes, we have seen men like that this evening. Oh, beautiful mountains, air so pure, were you created to preserve the life of such wretched creatures?

On the other hand, Hippolyte Taine (1855) is somewhat more scathing about the efficacy of the waters:

This town has several springs. The Source du Roi cured Abarca, king of Aragon; the Source de César, so they say, restored the great Caesar's health. One must believe in history just as one must believe in medicine.

… in the time of François 1, the waters of Eaux-Bonnes cured wounds; they were called the waters of the gunners… Now they cure chest and throat problems. In a hundred years perhaps they will cure other things. Every century medicine takes a step forward.

Cauterets to the Plateau du Clot

After breakfast, I repair my feet, line my stomach with chalk, and slather a layer of white cream on my knees before going outside. As I have only a short distance to walk today I have decided to visit the Maison du Parc National first.

The exhibition seems to be largely about survival. Not what to do when you trip over and discover that your toe bone is no longer attached to your foot bone. No, the exhibition is about surviving in the Pyrenees year-in year-out, over the millennia, be you human, animal, or plant life.

There are numerous places in the world where life is impossible, but very few in Europe – none at all in Britain; though Robert Macfarlane finds *Wild Places* (2007) in Britain, there are none where life is *literally* impossible. Only arctic wastes, deserts, the depths of the oceans, and the tops of mountains push life to its limits and often beyond. In the Pyrenees there are virtually no living things at 2900m above sea level. Remarkably, a few lichens and a pink algae manage to reproduce higher up, on the slopes of Vignemale, for example.

A little further down, below the death zone, life is played out in slow motion. Some *pins à crochet* survive for 1,000 years. The tadpoles of the midwife toad can take up to 10 years before they metamorphose into adults – not a very suitable subject for primary school nature study.

The human presence in the high mountains is also precarious: a summer adventure which started as the last glaciers began to retreat and hunter-gatherers followed wild herds out of the forest. By the beginning of the 21st century the adventure was drawing to a close, confined to the few shepherds who still practise transhumance and live in the summer pastures with their flocks.

I also learn that, in classical myth, the Pyrenees were created by Hercules in memory of a princess called Pyrène, but this image is quickly replaced in my mind with an alternative explanation. A series of cross-sections explains the orogenesis which took hundreds of millions of years. The first one is innocuous: layers of hot red mantle safely contained in a cool earth skin. But then something starts to go wrong. In the second drawing the skin layers are starting to move. In the third, the earth's life blood is pushed upwards and starts to escape. The skin is dislocated, bulging. It bursts, the blood vessels haemorrhaging in streams of boiling lava, leaving irremediable scars. Only the effects of time, measured in millennia, and represented in the fourth drawing, restore a semblance of order and calm.

It looks exactly like the diagram my surgeon drew explaining what might happen if I didn't have my hernia repaired before setting out.

Now I understand the Pyrenees. The mountains are trapped entrails. The sulphurous hot springs are suppurating pus. The paths, roads, and railways straddling the hills are a clumsy surgeon's attempts to stitch up the damage... But perhaps I am getting my symptoms out of all proportion. Even so, I had better get going before I erupt.

Once out of town, I saunter along the valley before zigzagging between the trees down to a bridge. A monolithic stone building and a nauseous smell defend the crossing, but a prominent sign reassures: 'Thermes des Griffons (Rheumatology). Smells caused by water containing natural sulphur.' I hold my breath and climb up the Jéret valley – an inexhaustible, bubbling, babbling, booming, thundering waterfall 3km long – to the Pont d'Espagne.

The Pont d'Espagne is a popular excursion destination for motorists. Once here, exhausted from the nerve-racking drive up the steep winding road which runs parallel to the waterfall, they collapse into the café-restaurant, gorge themselves, buy souvenirs, walk five minutes to the Plateau du Clot, and laze around all afternoon on the river bank sipping beer from the chalet refuge. Like me. One can also go rock climbing on the natural granite blocks, or take the ski lift to the Lac de Gaube (even in summer – skis are not obligatory), but even the latter seems too much effort.

Instead I chat to one of the guides thoughtfully stationed here by the National Park. His telescope, he tells me, is to look for *isards*, but there aren't any. In winter they will come right down to this meadow. Last winter, when the temperature dropped to –26°C, they came even further down into the valley. Today it is 50°C hotter so I settle for dangling my feet in the water, walking barefoot, savouring the grass between my toes.

In the fading evening light, I am eating *garbure* on the terrace of the chalet-hostel when a man and his dog appear. The man is wearing a black beret, a white tee-shirt, a pair of jeans, and an extravagant paunch as though it were a fashion accessory. Behind the man and the dog, a flock of perhaps a hundred sheep ambles into view, followed by a bottle-green truck. The man disappears into the bar and the dog runs off.

As soon as the shepherd has disappeared, the sheep start behaving oddly, for no apparent reason. Those in the centre of the flock are standing still but those at the outer edges start walking in an anti-clockwise direction around the ones standing still. The further they are away from the centre, the faster they walk. And those sheep which had somehow become detached from the flock return to it. It is like a giant woolly Catherine wheel but working in reverse: instead of projecting sparks as it turns, it is gaining stragglers. The dog reappears, silently putting the finishing touches to its work of art, and then sits down on a slight promontory to admire the result. The flock is now a compact, complaining mass, encircled by a single dog.

One sheep has escaped the roundup but only because it is in the back of the truck. I take it to be too ill to have done the journey on foot, so I go to look. When I get closer I see that it is not ill. It is a ram, being kept separate from the females. Tomorrow is his big day. I study his expression. Is it frustration, anticipation, disdain, boredom, or lust? Sheep don't give much away.

Plateau du Clot to the Bayssellance hostel

In the early morning dew, I climb through the woods to the Lac de Gaube, famous for its beauty and infamous for the number of visitors it attracts. I feel privileged: there is nobody to be seen, only the lake, the inclined strata diving into its cool depths, and the vertical cliffs and glaciers of Vignemale far away, blocking the head of the valley. For me, for many other people, this *is* beauty. But the view hasn't always been so universally appreciated.

When the abbé de Voisenon, a friend of Voltaire, visited the lake in 1761 he felt 'crushed' by the mountains.

One sees only pine trees, yews, and verbena, and those things which characterise the home of a black magician; there are no birds, the silence is only disturbed by the avalanches which fall from the heights of the mountains with a frightening noise. Nature seems to shiver with horror at herself. I was always thinking that she was saying to me: 'Why did you come here with your happiness? You are bold to dare laugh in this place!'

His reaction was typical. But now, 250 years on, the Lac de Gaube is considered truly beautiful. Why have our ideas changed so radically?

I credit it to a literary orogenesis that created a new kind of mountain where none existed before: the Romantic Movement. In my version – at least as far as France is concerned – Jean-Jacques Rousseau plays the role of God. He found beauty in the heights where others only found fear. His *Julie ou La Nouvelle Héloïse*, also written in 1761 at the same time as the abbé de Voisenon was being 'crushed', was the prologue. Just as the Lake District in Britain was transformed by Wordsworth, the French Romantics came to value the Lac de Gaube, the Pyrenees, and beyond.

The movement stressed the importance of individual emotion and imagination over intellect. It took nature as its inspiration. Mountains were no longer *horrible*. (This 'horror' was a Western concept. In the Far East, mountains had long been revered, Mount Fuji in Japan being a well-known example.)

The Romantic Movement didn't merely limit itself to transforming the physical landscape. Within a generation filthy peasants had become noble creatures whose faults were the result of contact with corrupt city dwellers. When Hortense de Beauharnais, Napoleon Bonaparte's adopted daughter, was on holiday near here in 1807, she was tricked by a young couple into promising a dowry so that they could marry. When she found out, she forgave them because the young man admitted to his lies. 'I complimented him,' she said, 'that having done wrong, he knew how to make amends.'

One didn't need to have read the classics to understand Romantic literature. Equally, scientific names were abhorred. In fact scientific accuracy was thrown out of the window if it got in the way of a good sentence. Hugo, for example, describes the Lac de Gaube as 'Thirteen hundred feet [deep]. Our old Notre Dame could be heaped up on top of herself six times before the high balustrade of her towers would appear at the water's surface.' The lake is 130ft not 1300ft deep.

Inevitably, as the movement was pushed further and further, descriptions became over-written, losing touch with reality, and reaction set in. In 1840 Flaubert, who had dreamed of seeing the Lac de Gaube by moonlight, regretted leaving. But by 1872, again in the mountains, he just wanted to get back to his green writing table: 'I would give all the glaciers in the world for the Vatican Museum. It's there that one dreams.'

Romantic literature is no longer popular, but something remains. As *Le Romantisme et les Pyrénées* concludes: 'The Romantics have bequeathed us a feeling for the mountains which has become truly integrated into the human soul.'

So, the Romantics transformed our mountains in the space of a century from ugly wildernesses into beautiful playgrounds. A visit to the Lac de Gaube became one of the three principal outings for the wealthy taking the waters in the Pyrenean spa towns in the mid-19th century (the second was the Cirque de Gavarnie, two days further along the Pyrenean Way, and the third, the Lac d'Oô, is a week away).

I continue walking. Above the lake, my path rises slowly as the valley opens out into a long water meadow. The stream fractures into numerous lazy rivulets which merge, only to split again. Fluffy tufts of white cotton grass shake their Andy Warhol haircuts in the breeze.

I am overtaken by a man many years older than me, running. Without stopping, he tells me that he is practising for the Vignemale Race which will take place a week on Sunday. As I watch him disappear into the distance, getting smaller and smaller, I feel diminished as well. But then who wouldn't? The record for the Vignemale Race stands at four hours and 24 minutes. I calculate that it would take me something like 18 hours.

The first edition was in 1904. Starting from Cauterets, the competitors followed the path I am now taking up to the Bayssellance hostel, across the glacier to the top of the Grand Vignemale, going back to their starting point by a different route – a distance of 55km, with over 2300m of climbing. The winner, Jean-Marie Bordenave, a guide from Cauterets, took six hours and one minute, and lost 6.7kg in weight. Nowadays, it no longer goes to the summit – the Glacier d'Ossoue is considered too dangerous.

Being more of a Romantic than a hard man, instead of running I merely plod on up to the Hourquette d'Ossoue, warily crossing a small patch of frozen snow and then go down the other side to the Bayssellance hostel. There's nobody around and the door is locked, so I inspect the structure from all angles. It is as if four rowing boats have been pulled out of the sea for the winter, dragged up the mountain by some helpful Gulliver, arranged in the shape of a cross, and then turned over to protect any passing travellers. The design also means that there is always one corner which is protected from the wind. I sit down in it and eat my picnic lunch.

I am soon joined by a tall man wearing a cowboy hat who turns out to be English. John has been rock climbing for 26 years. He has just returned from the Grand Vignemale.

'I just followed the footprints across the snow. Except just before the top, that is. I made the mistake of climbing up a steep snow corridor between the rocks. It was a little tricky, I had to use my ice axe but the snow wasn't really frozen enough. Then when I came back down I met a couple who told me that I should have stuck to the rocks.'

'You were on your own?'

'Yes. Mind you, at one point my leg disappeared into the snow. What if I had disappeared completely? The hostel manager said that the crevasses were only a problem at the end of the summer. On the way back I saw some kids and a dog just wandering around completely uncontrolled, without a rope. Some people are absolutely stupid.'

After lunch I climb the snowless *Petit* Vignemale and sunbathe at the top. A white-winged snow finch comes to beg some crumbs; two yellow-billed Alpine choughs circle overhead. To the north, I can see all the way back down the valley to the Lac de Gaube and beyond, to the plains choked by white haze. To the east, half-way down another grey-green valley the Ossoue dam is taking its tribute of the melt waters of the Vignemale glacier. The cars parked at the dam sparkle in the sun. Beyond them a slug-trail road wanders indecisively down to Gavarnie. In contrast, all around me the mountain tops are uncompromisingly harsh and jagged: bare rock or loose scree. Except just below me, to the south, where the glacier – the Glacier d'Ossoue – has polished off the worst of the deformities, covering them with alternating swathes of snow and ice.

I can see a few small figures crossing one of the bands of snow near the far edge of the glacier. There are perhaps 30 dots, semi-colons and question marks in several groups, descending. The first group reaches the edge of the snow and stops before risking the icy slope. They progress gingerly, but I see one of the dots moving fast, much faster than the others, overtaking them ungrammatically and then coming to an abrupt full stop. The other dots catch up in a typographic mess, and mill around. After a few minutes they all set off down the slope again.

At my table in the evening we are four French, two English, one Belgian, and three Spanish. One of the Frenchmen has two fingers held together by an ostentatious white bandage.

'I was bitten by a bear,' he says.

Seeing our sceptical looks he says: 'Would you believe me if I said a *marmotte*?'

'Not now.'

'Actually it was a lawnmower. You might not think so, but it is quite a handicap. Even though I don't need to use my hands most of the time, my feet don't seem to work as well. I keep on falling over.'

The conversation is excitingly multilingual. There is plenty of goodwill and lots of communication at a basic level – where have you come from? Where are you going to? How much does your rucksack weigh? But as soon as we start on more complex subjects, everything grinds to a halt in mutual incomprehension. Europe in miniature. Even so, Europe *is* being constructed here, in an isolated hut, a day's walk from the nearest road, just as much as it is created in the padded conference rooms of major cities.

Vignemale

At a quarter to eight in the morning, after a night disturbed by snoring, I am at the Grottes Bellevue. I put my rucksack down and look into the first of the three caves. It has been carved out of the native rock and might sleep four or five, uncomfortably. Although the floor is littered with shreds of silver and gold emergency blankets and an empty wine bottle, I regret not having slept there, *inside* the mountain. The second one is in the same state. The third one, which is partly protected by a wall, is occupied. The rustling and grunts suggest some kind of wild animal but when I stick my head cautiously into the entrance, I make out a blue sleeping bag. A voice says, '*Buenos dias*'. The occupant tells me that his companions have gone to climb Vignemale but his nose didn't like the idea. It had been gushing blood all night so he didn't feel strong enough. I ask him about the hard hat sitting on top of his rucksack. 'That was for the rock climbing at the end, in case someone dislodged a stone and it fell on my head.'

'Excuse me,' he continues, 'we camped near the hostel last night and what with my nose and the canvas flapping in the wind, I didn't get much sleep,' and he tucks himself back into his sleeping bag.

The caves look more suitable for bears than for human occupation yet they and four others just under the summit have carved out the legend of the man who financed their construction: Henry Russell, arguably the greatest Pyrenean of the last two centuries. The first biography I read about him was entitled *The Man Who Married a Mountain*, and the epithet is just perfect.

With an Irish father and a French mother, Count Henry Russell Killough was born in 1834 in Toulouse. He spent his early adult life adventuring across the world but came back to the Pyrenees definitively in 1861, at the age of 27, climbing Vignemale for the first time in that year. By 1864 he had become one of the founding fathers of the Ramond Society, dedicated to the scientific study of the mountains, though science wasn't at all his thing. February 1869 found him at the summit of Vignemale for the third time, with the guides Hippolyte and Henri Passet. In *Souveniers d'un Montagnard* he wrote:

> Never will I forget the short but memorable minutes which we spent up there in the heart of the winter with the certainty that no other man in Europe was breathing at our level [3298m]; childish pride, but pardonable… From the top of this celestial cathedral, I saw below my feet the Pyrenean range frozen from one end to the other. I was in the centre of a snowy paradise! I was madly enthusiastic.

By the end of his life he had climbed all the major peaks, written several books about them, and could claim to have conquered some 30 'virgins'. Evidently his achievements would have guaranteed him a bulky entry in specialist books, but paradoxically his almost heroic status – his legend – is built on rather less substantial foundations. Russell is known as the man who became obsessed by a mountain.

He spent 150 nights on Vignemale, the first three being in the open air. The experience persuaded him that he needed a shelter so, eventually, he had a cave, which he named the Grotte Russell, carved in the rock face at the top edge of the glacier near the summit, in 1881.

Vignemale

An Eskimo would have built in snow; in Switzerland they like
wood; and me, I only like rock. Nothing is as warm and as solid.

But he had not calculated on the variations in the thickness of the ice
which sometimes covered the shelter and sometimes left it stranded,
inaccessible, way above its surface. So workers were employed to
build, successively, the Grotte des Guides, the Grotte des Dames,
and the Grotte du Paradis, the latter only a few metres below the
summit, in much harder rock, necessitating dynamite. Finally he had
the three Grottes Bellevue built for times when the higher shelters
were unreachable.

In *Souvenirs d'un Montagnard*, he gives me the impression of being
an austere, somewhat misanthropic nature-lover. One formal photograph shows a tall thin man, wearing a tweed jacket, standing stiffly
to attention. His face is rectangular and strong-boned. In contrast, he
has a full moustache and a strangely playful wisp of a beard which
doesn't seem to fit in with the severe aspect of the rest of the photo.
There is something about him which reminds me of Lenin. Another
photo shows him in his favourite sheepskin sleeping bag, lying equally
stiffly on an irregular rocky slope.

As he freely admits, he contributed nothing to the corpus of
knowledge which was being assembled by his contemporaries. In
the Introduction to *Souvenirs*, clearly influenced by the Romantic
movement of his youth, he wrote:

Nature is not a laboratory: it is an entertainment and a school...
The things which are least understood are often those which please
the most. What is melody, harmony, love? What is Beauty? ... Will
we know in ten thousand years? Probably not, and we won't have
lost anything.

Although he sought isolation on the mountains, he also welcomed
company when it arrived – at least at first. In 1884 he spent nine

consecutive days in his eponymous *grotte*, sometimes contemplating alone, sometimes partying, sometimes praying. He had the *grotte*, and the mountain, blessed by three separate masses in a single day. There were 30 guests, most of whom evidently had to shiver in the wind on the glacier outside.

But this church 'wedding' was not enough for Russell. He wanted the symbolic equivalent of the civil ceremony conducted by the mayor. In 1889 he wrote to the *préfet* asking for a 99-year lease, which was duly accorded. He wrote in the *Gazette de Cauterets* 'Vignemale is my wife and my seven caves are our children.'

Yet he was by no means antisocial. In Pau, he lived a normal life for a bachelor of his background, attending balls – he was an excellent dancer – and concerts. He played the cello. His passion for the mountains was, it seems, a compensation for an unrequited love affair.

One summer Henri Brulle and other climbing friends carried a tent up to the hermit's retreat.

They organised three delectable days for me, in ideal weather, in Asian luxury... carpet, armchairs, bedding, oriental perfumes, lanterns, and vaporisers... Never in my small snowy empire, were seen so many beautiful things, without counting the cigars, the fine wines and a ham so big that it could have served as a bench or a cushion.

Several times, Russell built a cairn at the summit so that his betrothed would pass 3300m, but each time the winter frosts brought it down again. By 1894, at the age of 60, he was talking of his 25th ascent as his 'Silver Wedding.' Ten years later, after his 33rd visit he said a final goodbye. He died in Biarritz in 1909.

Meanwhile it is half past eight and I am still waiting for the guide outside the Grottes Bellevue. I watch as yet another a group of walkers arrives, says hello, and passes by without stopping. Most of them have helmets attached to their rucksacks. Another half hour, I say to myself. By nine o'clock, exasperated but relieved, I have just decided to go back to the hostel when a man arrives and introduces himself. Jean sports wraparound sunglasses, has the deeply tanned skin of somebody who spends his life outside, and evident self-confidence. Then again he is small, almost skeletal, not particularly muscular, and what remains of his hair is thin and snowy-white. He is carrying a tiny rucksack which seems to be half empty. He opens it and extracts a pair of crampons. Nobody has told him about the ice axe. In any case I won't need one, he says. He doesn't even have one for himself. Use your stick, he says. I don't dare ask about a hard hat. It is quite clear that there aren't any.

Jean is followed by a young couple and a family of four: father strolling along, mother red-faced and breathless, and teenage children bounding up the track. Mother announces that she is not going any further. Full stop. She will spend the day at the hostel.

The path leads us across rubble to the edge of the snow where we sit down to attach our crampons. Jean makes loops in his rope and passes them round our waists.

'The rope is a safety measure,' he insists. 'Crampons are a means of locomotion. In the Pyrenees, people often think that crampons are a safety measure, so they don't bother with a rope. If you go to the Alps you will never see climbers crossing a glacier without a rope. Just as you'll never see them walking alone.'

He leads, followed by the teenage daughter, the son, the father, me, a woman called Brigitte, and finally Gérard, her husband. Gérard is the only one of us with previous experience of glaciers.

We walk onto the snow. The crampons sink in and grip well. I can hear the sound of water gurgling under the crust: from time to time there are holes and we can see the stream. We arrive at the edge of the ice.

The glacier is uneven, and grey, like a semi-petrified lava flow. The ice has been crushed and churned, pushed and pulled, defrosted

Heading for Vignemale

and refrozen through thousands of years. Where it is in the shade, its surface is sharply chiselled into ice cubes, like a gigantic sheet of coarse sandpaper specially designed to polish hard mountain rocks – or like a cheese grater waiting to peel away soft human flesh. Where it is in the sun, it is slippery. Water is already dribbling down the slope.

'The most important thing is to walk with your toes pointing outwards,' says Jean. 'Otherwise you will catch your crampons in your trousers and fall over. Where it is slippery you need to stamp the crampons into the ice. It's called walking on ten spikes.' I look at mine. I can only see eight.

'I don't like this. It's not my kind of thing. I don't like heights,' says Brigitte as we progress up the western side of the glacier and the gradient increases. All the other groups, I notice, are following a snow drift on the opposite side.

'You'll be alright. It's not difficult,' says Jean. 'I've brought hundreds of people up here without a hitch. Just look at where you are putting your feet and you'll be alright.'

'When did you first come here?' I ask him.

'Over sixty years ago. Not to the top, at that time. Just to the hostel. The roof was made of stone and every winter the cement in the joints cracked so that it had to be repaired. When I was nine, I was packed off from the Pont d'Espagne alone with two mules. I had to go up and back again in the same day.'

The first few fissures are narrow and hardly noticeable. But then we arrive at a crevasse where we have to jump across. The opposite side is much higher.

'Jump as high as you can and plant your feet flat in the ice, one foot above the other. And then run up the slope like a duck without stopping to think. Don't try to use your toes,' advises Jean. He passes, the family passes, I pass, and then it is Brigitte's turn. She jumps, plants her two feet in the side and then stops there, frozen for an instant, before slipping into the void. It narrows rapidly so she finds herself wedged between the two sides a few metres below. She starts sobbing, shaking her head. Gérard and I haul her out by the rope. Her sleeveless black tee-shirt and sexy black Lycra shorts don't afford much protection: the knuckles of one hand are red and there are long bleeding gashes on her right arm and leg.

'It's not serious,' says Jean. 'But Steve and Gérard: you must keep the rope taut. Otherwise if she falls she will injure herself. The same applies to the rest of you.'

'I should never have come. I get vertigo. I don't want to go on,' complains Brigitte.

'Don't be stupid. You *did* say you wanted to come,' replies Gérard.

Brigitte hisses something under her breath.

The next obstacle is rather more difficult. The fissure is too wide to be jumped, but there is a vertical curtain of ice, hardly wider than my instep, which runs along the middle, lengthwise. From our side, we can jump to the end of the curtain easily enough but then we will have to walk along it, one foot in front of the other for several paces before it joins the other side.

Brigitte jumps onto the ledge: 'I can't move. I can't balance. My ice axe is too small.'

She is stuck at the end of the curtain, with a vertical drop on both sides, unable to move, held in a fragile equilibrium by the rope. Her husband and I pull it taut. She is right, her ice axe is useless. It is too short to reach the ground. What she needs is a stick, but we can't move to help her.

'Spread your arms out. It'll help you balance,' shouts Jean from the other end of the rope, but she doesn't budge. He scampers down the slope and passes her a stick which she wedges against the side of the fissure. When she reaches the other side she is trembling.

'I *really* would prefer to walk on the snow,' she pleads, pointing at the string of walkers casually following the standard route on the other side of the glacier.

'I prefer to walk on the ice,' answers Jean, firmly. 'It's less risky.'

'Don't be such a wimp. Let's get on with it,' grumbles her husband.

'It's no more dangerous than being on a city pavement with cars speeding past. It is just that you are not used to it,' I suggest, hopefully. She is unconvinced.

Brigitte has taken the role I had allotted myself. I was the one who was going to panic. But now, for me at least, the climb has become enjoyable.

I point out a couple of climbers spidering down the vertical south face of the Petit Vignemale and ask Jean about it. 'It's not difficult,' he claims. When pressed, he admits to having climbed the nearby Couloir de Gaube. This is *the* classic route up the north face of the Grand Vignemale. Only very experienced rock climbers attempt it.

Finally, we cross to the other side of the glacier and onto the snow. Sinking in at every step, the snow is much more tiring than the glacier, but we soon arrive at the foot of the rock face which separates us from the top. On our left I can see the entrance of the Grotte du Paradis and a lonely line of footprints climbing up a snow corridor.

Jean looks at the other groups descending from the summit: 'They're not making things easy for themselves. That's not the normal route,' he comments. 'All the better for us. We won't have to worry about stones falling on our heads. Take off your crampons and your gloves.'

We follow him up the cliff, hauling ourselves up with our hands, concentrating on the holds. After the glacier, it seems trivial. At one o'clock we are at the summit, sitting in a nest of rubble. All the other birds have flown. The sun is shining, the view extravagant, like yesterday. There is still no wind.

The return by the standard route, slithering across the ice and snow slurry, now more liquid than solid, is joyful. Taking off her crampons, Brigitte kisses her husband, beaming. She thanks Jean effusively: 'It was wonderful. I'm really glad I came. I was just a little bit worried at first but I'm really glad I did it!'

I stay in the Bayssellance hostel again.

Bayssellance hostel to Gavarnie

As I leave the hostel, the valley below me is full of cloud, its top surface sliced flat by the rising sun to reveal a hidden lining, reflecting the silver light. As I descend through the vapours, the sun rises, burning holes in the swirling mist, creating transient views of Vignemale and its glacier, now behind me. At the Ossoue dam, the clouds are thickening again but open up to allow me a last fleeting view of the mountain reflected in the dank lake.

By the time I reach Gavarnie it is raining hard. The famous

Marmotte *near to Gavarnie*

donkeys are lined up under their tarpaulin hangar. There are twenty or more, fully equipped with saddles, bridles, and stirrups expecting, it seems, a coach load of deranged but impermeable visitors to hire them and gallop off, *en masse*, to the *cirque*. The donkeys are none the happier for their day off. Nor is the shopkeeper opposite, looking out morosely from between his teddy bears and whistling polyester *marmottes*. I compare his shop with the one next door, trying to spot the differences. Identical teddy bears wear identical red berets. Perhaps there is a small difference in the range of sizes and prices. Similarly, there are plenty of possibilities of eating, but little choice. All the restaurants promise traditional local menus; all start with *garbure*. All are empty.

This is very unusual. Between 15 July and 15 September every year, the village sees 200,000 visitors. One thousand visitors for every inhabitant. Many don't get much further than the last café, stopping when they realise that the *cirque* is still an hour's walk away.

According to the tourist office, Gavarnie has maintained 'a balance between tradition and modernism. This valley has managed to preserve a certain authenticity, evolving in its ancient tradition of welcome (the rich invalids come to take the waters, the pioneers of mountaineering, the literary and political celebrities) and adapting it to the multitude of contemporary tourists' ... with all the finesse of a high-class call girl, her youth in the Parisian salons well behind her, adapting herself to the demands of a rugby team.

The rain slows a little so I walk up the valley out of the village towards the *cirque*. I am just behind a young couple, walking arm in arm.

'*Oh, la, la, que c'est beau* – it's so beautiful!' says the woman ecstatically, pointing to the river and the luxuriant vegetation. Her husband nods in agreement.

I pass by, but a few minutes later they catch me up at the humpback bridge.

'*Oh, la, la, la, que c'est beau!*' she exclaims, wide eyed.

At the foot of the waterfall I see them again.

'*Oh, la, la, la, la, que c'est beau!*' she says emphatically.

Irreverently, I imagine her and her husband making love. I can't see her keeping quiet.

Nevertheless, the *cirque* itself really *is* imposing, even when the heights are hidden in the clouds. It is an immense natural semicircle of vertical cliffs and horizontal ledges, carved out by glaciation, enclosed and dominated by some of the frontier's highest peaks. The *gave* bisecting the green valley floor, the stark rock face, the snow-covered scars, and the long, long waterfall have all contributed to the reputation of the *cirque* and its classification as a World Heritage Site. Victor Hugo called it variously nature's coliseum, a hippodrome, a Parthenon, a cathedral, boas rolled one above the other, the mouth of a volcano, a storm trap and, beginning to let his imagination run

Statue of Henry Russell outside Gavarnie

away just a little, a Tower of Babel turned over and imprinted in the earth like a seal.

The Romantic authors of the first half of the 19th century came here in order to view natural beauty, and in writing about it they defined it. Gavarnie was given a special place in the pantheon. Hugo's effusive admiration, the concord of other great French Romantics, and the pecuniary interests of the tourist industry have together created a myth. Gavarnie is not simply a stop on the traveller's route. It has become a holy place for mountain lovers. Indeed, for many people,

Gavarnie *is* the Pyrenees. Going to the Sanctuary of Notre Dame de Lourdes in the morning? Why not make a pilgrimage to one of the great natural wonders of the world in the afternoon? Bought a candle to remind you of the grotto in Lourdes? Buy a walking stick to remind you of the waterfall!

On the way back through the village to the hostel where I am going to stay the night I stop at the bookshop and weigh up the relative merits of guides to the Pyrenees. None are light enough. Then I go to look at the bronze statue of Russell which greets visitors on the road into the village. He is perched on a rock, a book in one hand, holding one of the inconveniently long walking sticks favoured at that time. The locals are justifiably proud of this work of art, symbolic of the role of Gavarnie in the conquest of the Pyrenees. However, they seem to have missed one obvious interpretation: Russell has his back turned to the village.

Gavarnie to Luz

It is going to be a long day, so I get up before dawn and sneak out quietly. The first glimpse of violet is just visible on the horizon but the stars are still twinkling; I switch on my head-torch. Like Russell, I turn my back on Gavarnie. As the sun rises, the undulating pastures are thrown into sharp relief. A red tractor is already heading for the half-mown meadow where yesterday morning's hay was abandoned to the rain in green-and-yellow corduroy stripes. The path runs horizontally, half-way up the hillside, overlooking a valley speckled with stone-built farmhouses and barns. Traditional stepped gables are complemented by corrugated metal roofs and satellite dishes.

The margins of my path are annotated like an antique cookery book. 'Add a few leaves of fresh water mint (from the side of the stream).' 'A bunch of marjoram (gathered from the *garrigue* just before it flowers) adds a musky perfume to any dish.' 'Carline thistles picked while still in bud can be used instead of artichokes. The golden flowers are inedible, but nailed to the door they will keep witches at bay.'

Later, walking through the forest, I look up. Many of the trees are festooned with white candy floss, the silky nests of caterpillars. I used to like the strikingly pretty pine processionary caterpillars which make them. Until, that is, I got to know them better.

They have a mottled brown body covered by a nice furry white duvet. But, however pretty they look, don't pick one up like I did to examine it more carefully. And don't touch the nests either. They sting, like stinging nettles, only more. Birds and other animals soon learn to avoid them. Thankfully, they are readily identifiable because, as the name suggests, they like travelling together, head to foot in a long convoy.

And travel they do. They are progressively eating their way across the Pyrenees. Their favourite meal is juicy pine needles. The trees where they live are reduced to a few yellowing spikes. In winter they forage at night, taking a siesta in their nest during the day, basking in the sunlight through the gaps in the leaf cover. In spring they journey down the trunk in search of suitable earth in which to make a cocoon, following each other in a long sinuous line. Although mature trees manage to survive their attacks, those which are heavily infested are desolate, as if some malevolent wind has randomly plucked at their foliage. It isn't clear why they have now started to proliferate, but the ONF is taking the threat seriously, bombarding them from helicopters.

As a result, I am rather relieved when I reach the edge of the forest and can follow a small stream to re-join the Gave de Pau. Here, the meadows are flat and parched, in contrast with their high-mountain neighbours. In the middle of one of them, a man is behaving very strangely, his jerky movements suggesting a mind and a body not quite in harmony. I watch him from a safe distance, just in case. He is picking up huge sheets of metal, raising them above his head, and then throwing them into the earth at his feet, cleaving the earth like a mad butcher. One, two, three. Pursuing his vengeance on the barren earth, he fetches a new set and attacks another part of the field. One, two, three sheets, making a thin rusty wall. Now, I can see that he has half a dozen of these walls distributed about the field. Water is seeping out round them, flooding out over the grass from invisible canals. So there *is* a logic in his madness: he is building miniature dams.

On the opposite side of the *gave*, water is also being harnessed. But the purpose is different, as is the scale. The purpose is electricity, and the scale is the scale of Greater London. The Pragnères hydroelectric power station is a concrete spider at the heart of a huge steel web of overhead pylons. But it is also the centre of a much larger and much prettier network of reservoirs: stretching from the Ossoue dam which I walked around yesterday to the Lac d'Aumar which I will reach in two days' time.

Later, I come to a junction where the different variants of the Pyrenean Way meet up again. Cauterets is only seven hours away by the direct route. It has taken me five days. Following the track in the other direction, away from Cauterets, I descend rustic stone steps to St-Sauveur, an outpost of Luz-St-Sauveur, and one of the most noteworthy of the Pyrenean spas of the 19th century.

The oppressive heat drives me on, to the Pont Napoléon, conceived in 1859, exactly 200 years after the signing of the Treaty of the Pyrenees. For the Pyrenees it was to be a momentous anniversary. In the eyes of Parisian society, the mountains burst into flower.

The flowers had been waiting their moment. The first tentative signs of the Pyrenean spring date to the Revolution when Ramond studied the botany and geology. Then the Romantics came, with Victor Hugo passing through in 1843. And in 1859 the railway network finally reached the foothills. Napoléon III and his Spanish wife Eugénie arrived on the inaugural voyage. It was their stay which triggered the Parisian interest.

Napoléon III had always paid great attention to developing France's infrastructure but the Pont Napoléon is more a monument to Imperial glory than of any real use. Now it serves mainly as a launching pad for bungee jumping. This seems to me to be particularly appropriate: in his youth, Napoléon had been something of an expert at metaphorical bungee jumping, launching into hair-raising adventures which bounced back on him, taking part in various attempts to seize power.

Victor Hugo was one of the MPs who stood up against him. He portrayed Napoléon III as '*Napoléon le petit*' and questioned his legitimacy, not only as head of state, but also as a member of the Bonaparte clan. 'The child of chance, whose name is a theft and whose birth a fake,' he wrote. Which brings us back to the Pyrenees, the summer of 1807 and the visit to Gavarnie of Napoléon's future mother Hortense de Beauharnais. The notoriously unfaithful Hortense, who made no secret of her marital problems, described her stay at the Hôtel des Voyageurs in Gavarnie as one of the happiest of her life.

Whatever his ancestry, the direct legacy of Napoléon's visit was a mixed bag: although the bridge was unnecessary, the *routes thermales* which he financed were a real boon. The roads not only linked the spas but also provided access to the great natural resources of the Pyrenees: timber and minerals. Now in the 21st century, the Pyrenees have changed vocation. The *routes thermales* have been re-baptised the *route des cols* and are now mainly known for the high passes familiar to Tour de France cyclists: the Aubisque, the Tourmalet, and others.

It was also under Napoléon III that the frontier with Spain was finally defined in the optimistically entitled *Acte final de délimitation* of 1868.

Today, the Pont Napoléon is flanked by an assortment of souvenir shops and cheap cafés. My legs are no longer elastic so I slump heavily onto a white plastic seat under a sunshade in front of one of the cafés. I have just ordered my beer and ice cream, when the inevitable miniature rubber-tyred tourist train rolls up. The waitress is slow and the train driver has already rung his bell, bellowed something unintelligible, and disappeared before I have finished my beer. So I am condemned to more walking: down the main road, then along a track, which irrationally climbs again, although Luz is well below me. The advantage of this route is the view of the town below. It is also sig-

nificant for another reason. On a bluff overlooking the town of Luz I pass in front of the Solferino Chapel, another relic of Napoléon's visit, built to commemorate the Emperor's recent victory at Solferino in northern Italy.

I limp down to Luz, capital of the *Toy* district in the blistering mid-afternoon heat. *Toy*, originally *thôys* in Gascon, is a child or youngster. Perhaps it was a reference to the stunted growth of the malnourished mountain dwellers.

In the evening I go to a concert in the fortified church of St André. The building is surrounded by crenellated walls, with a tall gate tower through which all visitors must pass. Inside, the men – it is a male-voice choir – are dressed in coordinated shades of brown – jackets and trousers, bow ties and berets – set off by stiff white shirts. They start with *Se canto, que cante?* – It sings, what does it sing? a popular Occitan song known throughout the length of the Pyrenees. It is followed by *l'Adour* (a local river), *Le Pic du Midi* (the nearest mountain), *Le Pays Toy* (their own composition), and a traditional Basque medley. They sing in perfect polyphonic harmony, in French and in the local dialect.

The conductor turns round to explain something of the choir's history. The *Orphéon*, he says, was founded in 1888. In recent years they have sung in Germany and Greece. But, he complains, there is only one singer who is under 55, and he is the son of another chorister. I look at the audience: it seems to be largely composed of tourists.

Barèges

I get up late and trundle down to the tourist office in Luz to meet Raymonde.

She drives me up the Barèges valley along the road to the col de Tourmalet, overtaking panting cyclists wishing to measure themselves against the greats. She parks the van at a hairpin bend and strides off in front of me towards the Pic du Midi de Bigorre, pointing out the

nificant for another reason. On a bluff overlooking the town of Luz I pass in front of the Solferino Chapel, another relic of Napoléon's visit, built to commemorate the Emperor's recent victory at Solferino in northern Italy.

I limp down to Luz, capital of the *Toy* district in the blistering mid-afternoon heat. *Toy*, originally *thôys* in Gascon, is a child or youngster. Perhaps it was a reference to the stunted growth of the malnourished mountain dwellers.

In the evening I go to a concert in the fortified church of St André. The building is surrounded by crenellated walls, with a tall gate tower through which all visitors must pass. Inside, the men – it is a male-voice choir – are dressed in coordinated shades of brown – jackets and trousers, bow ties and berets – set off by stiff white shirts. They start with *Se canto, que cante?* – It sings, what does it sing? a popular Occitan song known throughout the length of the Pyrenees. It is followed by *l'Adour* (a local river), *Le Pic du Midi* (the nearest mountain), *Le Pays Toy* (their own composition), and a traditional Basque medley. They sing in perfect polyphonic harmony, in French and in the local dialect.

The conductor turns round to explain something of the choir's history. The *Orphéon*, he says, was founded in 1888. In recent years they have sung in Germany and Greece. But, he complains, there is only one singer who is under 55, and he is the son of another chorister. I look at the audience: it seems to be largely composed of tourists.

Barèges

I get up late and trundle down to the tourist office in Luz to meet Raymonde.

She drives me up the Barèges valley along the road to the col de Tourmalet, overtaking panting cyclists wishing to measure themselves against the greats. She parks the van at a hairpin bend and strides off in front of me towards the Pic du Midi de Bigorre, pointing out the buildings of the Observatory on top of the hill. We have arranged to meet a shepherd in his *estive*. An hour later, we find Laurent and his wife Christine surrounded by a flock of sheep. Laurent has one wedged between his legs and is applying a cream to its gums which are caked with blood and soil. He lets it go, scans the flock, and threads his way through the wool. Suddenly he leaps forward, like a rugby player, grabbing a sheep by the horn.

'Real shepherds don't need crooks,' he claims. 'You've just got to be quick.'

Laurent, who must be in his 50s, has pepper-and-salt hair and a full beard. He is wearing a bright purple tee-shirt and has a pair of binoculars strung round his neck. He has 141 ewes, 6 rams, and 10 wethers (castrated rams), and comes up from his farm twice a week to check them out. Here, sheep are bred for their meat so they don't need the daily milking required by their Ossau-Iraty sisters. This morning he and his wife set out at five o'clock and, with their two dogs, Filou and Anise, have just finished rounding up the flock.

'They roam over an area of about 2sq km but I put salt cakes down here so most of them stay pretty close. When I brought them up from the valley in May they were grazing near where you parked the van but they climb higher as the snows melt.'

'You haven't shorn them yet. When I was in the Basque country they were being shorn in June,' I comment.

'No. We shear them in the autumn, when they come back down. Not too short, of course.' He uses the traditional scissors. 'If we did it in spring they wouldn't have enough protection from the weather up here.'

The sheep each have a label attached to one ear, with a number to indicate the *département*, the village, the farmer, the year of its birth, and its birth rank. This one, I can see, was the 14th lamb to be born in 2002.

'It means that you can trace the lamb you find on the butcher's slab back to the farm where it grew up. I have to keep a record of every sheep and if the inspector comes, I have to be able to produce each and every one of them.' He gets a subsidy of 20€ per year per sheep.

'What about the bears?' I ask.

'Did you see the Tour de France on the television the other night?'

'No.'

'I was there blocking the road. Papillon [a bear who died recently] cost the state 3,000€ per day when you add up the cost of the staff, the helicopter, and so on. And the compensation for sheep killed is pitiful. I would get about 250€ for the sale of a sheep. But if it is killed by a bear I would only get 150€, and losses from miscarriages don't get counted. Also, you've got to prove that the sheep was killed by a bear. How do you do that when the vultures clean everything up within a few hours? The only thing that the vultures won't eat is a sheep which has been killed by lightning, or by a viper.' He stops to grab another sheep and inspects its belly. 'When it's a viper, they turn blue,' he adds.

Asked about the financial side of sheep rearing, he tells me that he gets 4€/kilo because his sheep are *appellation contrôlée*, but this has extra costs: he can't use fertiliser for his winter hay and he can't use silage either. But if he didn't submit to the quality control he would only get 2€/kilo.

Some of the sheep have a semicircular mini-skirt of sacking stitched into the wool around their rear quarters.

'It's a chastity belt. Those sheep are due for slaughter this autumn so I don't want them to get pregnant. Normally, sheep farmers give them a chemical contraceptive but it's not allowed in organic farming.'

He comes from a long line of sheep farmers, but says that he will be the last of them.

'My son used to be interested in sheep until he found a girlfriend,' he muses.

We are preparing to go back down the hill when he asks me what I am doing here.

'The Pyrenean Way.'

'I hate walking. You'll never find me on Vignemale or at the Brèche de Roland. I do it because I have to for my work.'

On the way back in the van I ask Raymonde about the economic significance of sheep farming.

'It's just folklore,' she replies.

She drops me off at a café for lunch and I then spend a happy afternoon in the botanical gardens looking at plants I have seen in the mountains and putting names to them. Overhead, red and blue hang-gliders pirouette. Afterwards, I trudge back down the road to Barèges.

In the afternoon sun, the spa of Barèges looks pretty and welcoming, but it harbours a dark history. It is not simply a long thin village clinging to the hill slope alongside a river. It is also an internationally notorious avalanche zone. Avalanches are a problem throughout the Pyrenees, but the Barèges avalanches were an extreme case. It was hit in 1803 (11 dead), then in 1811, 1842, 1855 (12 dead), and 1856. However it was the avalanche of 1860 which finally made the authorities react. Just a year after the visit of the imperial couple Napoleon III and Eugénie to the village, the military hospital caring for some of the wounded from Solferino was destroyed.

The engineer Lomet had visited Barèges as early as 1794 and concluded that deforestation was the cause of the disasters:

In the past, all the mountains which overlooked Barèges were covered in oak… Men still living saw the few remaining trees and finished them off. The inhabitants of the plateau have destroyed everything themselves because these slopes, being the first to be freed of snow by the sun and by avalanches, provide the first spring pasture for their sheep. The day they take them there, they forget that at home in the winter they have shivered with the fear of being carried away by the avalanches which they have stubbornly provoked.

So replanting became a priority. In parallel, the military authorities conducted a series of experiments. The building of stone walls turned out to be the most successful idea, stopping the avalanche of a small area from dragging a larger area in its wake. Meanwhile the village continued to suffer further disasters, in 1879, 1882, 1886, 1889, 1895, 1897, 1902, 1907, and 1939, becoming almost synonymous with the word avalanche.

In Barèges there is a saying '*Un Toy ne craint que Dieu, les orages, et l'avalanche* – The inhabitants of the valleys fear only God, thunderstorms, and avalanches.'

Despite all appearances, it isn't the snow sliding down the mountains that causes the problem. Snow has always slid down mountains. When the Pyrenees were only inhabited by a few shepherds, avalanches were unimportant. The zones where they seemed likely were simply avoided.

In fact, avalanches are a man-made problem. It was only when the Pyrenees started to be occupied all year round that avalanches started to kill significant numbers. Then there was the exploitation of mineral wealth, with disastrous consequences for the miners of the Société des Mines d'Arre et d'Anglas. And the construction of the hydroelectric dams from the beginning of the 20th century had its share of disasters. But the main problem in the 20th century was the phenomenon of winter sports, growing prodigiously from 1960, and bringing with it both white gold and black marble.

In January 2005, two skiers took a short cut off-piste, just where I have been walking today. Only one survived. An eyewitness wrote on the Web:

> I work at the ski resort of Barèges… Once the rescue was organised, the dogs took nearly 30 minutes to find the son. Unfortunately it was too late… I ask you once again to be prudent. That day many people, including me, were carried away by avalanches.

The zone is known as one of the most dangerous in the area. The risk factor announced on the weather forecast was 4 out of 5. This, then, was a tragedy in the original sense of the word – a fate foretold. Yet at the same time, this professional was skiing in an equally hazardous zone. *And* he is asking others to be careful.

At the hostel in the evening, I meet somebody else who practices a dangerous sport, one of the men who was hang-gliding over my head at the botanical gardens.

'Three descents today from the col de Tourmalet down to the botanical gardens. I'm tired. It's not the hang gliding. It's carrying the kit to the launch point,' he tells me. 'I've been hang gliding for the past 15 years. Since I retired.'

Barèges to the Lac d'Orédon

In the morning, I shamelessly take a taxi back up to the botanical gardens, and then follow the path as it leaves the road and climbs the valley, visiting a series of small lakes, traversing fertile pastures, passing under twisted *pins à crochets*. After an hour's walking I am overtaken by a man in blue overalls. He is off to build a sheep fold on the plateau, he says. When I arrive, he has just woken up his colleagues who have camped the night: they are standing outside their tents, stretching and yawning.

Higher up, at the Lac de Madamète I sit down by the shore, take off my tee-shirt, and let the sun soak into my back. In the stillness, I can hear the blood circulating through my ears. From time to time tiddlers jump out of the shallows: plut, plop. The unnaturally smooth reflection of the sky in the lake is an prefect indigo. Opposite me three chestnut horses with white socks are munching steadily inside a temporary electric fence, their hooves leaving deep prints in the soft peat. Nearby there are a couple of tents but no other signs of life.

I struggle up to the Col de Madamète which separates the rivers which flow into the Gave de Pau from those which flow into the Neste d'Aure. This is not only a physical watershed but also a linguistic one.

Twin lakes: Aumar and Aubert

The passes are no longer *hourquettes* but *cols* and the rivers, the *gaves*, have turned into *nestes*.

I lumber down to the Lac d'Aumar and its twin the Lac d'Aubert. Our cartographers had a field day here. Both *au* and *mar* can mean lake so Lac d'Aumar could mean Lake of the Lake Lake, which makes the Lac d'Aubert, Lake of the Green Lake seem quite sensible.

I meet increasing numbers of day trippers as I approach the lakes. You wouldn't know it, but this is a nature reserve. Created in 1935, the Néouvielle Nature Reserve was once an isolated granite massif, freckled even in mid-summer by patches of snow – hence the name, meaning old snow. It has since become a major tourist attraction. Unlike the Lac de Gaube and the Cirque de Gavarnie, which are on the edge of the central part of the national park, these two lakes are in the very centre of the nature reserve. Their isolation was eroded by the creation of the road access for building the nearby reservoir at Cap de Long and then eradicated by the construction of a road specifically for tourists in 1970. Nowadays, each summer, the nature reserve has to cope with 150,000 visitors and their cars.

I follow the path down to the Lac d'Orédon where I book into the hostel for the night.

Lac d'Orédon to St-Lary

In the forest dawn, I hear a strange feral barking but it stops after a while so I continue. I reach the first pass before the sun and look down on the Lac d'Oule, another reservoir built in the first half of the 20th century. Just as snow had earlier become *or blanc*, the mountain streams were nicknamed *huile blanche* – white oil – oil being *the* symbol of unexpectedly discovered wealth in a world where the motor car was just beginning to make an impact.

On the hill opposite and overlooking the valley, the scenery is rather less natural. The ski resort of Le Pla d'Adet resembles a fortress or perhaps a prison: white, rectilinear, forbidding. The view *from* Le Pla d'Adet is said to be stupendous.

I walk through the comfortably old Vielle Aure to the less comfortably new St-Lary-Soulan. The decidedly modern church sets the tone. Its predecessor, dedicated to St Hilaire – hence, by deformation, the name of the village – was demolished in 1949. The replacement, with its vertical lines and steeply sloping roofs over the aisles, looks like a space ship ready to transport the faithful directly to heaven when the last trumpet sounds. Inside, it is a different story. Covering the whole wall behind the altar, a painting shows Christ rising between snow-capped mountain peaks. Below the mountains, the artist has painted a harshly rectilinear concrete maze. For him, this was the (difficult) path to resurrection. The mayor at that time evidently thought the same about his village.

At the time that the church was being rebuilt, the population of St-Lary was only a couple of hundred. The pastoral way of life and the ancient stone buildings were crumbling. Although the road from the plain continued a few kilometres beyond the village before petering out at the end of the valley, it only served a few insignificant hamlets. In the late 1940s, the construction of the dams had brought a short-lived boom to the village but the end of that was also in sight. The prospects of tourist development were remote: the village didn't have the necessary slopes for a ski resort, or the springs for a spa.

Now, 60 years later, the village has been resurrected. It has a permanent population of 1024 and numerous shops. Now, the road continues into Spain through a tunnel, bringing skiers in winter and clients for the spa in summer. St-Lary-Soulan has become the biggest ski resort in the Pyrenees with 545,000 skier-days per year. Permanent residents, should they decide to sleep around, could each have the choice of 24 different tourist beds.

The village's new found dynamism is celebrated in the name of its high street: rue Vincent Mir. Mir was personally responsible for changing the destiny of St-Lary. A well-known rugby player, in an area where rugby is *the* sport, and a resistance worker, he was elected mayor shortly after the Second World War. His first major project was the creation of a ski resort and his great achievement was to negotiate the cooperation of neighbouring communes to the extent that St-Lary was able to devour the commune of Soulan in 1963. (The name Soulan derives from *soulane*, the sunny side of the mountain, a name which explains to some extent the popularity of the resort.)

His second achievement was the construction of the Aragnouet–Biclsa tunnel. The first contacts were made in 1956 but it was 1976 before the first cars emerged from the tunnel, the only border crossing for a distance of more than 80km.

In the meantime his daughter Isabelle had become an international skier, training with the 1968 Olympic team on the slopes above her home town and going on to win a silver medal. The slope where the team practised commemorates the exploit with an ingenious reworking of her name: it is called the *piste* Mirabelle.

But the village lacked a summer season to compare with its winter bustle. What it lacked was a spa. The Thermes de St-Lary were duly opened in 1988; the water comes from the Sources de la Garet, way up the valley. As if this wasn't enough, the Maison de l'Ours was opened in 1991. As well as a multi-media experience, the exhibition includes Bingo and Apollon, two brown bears, rescued from a circus where they were being badly treated. At least, in this small concrete-walled prison, they are looked after.

So the village found its path to redemption through a maze of concrete. But there is a down-side. Even the victors in a rugby match leave the field with bruises and St-Lary-Soulan and its mayor are no exceptions. By the time of Mir's retirement the town was heavily in debt; in 1991 his business – specialising in public buildings and works – was placed in liquidation. Then there are the holiday houses, 4000 of them, empty for most of the year. And whilst there are some ancient buildings, many of the shop fronts on the high street look as though they would be happier with neon lights.

I go into one of the shops, the newsagents. Above the comics, above the cookery and health magazines, above the girlie magazines, there is a blown-up model. All the folds, all the curves, all the secret corners. The Pyrenees from head to foot in vivid three-dimensional splendour. Pornographic cartography. The lurid colours, the insistence on detail, and the plastic moulding are all revoltingly crude, like a plastic carp which sings as you walk by. But I want one nevertheless. Unfortunately, it won't fit discreetly into my back pocket. It won't even fit into my rucksack. I will have to send for it by mail order. I hope it arrives in plain packaging.

I am constrained to walking along a road this morning, but at least it provides me with some amusement. It is bordered by concrete wall posts capped by giant dice balanced on one corner in a perpetual unstable equilibrium. Some of the dice will fall on a six, but not all of them. Did the owner of the house pay for it with a win on the National Lottery? Are they there to bring luck in the future? In the garden, a grey-haired woman is deadheading her carnations.

'I don't know why they are there,' she tells me. 'It was the builder's idea.' She pauses to think: 'No, I don't know why. We had the house built 40 years ago. But I've never thought about it before you asked.'

Finally leaving the road, my path ambles slowly up to the top of the hill and then dives down the other side. My right knee says: 'Beware'! I stop, wait, then continue carefully down into the valley of the Louron to the village of Loudenvielle. Here, the designer-Pyrenees are safe, lush, and carpeted, like at Arrens-Marsous. Around Balnéa, the spa, even the grass is manicured.

According to the posters, Balnéa eschews any pretensions to medical utility to concentrate on soft-focus self-indulgence. The Héliantis pool, for example, is described as 'a playground in a unique wooden décor inspired by the Hoogan huts of North American Indians... Fun and laughter assured!' But it is closed for renovation so I continue, grumpily.

I have just left the village when my knee speaks again, this time shouting: 'No!' Tendonitis. Every time I jar my leg – almost every other step – I get an incapacitating pain. I carry on gingerly, wondering whether I should go back down to the village and get a taxi back to St-Lary-Soulan. The pain returns intermittently, unpredictably, and I make halting progress towards the hostel in Germ. Then one of my front teeth falls out. Unlike my leg, it doesn't give me any warning, but I eventually find it under the ferns, wipe it clean, and stick it in my pocket. I had a croquet accident 30 years ago, and the resulting gap was repaired with a crown. Why now? I'm falling apart. I dismiss the pain in my left arm spreading across my chest – I don't want to know – and look miserably up towards the hostel.

The Centre de Montagne de Germ, as it is called, is somewhat more than a hostel, as I discover, a little restored by a cup of tea. It has English-style gardens with pink peonies, hollyhocks, a freshly cut hay-smelling lawn, deck chairs, and a swimming pool.

In the evening a party of kids with hyperactivity problems invades the dining room, so the meal is gluten-free. Thankfully, for those who can eat it, there is some bread, so we walkers stuff ourselves on it.

At my table there are two men who are walking from Barèges to Luchon. Like Paul, they are tax inspectors but unlike him, they want to talk about it. They seem anxious to know what I might think of the French taxation system. They ask me to compare the English and French models. In detail. Like off-duty policemen, they really want me to say: 'It's a dirty job, but we like you really.'

Germ to the Granges d'Astau

On the way through the village I pass in front of a roadside oratory 'built and restored in memory of an ancestor killed by wolves'. I walk slowly, resting five minutes every half hour in an effort to save my knees. I am beginning to wonder if they really are clinically deformed: after all, despite fierce competition, I did win the first prize in my scout troop's knobbly knee contest, at the age of 15.

The path rises through heathers and ferns. There are prickly juniper bushes and long spikes of white asphodel and, further up, patches of alpine birdsfoot trefoil, in flower, sprinkled with seductive miniature red-and-yellow lips. The few rhododendrons are past their best.

I slip into the next valley and meet a young man wearing hipster jeans, accompanied by a collie dog. His face is white with sun cream, and he is out of breath from the climbing. He is a shepherd he tells me, waving his crook to confirm it. He is going on to the upper pasture where he will take a siesta. His flock, lower down the valley will make its own way up when it has finished dozing. A quarter of an hour later I find the sheep and a few goats, not dozing but grazing next to the Cabane du Val d'Esquierry. On top of a prominent rock a magnificent brown Billy goat looks at me suspiciously. I approach the flock and the nearest sheep move away, bells ringing in alarm. Suddenly, from behind me, I hear loud barking. I turn round and see a large white dog, showing all its teeth, eyeing my bare legs. *Patous* are not dangerous, I have been told, *unless* you come between them and their flock. I freeze, wondering what the etiquette is in this situation. He is certainly handsome – bulky but at the same time elegant, with a long wavy white coat, almost silky in appearance. But what impresses me most is his teeth.

Brought up with the flock as a puppy, a *patou* will protect it from attack (and even from innocent walkers – clearly, they don't like human company). Until the 19th century they were a common sight in the mountains but with the disappearance of predators their numbers dwindled. In 2006 there were only an estimated 66 in the Pyrenees. Although the name derives from the Occitan *pastre*, shepherd, they are not sheep dogs, strictly speaking. They don't round up sheep; collies are better at that. But when the flock moves to a new pasture the *patou* will precede it, looking for any danger. In a fight with a bear they would have no chance, but bears are rare. The real purpose of *patous* is to frighten off stray dogs.

Some shepherds are hostile to the idea of *patous*. Their return to the Pyrenees is financed by the scheme to reintroduce bears, and the shepherds don't wish to be bribed by the grants for purchase, vaccination, training, and even upkeep. In any case, experiences with *patous* have been mixed, some being too aggressive towards humans, others not staying with their flocks.

My *patou* is definitely staying with his flock. I hardly dare move. I apologise profusely to him and shuffle away stiffly. The barking stops.

The Pyrenean Way tumbles through a luminous forest, the sun painting the leaves a garish green, highlighting the tree roots as they slither across the path and attempt to trip me up.

Arriving at the Granges d'Astau, down in the valley, I am confronted by a large car park swarming with cars and camper vans, a souvenir shop, a restaurant, a bar, and a hostel. Amidst all this clamour I am surprised to see a quiet little oratory: 'restored in 1959' reads the inscription over the door. The front wall, under a projecting roof, has a painting labelled St Jacobus, St Jacques, suggesting that the oratory is dedicated to him. But although many people walk through the Granges d'Astau, this is certainly not one of the Chemins de St Jacques. The passes over to Spain are all very high and blocked by glaciers and the visitors return to the car park at the end of the day.

The oratory is one of those chapels which you can't enter but which you can inspect through a metal grill in the door. Inside, the walls are painted with figures from the Bible. All the usual iconography but with a marvellous medieval simplicity of line and colour – warm ochre, pale worn-out blue-grey, and dark mysterious green. This, for me at least, is more spiritual than any amount of baroque gold work in more recent edifices like the chapel of Our Lady near Arrens-Marsous. Here, on the wall at the back of the altar is a young Christ, the good shepherd, sitting on a rock amid lambs and sheep (after all, we are in the Pyrenees). To my left is Mary sitting on a throne balanced precariously on the top of a mountain, with the infant Jesus on her lap. Underneath is the Latin text *Mater dei custode nos in montibus* – mother of God, protect us in the mountains. This beautiful medieval chapel is completed with a couple of saints I have never heard of: St Germana Cousin and St Aventinus.

St Germana is holding her apron in front of her and letting the flower heads in it fall to the ground. St Aventinus has just overpowered a bear, saving a choir boy and a couple of worried-looking peasants.

I wonder who these saints are and why they are depicted here, but nobody can tell me, so when I get home I investigate further.

Oratory at the Granges d'Astau

St Aventinus is here because he was a local lad. He had his hermitage an hour's walk away, near what is now the village of St-Aventin. He was killed by the Saracens in 732. The connection with bears and choir boys remains obscure, though the village is still bear territory: a thoroughly modern bear (with a transmitter attached) passed through the commune in July 2006.

St Germana, I discover, was a shepherdess. She is here in the guise of patron saint of shepherds. The flowers falling from her apron? Crumbs of bread. Mistreated by her mother-in-law, she was accused of hiding stolen bread in her apron but when forced to open it – miraculously – rose flowers fell out. Her other claim to fame was that her body didn't rot after her death, in 1601. She was canonised in 1867. 1867? So the paintings I had taken to be medieval cannot be more

St Germaina Cousin and St Aventinus

than 130 years old? They were painted for the benefit of tourists, not pilgrims. It doesn't detract from their beauty but I feel cheated.

Granges d'Astau to the Lac d'Espingo

Replete after a large breakfast, I bypass the barrier which stops cars from going any further and follow the track as it climbs through the forest. There are regular path-side updates on progress, giving the distance from Luchon, the nearest spa: La Roche Soufrée, altitude 1220m, 14km 350m, Lacets de la Régulatrice, altitude 1442m, 15km 200m. *Lacets de la régulatrice* means the controller's shoelaces. The identity of the controller is not divulged, nor her role, but her shoelaces are visible ahead of me: the zigzag track which leads to the famous Lac d'Oô. Although there is nobody else around at present, later in the day the track will be full of tourists, as it has been for the last 150 years or so.

Walking up the Lacets, I can hear a regular dull hammering. As I approach the lake the noise becomes shriller and more defined: steel against stone. When I leave the forest, I can see the source of the racket: a pneumatic drill. The bridge over the river (altitude 1490m, 16km 200m) is being repaired. One of the workmen is struggling to start a concrete mixer in the dry river bed. The hostel on the other side is still slumbering, with deckchairs and sunloungers piled up against one wall.

When Ramond first came here at the end of the 18th century, only the village, way down in the valley below, was known as Oô. The lake was known as Lac Séculéjo and the waterfall which feeds it as the Pich de Séculéjo. They soon became the object of excursions from the increasingly genteel spa town of Luchon. The name Pich de Séculéjo was unintelligible to the first visitors who understood nothing of the local Occitan dialect. Until some playful soul let out the dreadful truth. Pich in Occitan can mean 'piss'. This was evidently too much for Parisian ladies. The Pich became the Cascade and the lake was renamed Oô. But what the valley lost in vulgarity it gained in tautology. Oô can mean 'lake'. Yet another Lake Lake was born.

A few steps beyond the bridge and its pneumatic drill I glimpse a tiny pond girdled by a wide grey band of gravel and loose rock. Above the stony girdle, the mountains are as they should be, and the pond itself replicates them faithfully, but the effect is ruined by the dreary grey scar. Even the waterfall is looking rather wan. This is said to be one of the most dazzling vistas of the Pyrenees, reproduced in innumerable postcards. I don't remember the photographs looking like this.

I walk on a little and sit down to eat a snack by the lake. Looking back, I can see the small concrete barrier which dams the valley and holds back the waters. Only, it isn't holding back any water at all now.

The bottom of the dam is exposed to the air and the lake is a couple of metres lower still, so that it must be about as big as it was before the construction of the dam; indeed, as big as it was when the first tourists arrived. Can this pathetic lake really have impressed them so much?

This summer, the reservoir has been emptied for the benefit of the plains around Toulouse and the sun has done the rest. The tide is out. This is not a diurnal pattern but an annual one, with a high tide – 12m higher to judge by the measuring stick attached to the back of the dam – in the spring, and a low tide at the end of the summer. Undoubtedly it also makes life easier for the workers repairing the bridge.

The workman has finally managed to start his concrete mixer, joining the pneumatic drill in a discordant duet. All in all, the original names for the waterfall seems reasonably appropriate.

I am ambling along a path paved with large flat stones, making walking easy, when I am rapidly overtaken by a couple of young men. As they pass, I notice that one of them has a small red portable fire extinguisher attached to the outside of his rucksack. Could they be heavy smokers, afraid of setting fire to the dry vegetation? Could they be apprentice arsonists, lighting fires, letting them burn until they are nearly out of control and then drowning them under a cloud of carbon dioxide? Perhaps they are apprentice fire-fighters. Same scenario, marginally different motivations. I try to catch them up to ask but they are going too fast. Eventually I decide that they must be afflicted by the increasing paranoia surrounding the bears: they have come up with an unusual defence in case of attack.

Higher up, on the terrace of the hostel at Espingo, it is a different, more peaceful world. I eat a second breakfast, *crêpes* and *café au lait*, while gazing at the irregular lake, the sluggish streams which feed it, and the uncompromising cliffs beyond, slightly softened by the enduring snow. I am going to sleep here tonight. For the last two days, I have been resting frequently to spare my knee and to stop any

Sheep near the refuge d'Espingo

further dental attrition. But it is only 9 o'clock and I can leave most of my kit here. The Lac du Portillon is a mere two hours away and, according to the hostel manager, there is not too much snow on the path so, despite the lack of a proper map, I continue.

On top of a rock at the side of the path there is an abandoned hat. I am just about to pick it up when Tax Inspector No. 1 appears and reclaims it. His sudden emergence out of nowhere surprises me. It is almost as if the hat were a bait and I have just been caught in a sting, revealing the source of my lavish lifestyle. However, he merely tells me that Tax Inspector No. 2 has gone on to Luchon today but that he himself has decided to go up the valley. Then he tells me that he *only* likes walking in valleys, not climbing peaks, which makes me suspicious again. I walk slowly to let him get ahead of me, keeping an eye on his progress so that I don't catch up, but then he disappears and I am left wondering if he is going to leap out from behind a rock, this time brandishing a copy of my last year's tax return.

The path merges into scree but I can see the snow-filled valley which leads up to the lake above. I can't see any tracks, but the route is pretty obvious. From time to time, I can hear water under the snow so I use my stick to see if it will support my weight. I make slow progress, sometimes clambering on rocks to avoid the biggest drifts. The valley gets progressively narrower and, although I can see the rudiments of a path chiselled into the steep side a few metres away, the snow banked against it prevents me from going any further. I am obliged to climb up a small but dangerously friable cliff to the plateau where the Portillon hostel stands next to the lake.

In the hostel I am served a Desperate Dan portion of *tartiflette*, half a loaf of bread, and a jug of wine. Despite the succulent potatoes, the gooey cheese, and my considerable hunger, I fail to finish off the *tartiflette* and make no impact whatsoever on the bread.

After lunch, lying uncomfortably on the rocks outside, I chat to Tax Inspector No. 1. He really does like looking at mountains he tells me, but doesn't feel any urge to master them. On a trekking holiday in Nepal he climbed passes at over 4000m – higher than any summits in the Pyrenees – and greatly enjoyed himself. He also tells me where to find the correct path, without suggesting that I am completely incompetent and a danger to myself and to anybody else who might have to come to rescue me. He's quite likeable really. He is called Christian.

Next to the hostel, the lake itself is still partly frozen. From here up to the frontier ridge much of the slope is covered with snow and ice though the glaciers look less extensive than on my rather sketchy map.

My knee hasn't complained again. Back at the Espingo hostel in good time, I take a siesta. For the rest of the day I chat to other walkers and wander around, aimlessly contented.

In the morning, I double back along the other side of the valley I climbed yesterday. Below in the night-shrouded valley, the Lac d'Oô is jet black, but today its rocky, off-white girdle suggests to me an altogether brighter interpretation: a tropical lagoon enclosed by a coral reef. The path climbs steadily to the Hourquette des Hounts-Secs, the pass of the dry springs. Having looked at the map last night, I have brought large quantities of water with me. I don't want to run out: I have been told that my knee problem might be due to dehydration, so I drink copiously. As a result, I stop frequently, marking the Pyrenean Way like a dog.

At the Coume de Bourg I finally emerge into the sunny sheep pastures to find a near-naked man lying on the ground at the side of the path, sunbathing. He tells me that he has been taking '*une petite promenade digestive* – a little walk to aid his digestion'. His car is 5km away at the ski resort of Superbagnères. Yes, it was a good breakfast, he agrees.

Continuing on towards Luchon, I can see the peaks on the frontier backlit by the sun, ranged in formidable rows, surging towards me, their black crests crashing down over the grey slopes, like waves breaking in the once-again-molten rocks at the end of time. Aneto, the highest rock of them all at 3404m, must be floundering around somewhere in there but I can't make out which one it is.

An unexpected noise startles me and the sunbather leaps past. 'Sorry,' he says. 'I didn't mean to frighten you,' and races ahead. He is wearing what looks like a woman's one-piece swimsuit, but what is probably the latest thing in running gear. My chances of arriving at Superbagnères in time to hitch a lift from him seem remote.

A little while later, at the wire fence which marks the edge of the resort I see a new sign placed prominently in view of those who might wish to leave the resort's well-trodden meadows. It warns: 'Walkers, you are entering an area of high mountains, without safety barriers.

You must have the knowledge and the equipment to assure your own safety.' The top half of the panel has small drawings of a friendly *isard* and a grouse. The bottom half shows a menacing bear and, separately, an unfortunate walker sliding uncontrollably down a steep mountain slope. A cynical attempt to protect the owners of the ski resort from possible legal action?

The plateau is dotted with what used to be called *canons à neige artificielle*, but on reading a notice I see, in passing, that they have been renamed *enneigeurs* and their output is now called *neige de culture*. A semantic twist: instead of firing (nasty) artificial snow from (nasty military) cannons, the resort is now cultivating it, in snow makers. I am re-entering 'civilisation': a place where words are *written* and where connotations are considered. Evidently, the Cascade d'Oô, the new name of the Pich de Séculéjo, was merely the preface.

It is hot, I am tired, and there is nothing worse for tendonitis than a long knee-thumping descent with a heavy rucksack. The town of Luchon is much lower down, through a forest with nothing to recommend it. So I sit on a wooden railing at the side of the road at Superbagnères, waiting for cars to come by. Opposite me is an immense cruise-liner hotel with a string of small shops and kiosks floating in its wake, but they are all firmly closed. There are twenty or so forlorn cars in the car park but nobody around. After half an hour no cars have passed and I have just resigned myself to walking when an elderly couple strolls up to me. To my disappointment they only ask me about short walks in the vicinity, with the result that we are studying the map, deep in conversation, when I see my salvation driving by.

But the forest is not entirely devoid of interest. About half way down there is a railway viaduct across a valley. Not a common-or-garden horizontal affair but running down a steep slope. A well-worn notice explains that this was part of the rack railway which linked Luchon to the Superbagnères ski resort, built by the Compagnie des Chemins de Fer du Midi, the same company which built the cruise-liner hotel on the plateau above, and the same company which ran the Petit Train d'Artouste. The panel lists the number of passengers: in 1950 (45,000), 1960 (24,000), and 1962 (21,000), but singularly fails to explain the decrease in popularity. Later, I read the following account:

The accident

Sunday 28 February 1954 at 18:10: the 17:40 train bringing more than 130 skiers back to the valley was never to arrive. It all happened half way down, at the points at Mi-Sahage which permitted the trains to pass, at an altitude of 1189m. An incident derailed the train which continued down the hill in a mad 300m race. The engine detached itself and ended up 500m lower down in the Soulan ravine. The accident killed 9 people, including an 8-year old girl who had a bad fall at Superbagnères and who couldn't be quickly brought to Luchon, as a result of the accident.

The accident was engraved in the collective memory of Luchon. The line was modified and the route reopened... but the opening of the road in 1961 sounded the death knell of the rack railway which ceased to run at the end of the winter of 1966.

Leaving the remains of the railway behind, it is not long before I arrive at the outskirts of the town of Luchon. There, the flagstone pavements echo my footsteps, making an occasionally 'gloup' as they move under my weight: through the gaps I can see racing water. The suburbs – old houses, cheerfully irregular – suddenly give way to the planned town and its high street, l'Allée d'Étigny, lined with linden trees and elegant white façades leading up to the spa buildings.

I find a doctor easily and she gives me more anti-inflammatory tablets and cream. Dentists are more of a problem. I ring all six but not one of them will take me within the next four days. I will just have to grin and bare it.

In the evening I eat at a restaurant in the middle of an identity crisis. It is called the Crémaillère and, logically, the walls inside are covered with sepia prints of the rack railway and Superbagnères. But the glass-topped tables harbour models of tropical islands complete with palm trees, sun umbrellas, giant turtles, and, in the sea, multicoloured fish, all naïvely executed in papier-mâché. Yet the menu relates to neither the Pyrenees nor the tropics, making great play of buckwheat *crêpes* and Brittany cider. Further down the high street there is a stand selling Ben and Jerry's ice cream, a shop selling '*produits régionaux*', and the inevitable display of whistling *marmotte* toys. Venerable – but recently modernised and extended – spa buildings and former grand hotels rub cornices with the steel hawsers of ski lifts. Luchon is like that: charmingly idiosyncratic.

Luchon

I so am out of step with the rest of the world that I have finished my breakfast and walked into town well before the shops and the museum are open. The only other person around is a beggar with a black Labrador dog, arranging his life in the shade on the pavement, so I sit down with him. His rucksack is enviably small, it can't weigh more than 6kg: I would like to be able to survive with so little. When he talks, I can see that his teeth are in an even worse state than mine: most of them are damaged or missing. He is Flemish, but speaks English, French, and a little German, as well as his native tongue. He shows me a septic wound on the sole of his foot, an oversized blister running from his toes to his heel. 'I'll have to go and see a doctor,' he complains. He sleeps in a nearby garden, in exchange for painting the owner's house. He drinks too much, he insists, repeating it several times. '*Mais*,' he says, '*chuis pas clochard. Chuis routard, comme toi.* But I'm not a beggar. I'm a tramp, like you'

Finally the museum opens. Unlike some of the nearby businesses it is quite sure of its identity. It has not changed for 50 years and shows no sign of wishing to do so. Perhaps I am missing something, but the most recent addition to the collections seems to be the panel recounting the life and death of the rack railway.

In the 1950s the museum must have been state of the art; by the 1970s it was starting to look drab; and by the 1990s it was a disgrace to modern museology. Now it has come full circle and, like bell-bottomed trousers, has acquired a new legitimacy. The deadline for refurbishment has passed, and now it can be seen that it wasn't even necessary. The museum has transcended all that, to become, in the best Pyrenean tradition of tautology, a Museum museum.

It could still do with a little dusting and better lighting but it is a fascinating artefact in its own right, redolent of the past, part guessing game, part treasure hunt. The guessing game starts in the entrance hall with a short marble column complete with plinth and capital and, on top of it, a die balanced on one corner. I deduce that this must be a reference to Luchon's casinos or to marble quarrying in the vicinity. I ask the curator but, like the woman near St-Lary, he is unable to enlighten me: it's just decoration, he thinks.

In the first room, the most obvious exhibit looks rather grubby and worn. It is a three-dimensional model of the mountains around Luchon at a scale of ten centimetres for each kilometre on the flat. The vertical scale is twice as large. The model is covered by a web of red cotton paths with the lakes represented by fragments of glass. The peaks are punctured by cocktail sticks supporting little labels giving their names and heights, and the frontier is marked by a line of pale green ball-head pins. The result is charmingly amateurish – unlike the crude but accurate plastic model in St-Lary – but impossible to clean. It has been collecting dust since it was first put on display in … 1855.

Let's put that in context. In 1855 there were *no* large-scale maps of the area; the army had only just started preparing one. Toussaint Lézat, who created the model, had to do all the surveying himself, over an area measuring 57km by 25km! As if that wasn't enough, he was also an intrepid mountaineer, founded the Compagnie des Guides de Luchon, and created the museum in which I am standing.

Much less obvious is the display case behind the door, devoted to the Monts Maudits – the cursed mountains – which are just to the south of Luchon. There is an account of a climbing accident and the remains of the victim: his four-pointed crampon, the sole of his shoe, a gaiter, and the bones of his right arm.

When I was an archaeologist – a grave robber with a clear conscience, in the words of Pierre Minvielle – I routinely handled anonymous skeletons. But there is something disturbingly macabre about this right humerus. I know its owner's name. I can almost hear his last words.

A hand-written coroner's report from the time of the accident explains the circumstances of his death and a newspaper cutting completes the story.

On 11 August 1824 Pierre Barrau, a guide from Luchon, agreed to accompany two young and adventurous engineers, Blavier and de Billy to the summit of the Pic de la Maladetta, one of the Monts Maudits. De Billy suggested, even insisted, that they use a rope. Barrau, who was 68 and much respected for his experience, replied that he had taken a German to the summit seven years previously on the historic first ascent and that a rope wasn't necessary. They were almost at the top of the glacier, within a few metres of their goal, but there was one last crevasse to be crossed. One of the engineers tested a bridge of snow with his stick and quickly stepped back: the snow was soft and ready to fall into the void. Barrau tested another bridge further along and, finding it solid, stepped onto it, only to disappear.

'I've had it. I'm sinking deeper' he shouted for two minutes. And then... silence, a cold silence which was to engulf Barrau for over a hundred years. The Luchon guides were so horrified by his fate that they refused to tackle the glaciers in the area, including the one protecting the nearby Aneto, the ultimate challenge, for another 18 years.

But that wasn't the end of Barrau. In August 1931, two guides accompanying a group of English tourists found a body half eaten by foxes, eagles, and vultures at the base of the glacier, 1400m from the crevasse. It was identified as the indefatigable guide, who had continued his peregrinations even after his death.

More remains appeared in 1934 and Barrau was finally interred. Or, to be more precise, most of him was interred. The bone in front of me has a luggage label attached: right humerus of Pierre Barrau, who fell in the glacier of the Maladetta on 13 [sic] August 1824, found on 25 August 1934 by the dogs of messieurs Baylac and Aurélien.

On the opposite wall of the museum is an ornately framed list recording the conquests of the Baron de Lassus, entitled '*Avec l'aigle et l'isard* – with the eagle and the *isard*', giving the date, the name of the mountain, and its height. The photograph which surmounts the list shows the baron, debonair but serious, leaning on his walking stick. Next to him are four guides in regulation gear – a uniform invented in the middle of the 19th century because 'the sober clothes of the mountain folk were not in keeping with the image which Luchon wished to project as a luxury holiday centre.' The Pyrenees were being transformed by intellectuals steeped in the Romantic vision of the mountains, who were 'rewriting local folklore, putting the finishing touches to the shepherd's customary garb, embroidering legends, and denaturing the message of the past.' The guides are holding ice axes which reach up to their shoulders, typical of that time. They seem to be wondering what they are doing there, each looking in a different direction.

The walls of the stairs up to the next floor are decorated with posters, including one for the 1926 International ski competition which unwittingly shows how new the sport was. The woman in the poster is apparently skiing, but with her arms outstretched horizontally to either side and her legs pressed tightly together, vertical and rigidly straight. The artist has clearly never seen anybody on a real slope.

At the top of the stairs one of the rooms is devoted to local fauna: stuffed *isards*, ibex (extinct), *marmottes*, foxes, eagles… and bears. There are two bear cubs, the size of teddy bears and just as cuddly. One is sitting in a very unnatural position, on its haunches eating a pear which is held between its two front paws – as if it were a human baby. The other is walking across a stone. This one has a scrap of paper next to it. The typing relates a sweet little story:

La Dépêche [a local newspaper] 27 May 1952

Capture of two bear cubs near to Luchon

Some tourists walking not far from the Hospice de France early this afternoon saw two bear cubs. Fearing that the mother bear could be in the area they quickly made their way to the Hospice de France and told the manager and reputed guide Odon Haurillon.

M Haurillon, some friends, and some policemen who were patrolling nearby immediately organised a hunt.

The cubs were found without difficulty, one allowing itself to be captured easily. The other climbed a tree but was soon captured as well. The two cubs, which seem to be aged one and a half months, were brought back to the Hospice where they were given a welcome present of a bottle of milk.

And afterwards they killed them.

The last, unofficial, hand-written addition has been crossed out, but the evidence is here before me.

They killed them. Is it true? Graffiti is raw, untamed information: I always take it seriously.

Only later do I reconcile the sugary official version with the harsh graffito. Jeannot Ladrix used to hunt in the area at that time. Now over 90 years old, he explains: 'they were kept in a sheep fold, then in a hut adjoining the Hospice for nearly a year. It was an attraction for

Bear cub in the museum

the whole valley, until one of the cubs died from poisoning. The other died a year later of diabetes.' So one might say they were welcomed; or equally claim that they were killed by captivity.

I spend all morning in the museum, before eating in another eccentric restaurant. Called the Maeva – meaning welcome in Tahitian – it sells ski equipment in the winter and serves Spanish tapas in the summer.

Then I go to the spa facilities at Sourcéa for what are called 'treatments', not that I expect them to do anything for my various ailments. I have chosen the *Rendez-vous énergie* in the hope that it will liven me up. The other clients are also healthy-looking – the afternoons are reserved for hypochondriacs and hedonists. If you are ill you come in the morning. The reception area, as might be expected, is a cross between a hotel and a hospital, with the background music and fluffy dressing gowns offset by the ubiquitous clocks and staff who are clearly nurses, in dazzlingly white, starched uniforms.

The first 'treatment' is a Jacuzzi bath. I lie in the bath with jets of water squirting at me but any attempt to relax is destroyed by the large electronic panel on the wall opposite. The LCDs display a series of incomprehensible numbers. The only one which I manage to understand is the clock.

Within a second of the end of the last jet, the nurse comes back in. 'That's it for now,' she says. 'You can go into the waiting room. Somebody will call for you at 15:30 for the cervical mud.'

At 15:30 I am led into another small windowless room. The nurse wraps my neck in linen bandages and then slaps hot mud onto them. I get to lie down, the heat and the mud soaking into my shoulders, in semi-darkness for precisely 12 minutes.

'You can go to the hammam and pool now, but make sure to have a shower first,' another nurse tells me. 'You must come back to reception for 16:40. There's a clock over the pool.'

At the appointed time I am led into a long, completely sealed room, tiled in white, with stark lighting. No soothing music here; I feel rather flaky after all the 'treatments' and would prefer to lie down.

'Go to the other end and stand under the arch, with your back to me, facing the wall,' says the nurse, a middle-aged woman with a rather abrupt tone of voice.

She stands behind a console in the shape of a church lectern, adjusts some controls, and points a high-pressure jet of water at me, aiming it up and down my back, from my neck to my ankles.

'Turn 90 degrees to the right and raise your right arm above your head. Hold onto the rail with your other hand,' she barks.

When I am sufficiently battered she turns the water off and orders me to turn round and show her my other side. I feel as though I am being examined with a critical eye. At least at this distance my gap tooth isn't visible.

I wonder what kind of bizarre experiment the doctors might be conducting here. I have just read that, in the 1930s, two radioactive springs were authorised for use in the spas – this being before the dangers of exposure to radioactivity were fully appreciated – and that doctors vaunted the health-giving qualities 'of radioactivity 15,000 times that of normal air'. Is the warder going to switch to ice-cold water and measure how many minutes I survive standing up? Is she going to turn up the pressure and flatten me against the back wall?

'Turn to face me,' she demands, 'and shut your eyes.'

When I am released, at 16:55 give or take a few seconds, a different nurse takes me up to the relaxation room in the lift.

'Are you alright?' she asks, installing me on a lounger.

I look up at the ceiling blankly.

That night, I sleep comfortably again at the Lutin. In the morning I decide to go home to get my teeth fixed. When I arrive there is a postcard waiting for me, from Paul, whom I last saw in Sainte-Engrâce. To judge by the postmark, he must have been walking just a couple of days ahead of me. I have also had an email from Grégory. He has written a play, but curiously seems more proud of the poster he did for it, than of the play itself. Yes, he says in reply to my question, Aimé finished *his* Pyrenean Way last year.

I am still a long way from Banyuls, I reflect. Strange how I hardly got to know anybody this year. Perhaps it will be different next time.

But I can't wait until next year to go back to the Pyrenees. And since I want to go somewhere interesting, there is only one choice.

Aneto

The summit is empty, elemental, the air thin. To the west I can make out the sea. No, it's not possible: the Atlantic is 200km away. It must all be sky – both the cold grey layer near the horizon and the warm baby blue layer above it. To the south, in Spain, the clouds are romping over the peaks *below* us, but to the north, France is melting under a fiery sun. Here, in the middle at 3404m above sea level, there is not the slightest wind. Beneath my feet there are jagged blocks of untamed primeval granite but no earth, no life. There is no water either, though we have just crossed ten thousand years of accumulated rain and snow to get here.

When I have recovered my breath and my heart has returned to its normal rhythm, I listen. Nothing. The last natural sound – a twittering bird begging crumbs – was left behind several hours ago. I look around at the serrated landscape of mountains waiting to lacerate any rain clouds that happen by. Here, on the highest peak of the Pyrenees, humans make no impact and nature no compromises. Almost.

'The main problem is the number of people. At the height of the summer season you get 200 people a day. They really ought to install traffic lights at either end of the Pas de Mahomet,' jokes our guide.

And, just for once, nature is feeling kind.

'You'll have a thunderstorm on your way there and another on your way back,' my friend Alice has warned me, 'and you'll be lucky not to be blown off the Pas de Mahomet by the wind.'

It's not supposed to be like this, then.

A month after leaving Luchon, encouraged by climbing Vignemale, I am back in the area with Claude, a friend from my walking club. We approach our grail cautiously, circling it on all sides in the car, without actually being able to see it. On the way, we notice some 'Aneto' tee-shirts for sale. 'Let's get them afterwards,' I suggest, not wanting to tempt fate.

Climbing up from the valley, we can soon see the Refuge de la Rencluse where we are going to spend the night, but not the peak itself. The valley was green and lush but here the hillside is almost barren. Standing talking on a hillock which still has a little grass, we are nosed away by a bad-tempered mare who wants to make more room for herself and her filly. Nearby, a stream disappears abruptly into the rock: the strata here are vertical. This is the epicentre of the Pyrenean hernia.

By dinner time our guide still hasn't arrived so I ask the hostel manager when he might turn up.

'*A las diez, las once, o mañana por la mañana* – Ten o'clock, eleven o'clock, or tomorrow morning. You have to get up at quarter past five, eat breakfast at half past and be ready to go at six.'

During the night I wake up several times. In the haze between sleep and wakefulness, I tell myself that I need to breathe more deeply to capture the oxygen. Next morning Claude eats steadily, quietly. I'm nervous.

At quarter to six a skeletal young man with a tiny rucksack opens the door. He is dressed in variants of khaki, with a black sleeveless woollen waistcoat. Short curly black hair. Angular features and the slightest suggestion of a moustache. He looks competent, sharp, and determined. He introduces himself. His name, appropriately, is Pierre.

Outside, it is completely black, but somewhere ahead of us there is a formation of four moving stars, flickering. Like the three kings, we follow them; we too have lights attached to our foreheads. There is no path through the giant pink-grey-white-and-black speckled granite cubes, and at the same time there are dozens of paths. There are cairns everywhere, but no sense to them. Every step has to be calculated. The blocks are unstable, an irregular un-worn clutter. *Chaos*, the French term for it, is totally appropriate.

The sun must be rising but we are wrapped in mist. Occasionally the atmosphere coalesces into drops of rain but I can see that the clouds are thin and will disappear as soon as the sun rises above the horizon.

'Will we be roped up for the glacier?' I ask.

'We'll see,' replies Pierre.

'What about the Pas de Mahomet?'

'We'll see.'

'Are we on time?'

'Yes.'

'How long will it take to get to the top?'

'Five and a half to six hours.'

Finally, we are above the mist. To the west, the horizon is tinged pink. To the south, the Pic de la Maladeta has a sparkling-white glacier bib. It looks pretty, but this is where Pierre Barrau disappeared into a crevasse.

When we reach the Portillon Supérieur, the 'doorway' through the ridge, we discover simultaneously the sun opposite us and an immense glacier sloping steeply downwards to our left. Between us and the sun there are layers upon layers of mountain cut-outs, printed in colours graduating from the darkest black to the palest grey. On the right, three peaks delineate the horizon.

'Aneto?' I ask, breathlessly.

'The furthest one,' Pierre replies.

We cross more scree and *chaos* to the edge of a small snowfield. It's not worth putting on our crampons but the snow is frozen and slippery so I extract my ice axe from my sack and hold it ready to hook it into the ground should I slip.

'You've never been to snow school, have you?' says Pierre.

'No,' I admit.

'It is a complete waste of time holding your axe like that. And you've got it in the wrong hand. In any case if you slip an ice axe won't stop you. You'll just create a furrow in the snow.'

'What's it for then?' I ask.

'Not much really. If you slip on snow you have to roll onto your stomach, stick your arms out and your hands into the snow, and use your hands to push upwards. If you are *really* lucky your feet will dig in and you will come to a stop.'

I promise to go to snow school next winter.

The glacier, when we get to it, is grey and slippery, quite different to Vignemale. We put on our crampons.

'We'll do some exercises before we start,' says Pierre.

We totter along for a few uncertain paces.

'Now we'll try running down the glacier,' Pierre continues. 'Put the whole weight of your body on the leg which is in front, bending your legs at the same time. Steve, you go first.'

This seems a little excessive, I think. We haven't yet mastered walking, and now he wants us to run. I lunge forwards.

'No. Not like that. Don't waddle. Run! You need to put your chest forwards as well, so that your weight is above your feet.'

I run like a drunken monkey, arms swaying.

'That's better,' he says. 'If you do get your crampons caught in your trousers the only way to avoid falling down is to leap into the air and land running until you regain your balance.'

He gives an acrobatic demonstration of the manoeuvre but doesn't ask us to emulate him.

'Hold the ice axe in the hand which is highest. Use it like a walking stick.'

'What do we do if we fall over?' I ask.

'Don't fall over,' replies Pierre, putting on his wrap-around sunglasses, rubbing sun cream into his cheeks, and looking up at the sky. 'Let's go.'

'I'd prefer to be roped up,' I suggest, hopefully.

'It's not really necessary.'

'I'd prefer to be roped up,' I repeat, more strongly.

'OK. But you must keep the rope taut.'

Pierre loops the rope round our waists and we set off. After a few steps he looks back.

'If you let the rope droop like that, Steve, when you fall you will pull us all down the slope with you.'

The glacier is fast disappearing, like all the glaciers in the Pyrenees. In 1870, altogether they covered an estimated 40 km², now there are less than 5km². The Glacier d'Ossoue on the slopes of Vignemale is still 50m thick, but it is shrinking by 1.8m every year.

There is no longer enough snow to replace what melts in the summer, and here on Aneto last winter there was even less than usual. I have seen photos where the glacier and the rocks are covered in snow all the way from the Portillon to the Pas de Mahomet near the summit. At the beginning of July, there is a comforting channel across the snow traced by hundreds of pairs of feet. It is now the end of August and all the snow has melted. There are no footprints.

'At least that means you won't fall into a hidden crevasse,' muses Pierre.

We walk across the glacier, hardly climbing at all, feet twisted uncomfortably to conform to the slope. Waddling like a duck, concentrating on every step, taking care to plant each crampon firmly in the ice, is a tiring process. We stop for a breather and I am startled to look around and discover a young couple sitting on a rock only a few paces away. Nobody else is on the glacier. This morning's stars must have been been heading for a different Bethlehem.

Claude slips but is stopped by crashing into my feet, which are firmly dug into the ice. She has twisted her ankle but it isn't going to stop her. A few minutes later I notice that my arms are behaving oddly. I look at Claude. Hers are doing the same thing. We are both walking with our palms facing outwards. I twist my arms back into a more natural position only to rediscover them, palms outwards, a few steps further on. There is nothing to be done. As soon as I stop consciously controlling them, my arms twist round. We are walking like ducks, with our feet splayed, and our arms following suit. Now I understand why the Spanish man at Bayssellance kept falling over after his encounter with a lawnmower. Hands and feet are linked by invisible strings so an injury to one affects the other.

Claude's crampons have worked loose, but the slope is now too steep to stop and it is only when we reach a flatter zone that we can fix them. Here, the ice is covered with a pink dust, a kind of algae which can live at sub-zero temperatures. At least there are now some footprints to follow.

At the top of the glacier we take off our crampons and rucksacks and wrench our feet back into a more normal walking position. We are only a few metres from our goal but between us and the summit there is a small hitch: the Pas de Mahomet ridge. The name dates to July 1842, when Albert de Franqueville, Platon de Tchihatcheff, and their guides became the first climbers to scramble up it. The ridge is a series of irregular granite blocks, like a line of giant dice which have been thrown by the gods onto the sharp edge of a blade. A few have come to rest with a flat surface on top but the majority have an edge or a corner sticking upwards. There is no path and on either side of the ridge the drop is vertical.

'It isn't difficult,' claims Pierre.

I insist on the rope. Claude says it would get in her way.

The first obstacle is a large almost cone-shaped rock which we have to cross by stepping delicately on the footholds in its side, clinging to its top. Then there is a crevasse to descend into and climb out of. I have half my body over the edge but I can't find the foothold.

'Look where you are going to put your foot first,' Pierre scolds me, wrapping the rope round a rock and keeping it taut.

'Not there. Your right hand is useless there. It is too low. Put it higher,' he tells Claude.

Then there is a flat block, narrower than I am, higher than any of the surrounding stones. I feel like a tight-rope walker. I look at where I am going to put my feet, concentrating hard on not seeing anything else, but I see it anyway. It is a long way down.

Claude skips along ahead of us. And then suddenly we are there, at the summit of the highest peak in the Pyrenees. There is nobody else. Claude and I kiss, grin at each other, and amble around, empty-headed.

The view is intimidating. Innumerable mountains clutter this dreamscape but the overarching heavens are bigger still. We are isolated, and at the same time at the centre of the world. Even for an unbeliever like me, there is something otherworldly here. Something eternal. I'm not sure what it is, nor what it might mean. All I know is that as soon as I leave the summit, this state of grace will disappear. I won't even be able to take a clear memory of it with me. It can only be experienced here.

All the works of humanity are reduced to their real importance:

Jésus, Pierre and Claude at the summit of Aneto

the only man-made things we can see in the distance are a few match-sticks which might be ski-lift towers at Superbagnères, and the town of Luchon, a miniscule smudge in a valley near the horizon.

Here nature is writ large. Which makes the artificial features of the summit – a curious collection of personal, religious, and political statements – seem all the more pathetic. In the first category is the graffito spray-painted in red on a rock: 'Santos 22.06.2003'.

Religion makes its claim in triplicate. The first is a cross that I have seen in photographs although only the torn shreds of the aluminium base remain. The second is an absurdly dumpy aluminium pillar with, on top, a disproportionately small, black statue of Mary and the infant Jesus. The statue is encircled by ribbons, one red, white and blue – for France I suppose – the other red and gold – for Catalonia. There are also a couple of tiny bunches of artificial flowers, a checked pink-and-white handkerchief, and a powder blue cotton baseball cap. The pillar is no longer vertical. A few more winters and it will go the same way as the cross. Finally, there is a trapezoidal aluminium box, like a small house, with, inside, a naïve wooden carving of Jesus on the cross. There was once a door, but only the hinges survive.

Politics is represented by the word '*Euskadi* – the Basque country' printed on the back of a tee-shirt which is draped over a concrete survey pillar, the only edifice which seems to be withstanding the elements. The mountain has been annexed by the Basques. But not for long.

'It'll be torn to shreds if it stays here,' says Pierre, stuffing the tee-shirt into his rucksack and sitting down.

'When I came here ten days ago,' he tells us, 'I found a kitten wandering around. It was exhausted. I took it down to the hostel.'

'How did it get here?' I ask.

'It could have followed someone,' suggests Pierre.

'Across the glacier and the Pas de Mahomet? Impossible.'

'Kittens have built in crampons,' says Claude imaginatively.

We stay a long while, nibbling, recovering from the effort, and watching the unchanging scenery.

When we get back to our rucksacks after re-crossing the Pas de Mahomet, Pierre attaches us both to the rope without being asked, Claude at the front, me in the middle, and himself at the end. We head directly down the steepest slope, with Claude walking so fast that I have to monkey-skip to keep up with her. The surface is wet and in places there are rivers of water to be crossed. I have time to look down the slope. On the way up it was easy to restrict my thoughts and vision to a small zone where the next foot was going to fall. Now my vision keeps slipping.

In the car on the way back Claude asks if I want to stop for a tee-shirt.

'It wouldn't be right,' I reply. You can't represent a state of bliss on something as trivial as a tee-shirt.

III

Luchon–Mérens: Ariège, *terre courage*

Non à l'ours

A year later I come back to Luchon for a short holiday at the end of April and unexpectedly find myself in the middle of a battle. Just outside the town there is a blockade across the road. Two tractors with digger buckets attached, a huge wooden barrel, half a dozen tree trunks, and a significant number of bales of straw are there to back up a banner proclaiming defiantly: '*Non à l'ours*. No to the bears.' There are eight men and two women warming themselves around a small fire, inspecting every vehicle before letting it through.

I stop my car just short of the blockade and get out. Despite their evident numerical superiority, they huddle closer together at my approach.

'I saw your banner and thought you might be able to tell me more about what's going on,' I say. The protesters look visibly relieved. They tell me that they are from St Béat, a few kilometres away, and Luchon. Between them, they have 2000 sheep in the *estives* around the Hospice de France, a little further up the valley. Although the government has reduced the projected number of new bears it is planning to import from 15 to five, they are not satisfied. They hope to stop the programme completely.

The first bear, newly baptised Palouma, was released in Arbas, four days ago. Nelly Ollin, the new environment minister, had wanted the event to be a celebration, but both she and the bear were greeted by a heavily mediatised chorus of bells, pots, and pans. She accused the protesters of 'having transformed a beautiful fairy tale into a nightmare.' The protesters replied that she was writing a horror story for them.

The next bear, Francka, arrived yesterday and, according to the *Dépêche du Midi* newspaper, the shepherds had the wool pulled over their eyes. Luchon was invaded by both protesters and policemen. The newspaper portrays the events as a clever bluff, with the police being deployed in Luchon to keep the protesters occupied whilst the bear was quietly being released at Bagnères de Bigorre, several valleys away.

I ask the protesters for their version.

'I don't think that that's what really happened,' says one man. 'Once the authorities realised the extent of the mobilisation they decided to go for their second choice. Next time round it will be different. On Friday [yesterday] we had 200 people here for lunch. But we have decided to split up, with spies along all the access roads. We'll know where they are going before they know themselves,' he claims.

A white van goes by slowly.

'That's the third time this morning,' explains the protester. 'They spy on us as well.'

'When do you expect the next convoy to arrive?' I ask.

'To get back to the mountains in Slovenia will take them 17 hours, but with a bear they will have to drive carefully on the return journey – about 22 hours. They could arrive as early as Tuesday.'

A mobile phone rings and there is a short conversation.

'France 3 is coming at 13:30,' someone announces. 'What are you doing here?' he asks me.

'Walking.'

'You know, in the future some areas will be out-of-bounds because of the bears, to stop them being disturbed.'

'But there have always been bears here and there weren't any reserves then.'

'The mountains aren't like they were 50 years ago. There are more people around. Just because there were bears here in the past doesn't mean to say that there should be in the future.'

'What do you think will happen next?'

'We know we can't stop them this time, but if we make enough fuss they'll think twice about trying again.'

Luchon to the Cabanes de Peyrehitte

Returning to the town six weeks later, the first thing I do is go shopping for food. I have some dehydrated provisions, but I want to keep them for when I am desperate. There are two criteria: weight and how well it will keep in a warm rucksack. I buy hunks of dried ham, good solid cheese, country bread, carrots, and apples – without thinking I have composed the kind of meals eaten in the mountains before the invention of refrigerators.

My rucksack is heavier than last year. I haven't packed a tent but I have equipped myself for sleeping in huts… if they are open, and the shepherds don't mind. If not I will have to sleep under the stars.

The next day I walk out of Luchon along the side of the river, past a fisherman hunched over the tranquil waters. The first village has flower beds at the side of a disciplined stream which runs next to its main street. The *lavoir* – where the women used to scrub their clothes – has been heavily renovated and planted with geraniums.

The path climbs through the forest and emerges two hours later into another world, at the village of Artigue. The name itself is significant. Artigue means *the* clearing. There are many Artigues coupled with qualifiers, like Bious Artigue – Bious' Clearing, but few which were so extensive that they became known simply as *the* clearing. In the middle of the 19th century when population pressure was at its maximum, creating new pastures from the forest was the last desperate attempt

At dawn, downstream from Luchon

by younger disenfranchised sons to make a life for themselves locally, before they turned to emigration as the final solution.

In the village, constructed by those who managed to stay put, there is holiday accommodation and even a restaurant, but this is a working community. Here, the barns smell of straw, and slurry dribbles out onto the road. I walk past the church and into the pastures where I am greeted by a row of home-made notices. Although polythene bags cover the paper, water has already penetrated and the letters have started to run; but the message is still clear.

Beware

You are in bear country. You can meet a bear at any moment. These new Slovenian bears are unpredictable. We cannot predict how they will behave when they meet humans. Be vigilant.

To our tourist friends

Do you want tidy mountains, maintained by sheep and cows? Do you want mountains without farmers, with daily danger?

The undergrowth will take over, with all its associated disadvantages (fires, avalanches, impassable footpaths), knowing that the damage to the flocks isn't just a question of the sheep which has been devoured (when it is found). There is also the stress, the injuries, the miscarriages and, of course, the work of the shepherd!!!!

In conclusion, farmers abandoning their jobs will have more effect than bears on the environment and tourism, and soon!!!

A bear has been released a few hundred metres as the crow flies from our commune, to which we welcome you, hoping that your walk doesn't finish as a nightmare!!!

Signed by the population of Artigue

> We produce lambs of quality,
> The best on all the markets.
> Sheep are our trade.
> They are our pride.
> We bring them up.
> We love them.
>
> They are not bait
> And we don't want
> Them to be eaten
> By a badly brought-up bear.

The population of Artigue was 168 in 1876; by the time of the last census in 1999, it had dropped to 34. Evidently, all is not well, but clearly the new bears can't be blamed.

Walking through the forest earlier I was already thinking about bears. What would I do if I saw one? What would I do if one attacked me? If I whipped off my rucksack and put it on backwards, against my chest, would it afford me any protection? I tell myself that I am less likely to be killed by a bear than by a car accident – nobody has been killed by a bear for over a century. But logic has no power over emotions. I can't stop thinking about what *might* happen. My walk has become polluted by bears.

My path climbs inexorably. I overtake three people who tell me that they are just going to the top of the first hill and meet one man walking the Pyrenean Way in the opposite direction, and then nobody. I feel isolated.

The heat is building up but so are the clouds, so that when I arrive at the Cabanes de Peyrehitte, I decide to stay for the night. One of the huts is labelled *Cabane du berger*. The other, labelled *Refuge*, has a rudimentary stone bench outside it. There is a cheerful yellow sun painted on a beam above the bench, and a moon on the door, but no other instructions.

I open the door. There is no window but I can see a rusty bunk-bed frame, with metal grilles to lie on. The floor itself is flagged; the walls are concrete. The chimney hosts a large amount of ash and a few sticks of wood – just enough for this evening. On the mantel-piece are several empty wine bottles, including a bottle of Taittinger, with the neck cleanly sliced off, as if someone had brought a sabre with them as well. Hidden in the corner, what is it? … a very burnt saucepan. But the real discovery is two notebooks, filled in by walkers. Many of the entries thank the shepherd for his hospitality, exclaim at the beauty of the surroundings, or complain about the fog which makes the huts difficult to find. But some are much more poetic.

15 May 2005. There are moments when life takes a strange direction. Signs, people, and places bringing us back to our destiny. This evening, in front of the fire, I know that I am not here by chance. I don't know where this is going to take me, but I know that I am on the right track. Outside the fog has lifted and the sun has appeared again. Thanks to Robert the Basque shepherd whom I met last week, and with whom I would greatly like to spend more time. Thanks to the shepherd who looks after this hut, absent, but to whom I transmit all my gratitude for the existence of this unique place of self-rediscovery, and for the love that he puts into doing this work. From the bottom of my heart. Angeline de Saumur.

Tuesday 6 August 2002. The destination of the voyage doesn't matter, what counts is what one experiences here and now. You have stopped here. For a moment? To eat? For the night? This is the sign that one should not let encounters pass by. Step by step, mountain pass after mountain pass, I smile at my suffering. I appreciate the instant because it exists and don't propose to string the stages one after the other like pearls on a thread to make a necklace.

Mentally, I add these thoughts to my collection of reasons for walking the Pyrenean Way.

When I arrived at the hut I could see the central ridge of the Pyrenees. Now the clouds have closed in. Everything is grey. It is raining more or less continuously and there are claps of thunder from time to time, some near, some further away. I'm just sitting here. Sitting on my rucksack in the doorway of the hut.

Now I can hear the bells of sheep coming down the slope behind the hut. Now I can see the dog and the shepherd, who is actually a shepherdess. She says I can make myself at home, and then charges off down the valley after the sheep and the dog. The big flowery motifs on her ankle-length yellow dress fade into the clouds.

After the storm at the cabanes de Peyrehitte

In the evening, after the storm – the painful labour – the valley is reborn in a mist which washes back and forth, softly lapping over the huts and then clearing again, under a sky of fast-moving cumulo-nimbus. The sun is timidly reappearing in the west; the grass sparkles, as if it too has been transformed by the lightning.

I inspect the shepherdess' hut from the outside. It is equipped with solar panels but the water heating consists of a black pouch hanging in the sun. There are troughs to collect the rainwater which falls on the roof. It has windows. Inside it looks cosy.

I'm feeling cold, so I retreat to my hut and eat morosely. It is getting gloomy when the dog nudges its way through the door. I feed it some scraps of ham and stroke it but the shepherdess soon returns as well and calls it home. So I light a fire and watch the endless flames into the dark.

For the first hour of the new day I traverse a gigantic purple bouquet: the hillside is covered in flowering rhododendrons.

Below me, shepherds' huts dot the slopes. Last night's shepherdess told me in passing that she looks after 1280 animals: the ovine population here must run into several thousand. Indeed, higher up at the pass the grass is scored by a hundred horizontal *drailles*, parallel tracks ploughed by systematic sheep.

The last part of the descent into the next valley, down to the Garonne river, should be a pleasant stroll between the trees to the sound of a cascading stream. The trees provide the necessary shade, the descent is only 20%, and the path is well made, dry, and surfaced in stone. But I have been warned, so I extract my telescopic walking stick from my sack and proceed with caution. Even so, in the space of half an hour I fall down four times and slip but manage to avoid tumbling a further six times. Normally, in a week's walking I wouldn't fall over once. This innocent-looking passageway must be the most dangerous section of the Pyrenean Way.

Down by the river, at the side of the path there is a notice mirroring the one at Artigue, but here the reflection is different.

Welcome to Bear Country
Hello I am a Pyrenean bear. With the ADET, I invite you to discover this walking country. In order to preserve our tranquillity and that of the herds, I ask you to keep your dog at your side and to stay on marked footpaths. Thank you. Have a good walk.

The solid wooden board is designed to last. At the bottom there are three logos. The first one is evidently based on the European Union flag, with the word 'Life' (in English). The second is the logo of the Ministry for Development and the Environment. The third, a schematic drawing of a bear against a mountain background, is symbolically surrounded by a lifebelt, and sports the wording 'ADET [Association for Economic Development and Tourism], Central Pyrenees, Bear Country'.

On the other side of the river, in the village of Fos, I look for the village shop, but am told that it shut definitively several years ago. For tonight it doesn't matter, but the nearest shop on the Pyrenean Way is several days into the future.

Walking along the main road through the village I see a sign for a Bear Country exhibition, free entry. Naturally, there is an effigy of a bear outside, but not what I might have expected. Although he is a realistic size for an adult bear and is standing up, there is nothing scary about this teddy. He has a small head, a big smile, and the proportions of a 40-year-old man with a beer gut – his stuffing seems to have slumped. An average two-year-old wouldn't be afraid. I can imagine the bear which would stand outside an exhibition organised by the village of Artigue on the other side of the watershed. If he had a big smile it would be because his teeth were clasped round the amputated leg of an unfortunate walker, blood dripping from his lips.

Inside, the exhibition is unsurprisingly positive about the reintro-ductions but I quickly gain the impression that, in the crude market economics of the third millennium, even bears have to justify their existence. The issue is not whether the bear community can reproduce itself, nor whether it can withstand the harsh Pyrenean winter, but whether it can survive the rigours of a cost–benefit analysis. In 2006 the reintroduction programme cost the state 2,246,818€. Compen-sation has to be found for the dead sheep and destroyed beehives. Shepherds have to be paid to stay with the flocks in the *estives*; and shepherds are no longer satisfied with the *orrys*, the dry stone huts of their grandfathers. New *cabanes* will have to be built, with enclosures to protect the sheep if there is a bear in the vicinity. *Patous* need to be trained. Helicopters need to bring in supplies. Then, in addition, there are the costs of the teams, at the Ministry for the Environment and elsewhere, looking after the bears' interests.

Those are the financial costs. The financial benefits are much more difficult to define and slow to materialise. The ADET sees bears as a vital factor in the development of green tourism. It is developing the concept of a 'Bear Country' label for a range of tourist activities which conform to its ethos, and encouraging sheep farmers to reorganise their production methods. If shepherds stay with their flocks in the mountains as they used to do, says the ADET, the sheep will be better cared for and benefit fully from their time there.

One thing is clear, however: if bears insist on a first course of tender young lamb followed by a dessert laced with honey, they will have to pay for their supper by attracting tourists to the region. They will not be allowed to live on state benefits indefinitely.

I continue round the exhibition. Despite the promise of the teddy bear at the door, there is nothing inside for kids. No, that's not quite true. Children can make casts of real bears' paw prints, a full-size one attributed to Pyros, 235kg, or a tiny one, no bigger than my thumb-print, from a newly born cub, 0.4kg. This reminds me that the bears which arrived earlier this summer were reported to be pregnant.

'Have they had their cubs?' I ask the woman behind the counter.

'No…' she replies. She sounds evasive.

'But they were pregnant weren't they?'

'Maybe. We'll only find out next spring. If they give birth.'

'Then why did all the newspapers say they were pregnant?'

'Because they probably *are* going to have cubs, but they are not like humans. They copulate in Spring but the pregnancy doesn't start until December, when the bear is in hibernation. And then it only starts if the bear has managed to eat enough in the summer to have a chance of surviving the birth and bringing up the cubs.'

The birth, if it happens, will inevitably result in the death of more sheep. But the statistics need to be kept in proportion. Looked at on the scale of the French Pyrenees the number of deaths is relatively small. Jean-Jacques Camarra, a specialist, points out that bears are implicated in the deaths of 100–200 sheep each year in the French

Pyrenees. Yet dog attacks, disease, thunderstorms and other causes account for 10,000–20,000 fatalities.

On the other hand consider the proportions viewed through the eyes of a shepherdess, Violaine Berot:

27 September 2001… Gilbert has a herd of 138 sheep on the mountain. That day 44 will be killed by a bear, 20 will go missing. The beasts are scattered over more than 300m, lying on the soil, ripped open. Horrible vision, those massacred sheep, disembowelled. Unbearable vision for the farmer, however hardened he might be.

And what about global warming? Nobody seems to be addressing the issue, though it must have a significant impact on the viability of the bear population in the long term. Will it make life easier for them, or destroy their habitat?

Leaving the exhibition, I walk along the main road through the rest of Fos, clinging to the walls, hiding from the incandescent sun and the hulking lorries. This is the main cross-frontier road into Spain in the central Pyrenees. From here on eastwards there are no crossings for 90km as the vulture flies, until the other side of Andorra.

Within spitting distance of the border post, I see another reminder of the battle for the future of the Pyrenees, on the tarmac: '*Vive l'ours!*' '*Non à l'ours!*' Turning round I see an advert for Maya, *medium international, divination*. She has her offices here in Fos. Should I go and ask her what the outcome will be?

Instead I follow the track up the hill. Just outside the village of Melles, in a field where sheep are grazing, I meet an old woman who is knitting, standing up.

'Is it your own wool?' I ask her.

'No,' she laughs, 'though I've got a room full at home. I can't sell it, but I still have to have the sheep sheared every year.'

'What about the bears?' I continue. 'Do they cause you problems?'

'No, because the sheep go back to the farm at night. I'll be taking them down shortly,' she explains as I set off again.

In the village a small ceremony is in preparation. Flowers are being placed round the war memorial and the mayor, identified by his *écharpe*, is unpacking a loud-speaker. It is 18 June, the anniversary of de Gaulle's rallying cry after the occupation of France in 1940. After the ceremony I talk to the mayor, André Rigoni, and ask him about the continuing local resistance to the presence of bears. Quite by chance, I have unearthed one of the key actors in the story.

It was here that Ziva, the first of the newcomers, was released in 1996, at Rigoni's suggestion, in the first wave of reintroductions. Later she was to be followed by Mellba and Pyros. A recent book recounts the events:

That morning the Pyrenees changed era... The French state decided to reinforce the Pyrenean bear population, at the initiative of five communes in the Haute-Garonne. And thus the Pandora's box was opened...

It won Rigoni many political enemies, with cynics claiming that he knew the bears would soon leave his commune and that he wouldn't have to live with the consequences.

Today, Rigoni is wearing a dapper broad-striped shirt and a light-coloured suit. I take him to be in his 50s but later learn he is 74. For him 'bears are part of our national heritage just like the Eiffel Tower or the Louvre'.

'I have been elected six, or is it seven times, and have been promoting the existence of bears since 1989. So if a majority of local people were against it, I would have been replaced long ago. There are shepherds in the commune who are in favour. What you see in the media is a well-orchestrated campaign by a few determined individuals.'

A poster on the town hall shows a picture of a bear with the caption:

Mellba died on 27 September 1997, killed by a 7.64mm bullet. Coming from Slovenia, she was brought to the Pyrenees on 6 June 1996. She had given birth to three cubs... The death of Mellba is the death of an idea. Intolerance sometimes brings men to kill bears as they kill ideas.

Opposite the war memorial is the Auberge du Crabère, where I am staying for the night. An elegant building with a decorative façade and ironwork balconies, it looks out of place amidst its bucolic neighbours. Inside, the furniture also looks out of place but for a different reason. The double doors leading to my bedroom, the windows, and the wardrobe all look as though they were intended for a full-size chateau although the building itself is quite small.

While drinking an aperitif, I talk to the chef, Patrick Beauchet. He has a jovial manner, a bushy moustache, and evidently enjoys eating – never trust a thin chef – so I am hopeful for tonight's meal. Although he is quite small, in his youth he played rugby against England. He then went to sea, as a ship's cook, working on *Le France*.

'I gave it up because I couldn't stand everything rolling about in the Bay of Biscay,' he tells me. 'We've been here 16 years now. At first we used to be full all the time, but now it's hard to make a living. There are only two of you tonight.'

'What's changed?'

'I'm not sure. Breathalysers partly. Also people think that self-catering accommodation is cheaper – it isn't. And then they don't like simple hotels anymore. They want televisions in the rooms.'

The inn doesn't have any stars, but is perfectly comfortable. And it is homely, unlike those antiseptic star-studded modern hotels. Bed, breakfast, and evening meal for 32€ must be difficult to beat.

'I used to do gastronomic meals, which worked well, but I'm not sure if I'll do any more,' he adds.

He passes me a book of press cuttings and menus. It includes 'A tribute to Bocuse', a reproduction of one of the great chef's meals, faithful in every detail except the price.

He has written several books of recipes and has been commissioned to write one about his life on board ship. He asks me if I know anybody who can rescue it: his computer has just been struck by lightning.

Patrick's wife comes in with a patou, Tammy. She is as big as the dog I saw near the Granges d'Astau, but a pet. She barks suspiciously at me, once, before lying down under the table, her head sticking out at one end and her legs at the other. She needs a full-size chateau. The woman disappears.

'That's Annie,' says Patrick. 'She looks after the guests. I do the cooking.' He changes the subject: 'You're walking on your own, aren't you? It's not a good idea you know.'

'You see more, and you can think about things,' I reply.

'You think *too much*. I wouldn't like to do it. Walking in company could be good fun, but I wouldn't like to walk on my own. No.'

Sitting at the next table is a gorilla of a man, the other guest, who introduces himself as Maurice. *'Comment tu t'appelles?'* he asks me. He is big, very big, with sequoia legs. There is hair sprouting out of the back of his tee-shirt collar, but less on his head. He is wearing thin-rimmed glasses. His face, his eyes, look solid, uncomplicated. He is also walking the Pyrenean Way; 20kg; Hendaye; four weeks. A retired engineer, he is due to meet some friends in Mérens in two weeks' time.

Patrick serves us a meal that is both copious and tasty. It starts with a tureen of *soupe ancestrale*, a soup that has been redefined daily, but never quite eaten up. On its own this could constitute a meal but there are four more courses. Maurice downs everything put in front of him and a whole bottle of wine without any noticeable side-effects.

I leave the *Alice in Wonderland* inn with a packed lunch, wondering if eating it will shrink me or make me grow. It is still hot from yesterday and I am wearing only shorts and a tee-shirt. I can feel – but not see – spiders' webs breaking on my face as I slip through the dark forest. Back in the open air, I sit down for a second breakfast next to a stately – and highly poisonous – common monkshood, flowering blue amongst the rhododendrons which, here, have finished their summer display.

I detect a movement on the slope nearby – an animal which looks like a fat *isard*. But it isn't an *isard*. It has long, thick, curved horns arching backwards, the pointed ends virtually sticking into the brown fleece on its neck. It must be a *mouflon*. These are wild sheep brought in by hunters some 50 years ago.

At first I thought it was an ibex (*bouquetin*), but I quickly realised that it wasn't possible: the last Pyrenean ibex died in AD 2000. There had been ibex here for over 12,000 years. But by the start of the 21st century, of the 22 species or zoological genera identifiable in the Palaeolithic caves, only eight survived. And then there were seven.

Yet few people are kicking up a fuss, even though ibex are an ideal candidate for reintroduction. They are inoffensive herbivores. They could even serve to nourish the bears if there were ever enough of the two species for them to have the chance – or bad luck, depending on your point of view – of meeting up. There are some further south in Spain but the Spanish are not interested in letting them go.[*]

Are there any truly wild animals in the Pyrenees? Any which have escaped our Pygmalion hands?

After breakfast I climb up to the plateau above. There are sheep everywhere, 6-month-old lambs and their mothers, two flocks mingling, stars for some, hearts for others, but unified by their distinctive coiffure: long back-and-sides with a razor-cut belly.

---

[*] The Spanish eventually relented with the first reintroductions arriving in 2014.

This is where the Haute-Garonne *département* becomes Ariège. Walkers whom I have met coming the other way describe Ariège as the most difficult section of the Pyrenean Way. Although the mountains are less dramatic, there is a distinct lack of facilities for hikers. The rare beds or meals are not to be sniffed at.

A blue emergency-services helicopter passes overhead as it descends towards the Lac d'Araing, scattering the sheep in its noisy wake. By the time I arrive at the hostel on the shores of the reservoir, it has flown off. It came for a man who had a minor accident yesterday, knocking his head, I am told. He appeared to have recovered, but in the night he started vomiting repeatedly.

The hostel looks like a big slab of milk chocolate with a small entrance made by nibbling mice. Officially it is run by Anoura Barre but there are half a dozen friends involved and I can't quite make out who does what, or indeed which one Anoura might be. I eat lunch in the sunshine and then go to take a siesta in the dormitory. Less than an hour later the sound of thunder and torrential rain beating on the aluminium structure gets me out of bed. Maurice is here, having arrived just before the storm. The door opens and an elderly woman comes in, dripping.

'Hello Julie. You're not a moment too early!' says Maurice, helping her to remove her rucksack. 'No. It's a long way from Fos,' she replies, grumpily.

'You stayed in Fos! I wondered why you didn't show up at the Auberge du Crabère.'

'I did. But when I arrived, the woman said that it was fully booked for the night. She didn't look too pleased to see me. I think I must have disturbed her siesta. So I had to go down to Fos again and climb back up this morning.' She looks out of the window: 'I hope it's not like this tomorrow.'

'Don't worry, the storm will stop soon,' Maurice reassures her.

Julie is from Quebec. Retired, she is walking the Pyrenean Way, but is travelling light, with neither sleeping bag nor cooking equipment, so she has to stay under a roof each night. She is going to skip the rest of Ariège and rejoin the path at Mérens. Maurice has met her *en route* on various occasions.

The door opens again. This time it is a fat man wearing nothing but a spare tyre and a pair of shorts, soaked to the skin, with a sodden poodle by his side. He mutters something to himself in German, drags a towel out of his rucksack, and dries the dog. We ask him the standard question. 'Melles,' he replies.

Maurice asks another young man: 'I suppose you are walking, too?'

'No, I came by plane. We don't all have the same ideas,' he replies.

'Really! What sport do you do then?'

'I was joking. I work here. But every day I get asked where I have come from. I don't *even* have time to go walking.'

'That's a pity. But you could have arrived by plane. I'm a parachutist,' Maurice explains.

He does precision jumping. You leap out of the plane at 4000 metres. All you can see is the runway of the aerodrome, a linear concrete blur. As you descend you look out for the yellow target. You open your parachute. You aim for the black bull's-eye, 1 metre across, in the centre of the yellow target. If you get it right, you land with one heel on an electronic pad three centimetres in diameter in the centre of the bull's-eye. He also does artistic jumping – the competitors have to execute acrobatic figures – whilst descending in free fall at 240km/h. He started at the age of 38. Maurice is evidently pleased to have found an audience.

'The rain will stop soon,' he repeats.

He is right. After the storm I go to sit on the bluff behind the hostel. The last of the thunderclouds are being chased down the valley by the wind. At the bottom of the slope, somewhere way out of view in the forest, must be the road. Above it vast swathes of rhododendrons lap over the pastures. An unchanging landscape, it seems, indifferent to the tempests which shake humans to their core.

And yet, the landscape is changing. While it was raining outside, I was reading a dissertation written by Anoura for his Mountain Guide Diploma. Despite all appearances, the rhododendrons are not sleeping in their beds, they are in the process of colonising the hills. As sheep disappear, the pastures are replaced by rhododendrons and gorse, to disappear in turn under scrub and then forest. The flowerbeds have doubled in size over the last 30 years.

So the mountains are not immutable, changing only to the rhythm of some geological metronome, but in continuous flux, and the changes can be seen within a shepherd's lifetime.

Anoura also reports the reflections of Yves Garel, his predecessor. When Yves first started working in isolated mountain hostels, every drop of hot water was precious, an unexpected pleasure to be savoured. Now walkers expect free hot showers, although the hostels haven't moved any nearer to the pylons. The evenings were convivial, with the remote situation and the common experience of walking bringing people together, creating exchanges which wouldn't happen in a city hotel. Now, walkers increasingly want private space, to retire to their own room. In the common room, increasingly they keep to themselves, Yves regrets.

Lac d'Araing to the Cabane de l'Arech

I climb up to the pass, where a few metres of rusty railway and an electricity pylon betray the former presence of industry: the top end of the Bentaillou mine. Way below me on the ragged scarp slope, I can see the decaying remains of the workers' accommodation and mine buildings clinging to a rocky knoll, in a windy Machu Picchu setting. Around the mine, the entrails of the mountain have been vomited over the grassy carpet, the spoil tips staining it irrecoverably.

The end of the Bentaillou mine was just as final as that of the Mines d'Arre et d'Anglas between Gabas and Gourette, but played out on an

The Bentaillou mine

altogether different time-scale, with roots going back, quite literally, millennia. For Roman authors the Pyrenean rivers ran with silver, and gold was just as easily extracted. The rediscovery of ancient mines at Aulus in Ariège in AD 1600 contributed to the reputation in a Europe about to embark on an Industrial Revolution. The natural resources of the Pyrenees began to be exploited once again. '*L'Ariège produit des hommes et du fer* – Ariège produces men and iron' is the description attributed to one of Napoleon's officers.

He could have been talking about the Biros valley here. By 1850 the valley was overcrowded and emigration was the only future for many youngsters, so the opening of a new mine at Bentaillou was a welcome alternative. But it was to bring problems in its wake: the extraction of zinc, lead, and silver, from 1853 onwards, was to be financed by capital from Bordeaux. And the miners' adrenalin rush at the exposure of each new seam was often dissipated when they were confronted with the cruel reality of the dislocated geology of the mountains.

The scene was set. As in many valleys, the opening up of the mines was the first act in a tragedy which would eventually deprive the valley, first of its independence, and then of its population. Initially, the farmer-workers combined their pastoral activities with occasional employment in the mines, a day here, a day there – a kind of multi-activity before its time. But then workers from outside were brought in, as control passed from Bordeaux to Paris and then to England. By now the owners would only take on full-time staff. This was the end of the first act.

Then in 1879 a technological innovation was to transform the economics of the mine: a cableway was installed. This simple idea eradicated one of the major problems: the relief. The production increased dramatically. This was the beginning of the second act. (Incidentally, throughout the Pyrenees, cableways enabled the extraction of minerals and timber on a new scale and, with the arrival of winter sports, they became a vital part in the exploitation of that other emerging resource: snow.)

Back in the Biros valley new sites were being opened up. By 1904, the mines were employing 400 people, but the ore was becoming progressively more elusive. Bentaillou went through a series of owners until it was finally closed down in the 1950s: 600,000 tonnes of ore had been extracted. The valley had been transformed both physically and socially. It couldn't return to its former autarchy. Nor did it have the resources to develop in a new direction. It didn't even have the resources to clean up the mess left behind by a century of colonial exploitation. By the time the mine closed, 30% of the arable surface in the Ariège mountains had already been abandoned. The population dwindled. The commune, Sentein, had 1362 inhabitants in 1856 but just 150 in 2004. This was the final act of the tragedy.

A small marble monument by the side of the path is a reminder of another drama which took place here.

In memory of
Anglade, Fortuné
Perrissé, Alphonse
Seube, Henri
Electricity Board workers
29 December 1960

There is no other explanation but the date and the relief suggest an avalanche.

I head down to Eylie d'en Haut, a pleasant village, with a refreshing stream and buddleia bushes, only locally defaced by the remains of the mining industry. It is here that the ore was crushed before being transported down to the plain.

Going up again amongst ferns and flowers, the sun is intense, and although I filled up with water in Eylie I am consuming it rapidly. Opposite me, the pastures are parcelled up by hedges grown up into trees, each package with a postage stamp barn in the corner, testimony to the density of the habitation and the need to extract a maximum of hay from the lower slopes in summer whilst the sheep were in the *estives*.

The hostel has prepared me a packed meal. Although the sandwiches are dry as only *pain de campagne* country bread can be, I have to eat every crumb of them. It will be three days before I reach the next hostel and I only just have enough food. Pour water on one side, says the recipe. Turn the sandwich over and repeat. Leave for five minutes. Accompany with a bottle of tepid water. Anoura has also sold me a large lump of *pain de campagne* and some Bethmale, a local cow's milk cheese.

'We don't really do provisions,' he told me. 'We often get asked, because there is no alternative. But it all has to be brought up from the valley in a rucksack so it is very expensive. I'm always embarrassed at the price.'

The cheese is 30€ for a kilo, but I would have paid more. It *is* very good.

The clouds are building up menacingly so I cut my lunch short. Within a few minutes I have arrived at a bifurcation. To the right, the path continues to the Mail de Bullard, another high-level mine. The seam was rich but the access dangerous. The owners called it *La reine des Pyrénées* – the queen of the Pyrenees, the workers called it *La mangeuse d'hommes* – the man-eater.

My path, however, turns in the other direction and descends a little, to the Cabane de l'Arech, five minutes' walk from the ridge. *Priorité au berger*, a notice says. I knock, and then try the door. It isn't locked. Inside, the ash in the hearth is still warm but there is no other sign of recent occupation. There is the usual collection of bottles – though none of the quality of the Cabanes de Peyrehitte – but at least there is a table. There is a single bed on the ground floor with a mattress; *but* it is decorated by a series of circular stains. Upstairs, under the eaves, the three mattresses are clean, and there are some slippers which fit me. But for the moment the attic is stiflingly hot, so I go outside.

I am thirsty, and my water has run out so I go in search of a spring. The one marked on my map is dry, but I discover a sheep trough with a black plastic pipe leading into it and fill up my bottles adding some dehydrated water tablets. Of course, they go under the name of water *purifying* tablets, but I never liked the idea. It was only when I realised that they were really *dehydrated* water that I started to believe in them.

The angry clouds have now dissipated so I lie down and sunbathe: a contented baby taking his afternoon nap, nestling down into the thick grass, dozing from time to time, in a grandiose natural cradle.

The uncoordinated sheep on the slopes above me graze from pasture to pasture, but as the sun descends one after another they fall into line behind a leader. Another group does the same, behind a different leader, and they start to come down the hill, lines coalescing like fleece on a spinning wheel, until they form a single yarn, returning to the salt cakes strewn around the hut.

I get dressed and am just sorting out which food dust I am going to eat when Maurice arrives, waving his hands, showing the purple-stained palms.

'Bilberries,' he says. 'I've also got some mushrooms,' he adds, waving two plastic bags in front of me. 'Did you see the raspberries near the mine?' he asks.

'No. I saw the bilberry bushes in the forest but I didn't see any fruit on them.'

'You shouldn't walk with your eyes on the ground all the time. To really appreciate the walking you've got to stop and look around.'

He unfolds his tent, explaining: 'I snore, and I don't want to keep us both awake all night. I'd keep you awake when I snore, and myself awake trying to avoid keeping you awake.'

'Are there any hunters here?' he asks me, unexpectedly.

I look at the empty hillside: 'No, I can't see any. Why?'

'When I told my friends I was coming here, they said that I'd better be careful,' he says, taking his tee-shirt off and turning round. His back is covered with a mat of black hair.

'I don't want be mistaken for a bear.'

We each prepare our meal, Maurice sharing what he says are girolles – they look rather odd to me but I feel obliged to eat them, at risk of being poisoned – and the bilberries.

'Why are you walking the Pyrenean Way?' I ask him. I am half way along it and I still don't know what my answer would be.

'*Parce que c'est mythique* – it's mythical. It was my wife who introduced me to walking – and the Pyrenees. She's left, but the walking has stayed. It's a challenge and I wanted to see if I was up to it. I've been walking 80km a week in preparation but it isn't just strength. It is a question of the head and the mule. Divided at the neck. You need both, of course. But if the head leads the mule will follow… And there's the muscular exhilaration. It's like a drug, I think.'

He spots a couple of walkers coming down the path. A thin young woman bouncing along in front. A man trudging along after her, carrying a rucksack which extends out behind him in all directions.

'Have you seen the size of the rucksack?' Maurice exclaims. 'They must have one of those instant tents you can get from Decathlon. They weigh a ton.'

'The head and the mule?' I suggest.

When they arrive, we see that their tent is not a Decathlon special, but the rucksack is still overflowing.

'We are camping,' Martin tells me in English. 'We are students so we don't have much money, but we do have plenty of holidays.'

They started at Luchon this year, having walked there from the Atlantic two years ago. They camped near the Lac d'Araing last night, though I didn't notice them. Martin has just graduated. Sylvia graduated last year, has taken a year off, and is going to do an MA in September.

'I'm hungry,' Martin complains. 'She won't let me eat, except at lunch time.'

'I don't want you to get any fatter,' Sylvia chides.

'It's true that I've put on weight. I'm finding it much more difficult than the last time. I'm exhausted at the end of the day,' he explains.

Martin goes off to wash at the sheep trough, shouting joyously as he splashes himself.

'If I had no clothes on, I wouldn't go announcing it to the world,' comments Sylvia.

She goes and washes more discreetly. It is getting late so I light them a fire to cook on.

'What would you like to eat?' Sylvia asks Martin. 'Tomato soup or vegetable soup?'

'Whatever you like,' he replies.

'I asked you what you wanted. I don't mind.'

'Tomato then, but we can have the vegetable if you like.'

'Ok. Let's have that.'

They eat the vegetable soup, reconstituted with a minimum of liquid to give it a thicker consistency, and finish off the meal with a bit of cake. Then they have a bowl of tomato soup. We all sit around the fire chatting, with Sylvia and me translating.

'I want to see a bear,' she insists.

'I don't. I don't want to be attacked,' says Martin. 'I think they should be exterminated. The government should get rid of them.'

Sylvia and Martin have just reached the edge of their map and are going to have to rely on a guidebook which covers all the major Pyrenean paths in a pocket-sized volume, with maps drawn by a spider which has just climbed out of an ink bottle.

'He walks so slowly,' complains Sylvia.

'So you carry the food, like a carrot, to make him walk faster?' I ask.

'Oh, no. He has the food.'

'But if you carried more, then he could walk faster.'

Neither of them thinks this is a reasonable idea.

Having seen the mattresses upstairs, they decide to spend the night in the hut. I sleep downstairs.

Cabane de l'Arech to the Cabane d'Aouen

I want to walk as much as possible in the shade, while the sun is still hidden behind the mountains, so I get up first. The path follows a track for a few minutes before it leaps head-first into the valley, only slowing down when it hits the edge of the forest. Although the sun has officially risen by now, under the tree cover it is still sombre, indeed sinister.

The winter here must have been very dry as last autumn's leaves have not decayed, rustling with every step. Normally, I like walking along kicking at the leaves, but today I feel uneasy. Can I hear another noise? Another rustling? I stop. Nothing. I try to walk quietly. I'm sure there is a rustling noise somewhere ahead. I stop again. It stops. There is something there, watching me. But I can't see it. I walk a few wary paces further and the rustling recommences, then develops into a frightening crescendo, a noise like the vapour escaping from the pistons of a steam train as it gains speed, faster and faster. And then it stops dead. Silence. But my eyes have followed the sound. At first all I can make out is a white backside, but then the beast moves into a patch of light. It is only an *isard* running away from me up the slope.

The path crosses the river and then cruelly climbs up again on the other side. On the subsequent ridge I get lost, following a path perfectly marked with red and white waymarks, but not the Pyrenean Way. By the time I have retraced my steps, the sun has turned into an instrument of torture. I hide from it in one of the many huts which mark this part of the route, enjoying the chance to lie down in the dark with my eyes shut.

The path crosses a second valley, the Ribérot, and climbs again, back into the shade of the forest, but by now even the trees are sweating. At every stream I slop water over my head. At every spring I refill my bottles.

A small collie dog scurries up to me, gives me a quick sniff and then continues on its downhill trajectory. It is followed by a young woman in sports shorts and an elastic top, running directly down the slope, ignoring the path, using her long stick like a rudder behind her to steady her descent.

The Cabane d'Aouen, where I intend to sleep the night, is already occupied by a man from Bayonne who offers me some freshly brewed tea, in a choice of several varieties. 22 kg; Eylie d'en Haut. The shepherdess, he tells me, has just left. I would have seen her on my way up. She has two-thirds of the hut. There is still space for me in the separate room reserved for walkers.

The double bed takes up practically the entire room so I unpack my rucksack outside, and then go off in search of the spring. There are no sheep and the grass has grown high, perfumed like a flower shop by the wild carnations, there are so many of them. Opposite me, determinedly vertical but unusually stunted pine trees cling by their toenails to the cliff face. Further away, I can make out patches of snow on the slopes of Valier.

Maurice arrives later and pitches his tent, but Martin and Sylvia haven't got this far. Fearing neither sun nor lightning, they prefer a morning lie in, they told us yesterday.

Maurice and I agree that the next stop has to be Esbints. It is a real hostel, but more importantly, it sells provisions. I thought I had packed too much food, but I calculate that I will only have sugar cubes and coffee left after tomorrow's wild raspberry and reconstituted dust breakfast.

Cabane d'Aouen to Esbints

At first light, I walk along a path high above the valley of the Ribérot. Below, clouds slopping from shore to shore push up from the Toulouse sea, its liquid surface glistening in the low light. The Pic de Crabère – named after the female *isard* – casts a witch-black shadow, filling the horizon. Above, the heavens are empty; the sun is still struggling to disperse the night's damp legacy. The pastures are being tended by horses, cows, and sheep, in separate battalions, advancing in long lines across the vegetation.

On the shores of the Étang d'Ayes I scoop up the lake water with my hands and pour it over my hair. Then I plaster my face with sun cream and search out the spring marked on my map. The sun has captured the mountain tops, but I soon discover that it has not yet captured the slopes. Passing onto the northern side of the hill, I am suddenly enveloped in cold fog, with visibility down to a few paces, the air so thick that I can stick out my tongue and lick it.

Back in forest, the clearings are covered with St John's Wort and *geranium des Alpes*, yellow and purple five-petalled flowers intermingled as far as the eye can see, which is not very far. Nearby, shallow scoops in the ground signal the recent presence of wild boar looking for roots.

By the time I arrive at the Col de la Core I am frozen through. I hide behind an abandoned roadside caravan, which in better weather might have served me a snack, and light my gas stove to make some coffee. Maurice materialises with Jean-Michel, a walker he has just met. 12 kg; Hendaye; 22 days ago. We set off together down the hill.

We are soon below the clouds and, although the sun is still invisible, we heat up, going faster and faster in one of those puerile games favoured by men who have just met in the context of a sporting activity. There is also the incentive of lunch. If we are too late we will have to starve for another seven hours until the evening meal. We stop to take our anoraks off.

'Ow!' cries Maurice, slapping his thigh.

'*Merde*. What's that?' asks Jean-Michel, scraping a squashed brown insect off his arm.

'A horsefly,' I reply, brushing one off the back of my neck.

A swarm of them is chasing after us. We put our rucksacks back on and start running, cursing. Three men with big rucksacks running down the mountain, madly jumping and skipping for no apparent reason. Slapping themselves and each other, shouting loudly, occasionally yelping.

We hammer desperately on the door of the hostel but there is no answer. I lie on the grass, reasoning that at least my back won't get bitten. Then a car arrives and somebody gets out.

The woman who comes up the steps is fair-haired, tanned, and smiling. She introduces herself as Gila.

'I don't do hot meals at lunch time,' she tells us, with a slight German accent, 'but I can put something cold together, if that would be alright. Go and have a shower first if you want. Would you like to sit outside or inside?'

The horseflies having disappeared, we opt for outside.

She fetches tomatoes, with basil and garlic cloves to spread on top of them; melon, pâté, cheese, yoghurt and fruit; wine and beer; and home-made rye bread.

'It's burnt on the bottom, because that's the way my grandmother used to make it and I like the caramelised taste, but I advise you to cut it off.'

She brings us tea and coffee afterwards and Maurice invites her to sit down and have a cup for herself.

'Did you have any trouble finding your way in the fog?' Gila asks.

'No. The only point where I hesitated was at the Col d'Auèdole,' replied Maurice.

'There were signs pointing in every direction except towards Esbints,' I add.

'Since the *département* has taken over, things have gone downhill,' says Gila. 'What about the path?'

'It was fine. Just after Eylie d'en Haut, somebody had recently cleared the undergrowth.'

'So the council *has* taken some notice of our complaints.' Gila continues: 'They're not very keen on maintaining existing paths. They're more interested in creating new ones, because they can get grants for that. But even the new ones are not always very well thought out. Last year two people were killed on a path near here, so they've had to improve it… We're very reliant on the Pyrenean Way but the number of visitors has decreased. Walkers by-pass Ariège because there aren't enough hostels and the council does nothing to encourage new ones.'

She continues: 'Or they get lost, stupidly. Recently two walkers arrived at my door, asking to use the phone. Their friend was ill, they said. I told them that the police wouldn't do anything unless he couldn't move, and sent them back. They reappeared later with the friend. The next day I found out the real story from the man himself. He hadn't been ill. He was just extremely tired and got left behind. He had been following the path when he found that it was barred by a bit of blue string. So he assumed it was the end of the path, and went off across the *garrigue*. He got himself into a thorough mess, so he decided to pitch his tent. Then he got down on his knees and prayed. God's reply was thunder and lightning. Even more worried, he packed up his tent and went back to the blue string, which is where his friends found him. The blue string was an electric fence to keep the cows in!'

A hen suddenly starts clucking.

'She's singing,' says Gila. 'I will have to go to find the egg. Feed the scraps to the pig.'

The pig is waiting on the other side of a wooden gate. She is Vietnamese, very black, and very pot-bellied.

'When are you going to eat her?' I ask.

'Never. My husband and my son would like to. But Zita is my pig so we are not going to eat her.'

It's like bears, I think. Giving them a name protects them; makes killing them less acceptable.

Maurice and Jean-Michel put up their tents and I go for a siesta in the building reserved for walkers. When I wake up, Gila's son, Mathias, is coming back down from the meadow with a haystack on his head. I can hear the sound of an accordion being played in the house.

Martin and Sylvia have arrived.

'There is somebody lost on the mountains in the fog. But they heard the accordion music and somebody is going to search for them. I think,' Martin tells me.

Come dinnertime, I am sitting at the table in the corner of a room in the main house. The table is not a piece of furniture, it is part of the structure. Although, theoretically, it could be moved it seems improbable that this has happened since it was built in this very room some lifetimes ago. It is square and could comfortably seat four on each side, though there are only eleven of us eating. It is piled with food, dominated by dishes holding the various elements of a *couscous*. The rest of the room is in keeping: the hearth and neighbouring bread oven; the beams which span its entire width; even Gila's more modern kitchen which runs its length.

'What happened about the person who was lost?' someone asks Gila. 'Did they find her?'

'Yes. It was Christine,' Gila replies, indicating a thin, pretty, young woman with curly red hair.

'I think I've worked out what happened now,' Christine tells us. 'Gila gave me instructions from the Col de la Core but as I was walking up the road somebody stopped to give me a lift. They thought they knew where I should go, so they dropped me off at a path. But it was the wrong path so I was lost from the start.'

'Where were you when you heard the music?' I ask.

'I didn't hear any music,' replies Christine, doubtfully.

'I was playing the accordion this afternoon to calm myself down,' clarifies Gila. 'If she had continued she could have fallen off a cliff. But she couldn't have heard me where she was.'

'How did you get back then?' I continue.

'I kept on trying to ring up on my mobile but it couldn't find the network. Then finally it worked. Mathias came to fetch me.'

Christine was going up to see Gila's husband, Francis, in the *estive* on Valier, and intended to stay there for some weeks. She wants to see what life would be like as a shepherdess.

'But I'm not going up into the mountains again on my own,' she says, emphatically.

'You'll have to wait until Wednesday, when my son can take you,' says Gila. Today is Saturday. 'I'm too busy at present, but you can see how the farm works in the meantime.'

Christine tells me that she had tried everywhere before she found someone who would take her on. Eventually she found Francis on the Internet.

'It's difficult if you are a woman, and not from round here, to find an opening,' explains Gila. 'I know that from when I first came here 28 years ago. When I did my training there were no shepherdesses. Young women simply didn't go up into the mountains on their own. What would an honest woman be doing up there with all those virile men? You should have heard the tales they told about me at the fair in Foix. Horrible! I could have cried but it was so ridiculous, I decided just to laugh it off. But I had a different life then. I used to walk barefoot.'

She tells another story: 'One morning I was bathing in a stream a little way from my hut and I saw the helicopter from the *gendarmerie* circling overhead. It just kept on circling round and round. All my clothes were in the hut. *Hallucinant!*'

Maurice recounts our descent from the Col de la Core pursued by horseflies.

'I killed three of them with one swipe,' he boasts.

'I don't kill them,' says Christine. 'I like insects. There are so many you could never kill them all, so it doesn't help to kill them. I just brush them off.'

She shows me her bulging wrist where she was a little slow in reacting.

'How long have you been here?' I ask Gila.

'Ten years. It was a hostel already but we have done lots of restoration. We needed something to supplement our income from the sheep. Multi-activity. The idea was that we would share the time in the *estive*, with one of us in the mountains and the other here. But Francis isn't renowned for his cooking so I asked him how he was going to cope. "I'll open a few cans," he said. I told him that it wasn't good enough. So he is up there with the animals and I am here with the walkers.'

Francis is a rare breed – an owner-shepherd. Most pastoralists are either sheep farmers who employ shepherds, or shepherds working for one or more owners. Francis is looking after 800 sheep, of which only 80 actually belong to him. For each of the four months in the *estives* he receives 1€ per sheep. He also cares for about 25 cows which are paid a little better. Naturally, he has a *patou*.

He is also a rare breed in another sense. A shepherd who sees bears as part of the Pyrenean landscape. On a pro-bear website he is quoted as saying:

Fundamentally, profoundly, as a human being and a Pyrenean I believe that our mountains will no longer be the same [if the bears disappear]; that they lose a little of their splendour every time a bear dies. The bear is a legendary symbol of our region; he has always been an integral part of it. More concretely, he is also the proof that our countryside remains natural. Here biodiversity is still possible. The countryside is not simply a semblance of nature made for and by man.

I go back to Esbints at the beginning of October 2010. Francis has just brought the animals back from the *estives* and the first lamb of the season has just been born. After four months essentially alone, he is in an expansive mood. Since the reintroductions in 1996, he tells me, he has lost a total of three sheep to the bears.

'I once met a group of Canadians,' he continues. 'They asked me why there was so much anti-bear graffiti in the area. How many were there? I felt a bit ridiculous when I had to tell them that there were twenty in the whole of the Pyrenees.'

'Have you seen one?'

'Never, although I have seen footprints around my spring just above the hut. It's the only one on our mountain and the bears drink there like all the other animals. I get up early, but bears are nocturnal.'

'Aren't you afraid?'

'That's an interesting question. I have always asked myself how I would react to a bear. It's a waste of time to run or to cry out, but...'

Francis and Gila are trying to adapt to the new economic and social conditions. Consumers are prepared to pay for quality but also demand certified organic labelling. So the farm went organic in 2000. To increase their margins, they sell directly to the consumers. And they produce *broutards* – lambs fattened in the *estives*.

Most of the sheep in the French Pyrenees (except in the Basque country) are raised for their meat. In general the lambs are sold soon after birth for a low price to Spanish or Italian farmers. Lambs which have been brought up naturally are then fed whatever is necessary to get them onto a plate as quickly as possible. The *broutards* are more work but, since they are organic, the extra effort is rewarded. I ask Gila if the system is economic.

'Not without the subsidies, no,' she replies.

Although Francis and Gila have found a work-around, the main problem for other shepherds is the lack of an officially recognised system for fattening organic sheep. As Corinne Eychenne writes in her thesis:

> The farmers find themselves in a paradoxical situation. They are proud of their skill in raising sheep in the extensive mountain pastures and the resulting quality of their produce. But then they are obliged to sell the animals to merchants who practice intensive fattening with no interest in a quality end product.

Back to the Pyrenean Way and my first evening at Esbints. Gila advises the seven of us who are heading east to follow the main path up to the Cabane d'Aula even though it is a long way round.

'It's beautiful up there, and the short-cut is dull.'

The over-riding advantage of the short-cut, however, is that it passes through Seix, where there is a shop. The monolingual Anglophones, unable to distinguish between the pronunciation of Seix and sex, whisper amongst themselves.

In the end, only Maurice and I, not interested in the Seix shop, decide to go the long way round.

Esbints to the Cabane d'Aula

Breakfast is at the same table. While I am eating Gila prepares me a packed lunch and provisions for the next two days. Four hens come in through the open door.

'They've come to ask for their breakfast as well,' says Gila.

Seeing them I ask: 'Could I have some boiled eggs to take with me? It would be nice to have some really fresh eggs.'

'You can have some boiled eggs but they will be from the shop. The fox attacked our hens so I'm trying to build up the flock again.'

She gives me two hard-boiled eggs and I set off along the tarmac which the Pyrenean Way follows here. Later, when finally the road stops and becomes a path, I see a multilingual sign inciting walkers to take their rubbish home. It is covered in red paint, graffiti: 'Keep walking. Alaric, see U at cabin. Happy 17th. Luv H+J xx'. The graffiti is written in English, though Alaric is exclusively a French name.

Further along, in the woods, I read: '*Mort aux écolos de l'ours* – Death to the bear-loving ecologists.' Francis has his *estive* higher up the valley. Is this graffiti aimed at him?

An hour later, I come upon a clearing which smells of wood smoke. A barn by the side of the path is so chock-a-block with timber that it is falling out of the window under the eaves. The building next to it is being renovated. Two workmen and an old man, whom I take to be the owner, are standing outside, so I say hello. The old man looks at me suspiciously without replying. A young woman rushes out of the door with an Alsatian on a lead. The Alsatian doesn't like me either. I quickly say good-bye.

In the middle of the woods there is a huge block of stone perched precariously above the path. Under it there is a flower pot with a few very dried-up flowers, and a plaque.

Eric Garcia 1971–1994. Your life was full of nature and mountains, the object of all your studies. Your passion for life was stronger than yours. The memory of you will remain for ever engraved in our hearts.

An arrow points up at the block of stone.

The head of the valley is filled with clouds. I can't see from here, but I can guess where Francis has his sheep, way above me on the valley side. It can't be much fun up there today. But as I climb, the clouds climb too and I arrive at the Cabane d'Aula at the same time as the first sun of the day. The hut is at the very end of the valley, on the last flat pasture. Nearby, some cows are grazing peacefully.

To one side, the ragged summit of Valier is breaking up like a rotten eye tooth exposed to the extremes of heat and cold, shedding unwanted enamel on the slopes. In front of me, the frontier ridge has long since buried its feet under still-mobile scree. On the other side, the pass which the Pyrenean Way traverses seems hardly lower than the mountains which flank it. But that is for tomorrow.

I inspect the inside of the hut. Rough concrete walls, a corrugated iron roof. An old notice complains about vandalism and asks walkers to respect the building, but it is too late. The remains of the facilities are now ash in the chimney. The only surviving furniture is made of metal: rusty bunk beds, a few wobbly stools, and a table. The window is broken.

Outside, the view down the valley is clearing, and I can see Maurice lumbering up.

'I've lost my hat,' he complains. 'I left it on a rock. When I realised, I went back, but by the time I got there it had gone. I've had it for 20 years.'

We construct a table outside from a flagstone and a couple of stools, and eat rye bread, cheese, sausage, and apples, for the second time today, surveying the empty landscape. Maurice points at Valier.

'It must be somewhere there that she fell,' he says. He doesn't need to say more for me to understand.

Gila told us about a woman who nearly came to grief returning from the summit. She was walking alone and became disorientated in the low clouds, but she kept on going down, until she reached their base. Way below her, she could see the shepherds' huts in the valley Maurice and I have just walked along. There wasn't much vegetation because the slopes were steep, so although there was no path she made good progress. Then she fell, breaking her pelvis. She had been trying to descend a face normally reserved for rock climbers with ropes. For four days she dragged herself through the rhododendrons, across scree and broken rocks. The mountain rescue helicopter flew overhead seven times without seeing her.

That might have been the end of the story, but one of the shepherds in his *estive* half-heard an unusual noise. Without knowing that there was someone missing, he had the feeling that something was wrong: shepherds need to pay attention to their senses. He went to investigate and noticed a patch of rhododendrons which had been compacted like a nest, so he continued searching until he found the woman. But he realised that his sheep were grazing on the slopes immediately above. They could easily create a landslide, he thought, and he went off immediately to move them to safety.

The woman, in her confused state, thought her last chance of rescue had disappeared. When the shepherd returned he found that he couldn't move her so he went to the local police station – mobile telephones don't work over large areas of the Pyrenees. It was night and he was agitated. He rang the door phone and talked to the policeman inside. His tale seemed so unlikely that the police thought he was drunk or deranged and refused to open the door. Until the shepherd said: 'If you don't come out and do something, I will break the door down.' Finally convinced, the police set the rescue services in motion.

With the story still in our heads, we clear our things off the table and leave the salt-loving cows to lick it clean. I light a fire in the hearth and we sit next to it, Maurice reciting the *FFRP Guide* in detail, calculating the number of hours walking from here to Mérens, and where to stay the night. At the moment when the last light disappears from the sky we hear peculiar squeaking noises coming from outside:

pwiiiu…pwu…pwiiiu… pwu… pwu… pwu

It is too dark to see anything but the sound is circling above us and then coming to rest on the cliffs. Two birds certainly; three, perhaps even four. They sound like bearded vultures – but I'm no expert – coming home to roost. One of the rarest carrion-eaters in Europe, the bearded vulture intervenes after all the others, nourishing itself on the bones, which its stomach juices can dissolve. The larger bones, it carries high into the sky and drops against rocks to break them. Are they really bearded vultures? We will never know. At first I feel frustrated but quickly realise that it doesn't matter. Whatever they are, they have enchanted us anyway with their twilight magic.

Cabane d'Aula to Rouze

The sky is beautifully blue, or would be if there was enough colour in it to be any colour at all. I think it is Monday morning, but I might be wrong. Down below, the valley is partially veiled, but the red band of sunrise is already showing. The wind is warm and my rucksack seems light, but the path up to the pass makes no concessions to the early hour and my legs are heavy.

It is 7:30am. Just beyond the pass, a bright blue van is parked at the end of a gravel track. The back door is swinging open but there is no sign of an occupant and neither humans nor animals in the vicinity. Two unopened bags of salt and a sleeping bag on the passenger seat are the only clues as to the owner.

Turning round, I can hear a faint metallic noise in the distance. I can see something now, at the top of the hill on the opposite side of the pass. A small white handkerchief coming towards me. Some black specks running around the hem, barking. A taller blob behind. Some other black specks hovering overhead.

I'm not sure if it is the birds, the dogs, or the shepherd which are encouraging them the most, but the sheep are now almost running

Shepherd's van with Valier in the background

down the ridge. Finally in the valley, the dogs corral them into a neat rectangle and sit down.

I continue. An hour later, the path surmounts a small hummock and heads in the direction of the sun. Blinded, I can hardly see anything, but there seems to be a helicopter, a large tent, a humming generator, and a white van in a temporary enclosure. There are several people milling about. Has there been an accident? I can't understand what is happening, until I get closer and notice the cows. The shining dome is a refrigeration unit. The tent harbours a mobile milking station.

'As far as I know we are the only people to work like this,' the man tells me. 'We have 39 cows. As they go up the hill in search of new pasture we follow them.'

'Where have you come from today?' he asks me.

'The Cabane d'Aula.'

'Where's that? We've only been here since November.'

I explain. 'Where were you before you moved here, then?' I ask.

'Near Le Mans.'

He tells me that they were attracted by the subsidies, which are not available in northern France.

Lower down, at the Col de Pause, I take a break, walking a little off the path to find some shade. Much further down the valley, when the Pyrenean Way has joined a tarmac road, I meet a white-bearded Rumpelstiltskin with a rucksack even bigger than Martin's. He is hobbling, not because he has stamped on the ground in anger as in the fairy story, but because his walking stick is too short. In fact it isn't a walking stick; it is a brand new ice axe which barely reaches up to his knee. In order to use it he has to bend over to one side. He looks decidedly unstable. We don't swap names.

Then I walk through a couple of chocolate box villages down to Couflens, a village – and a valley – which seems to have missed several opportunities, for better or for worse. The Port de Salau at the head of the valley is one of the lowest passes into Spain in Ariège. According to Joanne, writing in 1858, 26,000 people passed through here each year. There were even projects for a cross-frontier road and a railway in the 19th century but they came to nothing. Then there was the paper factory – which closed in the 1920s – and the tungsten mine – which closed in 1986. But now there is not even a shop.

Maurice is already here – he must have passed me at the Col de Pause – eating lunch in a *lavoir* which has been converted into a covered picnic area. A female cyclist, met by chance, is telling him the intimate details of her double hip replacement. Not wanting to disturb them, and scenting the proximity of the public toilets, I decide to race for Rouze in the hope of finding sustenance at the hostel there.

The track up to Rouze is typical of the Ariège foothills. The path rises slowly through the trees – half of Ariège is covered in forest – following a small stream. Although we are well into summer, the ground is squishy from recent storms. Underfoot, ferns and grass alternate with cow pats and horseflies. Former habitation is represented by remains ranging from nettle-covered mounds, through piles of stones, to ruins. Where the path approaches a road, the ruins have been renovated. The numerous electric fences have insulated handles to allow walkers to unhook the wire and pass through unscathed.

At the hostel in Rouze I am supplied with a very large, very red, very juicy tomato – which soaks up the enormous quantities of salt and garlic I sprinkle onto it – some bread, and some goat's cheese, before being shooed away from the table on the terrace outside the house.

'There's a table outside the dormitory just up there, which will be more convenient for you,' says Jean-Pierre, the farmer. 'I'm going away for the afternoon, but make yourself at home.'

Maurice arrives while I am eating. He had intended to go further but the heat and the lack of a hat have discouraged him. The heat intensifies but clouds start to arrive from Spain, billowing at first, then blackening. By 4 o'clock it is raining. Through the window of the hostel, we can see the lightning striking Valier. Half an hour later the farm is awash, the lightning and thunder all around. Maurice comments: '*Il pleut comme vache qui pisse* – It's raining like a cow pissing.'

A voluminous, agitated mass runs up the steps outside, taking them two at a time. The door opens and the mass divests itself of its outer layers leaving rucksack, anorak, pullover, and boots in a sad, damp, inert pile on the floor, and a jumpy, shivering man in front of us. It is as if all the energy has been sucked out of the discarded shell of clothes and concentrated in the man himself.

'… twenty minutes from Couflens,' he gasps. It took *me* thirty and I thought I was doing well.

'Sit down and have a cup of tea,' I suggest.

'Yes,' he replies, but he remains standing up, jigging from one leg to the other, shaking his head, distributing droplets around him.

'I don't understand it,' he continues. 'I don't normally get electro-

Goats at the Rouze hostel

cuted by electric fences. But every one of them between Couflens and here gave me a shock.'

'You did use the handles, didn't you?'

'Yes, but I don't understand it. There were nine fences. I counted them. Each with two wires. Eighteen shocks. By the time I saw the farm, I was dreading each new fence because I knew what was going to happen as soon as I gripped the handle.'

'It must be the rain. The handles were wet so they were conducting the electricity.'

'I don't understand it,' he repeats mechanically. 'I don't understand it.'

Yann has come directly from Seix this morning, taking eight and a half hours to do the journey which took Maurice and me two days (on the alternative path). He left Hendaye ten days after Maurice! This is his second time. Last time he had a heavy sack. This time he is relying on walking fast and short cuts to get him to a hostel each night.

In the evening Caroline, the farmer's wife, serves us a meal which includes goat, the unfortunate son of one of those bleating in the barn outside.

'Have you lost a hat?' she asks Maurice.

'Yes,' he replies, surprised.

'Gila has just rung me up. She has been given one which was found on the path. She recognised it. She will bring it to the shop in St Lizier d'Ustou for you tomorrow.'

Prompted by the distant rumblings in the sky, Caroline tells us: 'There's one good thing about the thunderstorm. It will get rid of the horseflies. They used to be even more of a problem for us before we had the Pyrenean Way diverted. At first we thought it was a good thing to have it pass directly in front of our door. Walkers couldn't fail to notice us. But the walkers brought their horseflies with them – they are attracted by the sweat – and sat down at the table on our terrace just outside our front door. They either went on walking, or they stayed in the hostel, but in both cases they left us their flies.'

While we are eating the pineapple and watermelon salad Maurice asks: 'Is it always like this or do you have more guests usually?'

'From next week we are full up for the rest of the season. But we are really handicapped by the Cabane d'Aula. Nobody wants to stay there. So they take the short cut and then don't come here. There has been money earmarked for renovation for the last ten years but one of the shepherds up there doesn't like tourists so it has never happened. Sometimes we are nearly empty,' she shrugs. 'One night last week there was only one person here. A man doing the Pyrenean Way like you. A nice chap, we had a good chat. A hunchback from…'

'What was he called?' I interrupt.

'I don't know. He was retired, with silver hair. Small.'

'It must be Paul.' I explain that know Paul from two years ago. 'Which night did he pass through?'

'Last Thursday.' Today is Monday. It is unlikely that I will catch up with him.

Rouze to Aulus

I have miscalculated this morning. I have become so obsessed with avoiding the afternoon monsoon that I get up even earlier than yesterday. But the path dives directly into the forest darkness and I have to put on my head-torch for the first half hour. Although it is refreshingly cool to start with, by the time I arrive at St Lizier d'Ustou I am wilting.

I can see a Heineken sign. As I approach, my Pavlovian reaction is discouraged by the sight of a menu with prices still in francs, and eliminated when the door refuses to budge. On the other hand, the village shop *is* open. The baskets outside are filled with fruit and vegetables and the smell of fresh bread fills the air. It is the first shop I have seen since Luchon.

According to the *FFRP Guide* this is the actually the *only* shop on the Pyrenean Way in the whole of Ariège, even though the path passes through several villages. Indeed, with one or two notable exceptions, the Ariège mountains are where rural redevelopment stopped: the effects of the late 19th-century exodus are still visible. To what extent can this be blamed on the difficult terrain? Can it all be put down to missed opportunities, as in the Couflens valley? Or is it deliberate – how representative is the shepherd who doesn't want walkers in his valley?

Certainly, Ariège is *authentique* and it wants to stay that way. *Authentique* is a word which goes a long way here. It encompasses the landscape, the buildings, the people, and their ideas. Above all it means: leave us to make our own decisions. Paris is to be kept at a distance. After all, the language spoken here until well into the second half of the 19th century was not French but Gascon: an 1864 survey revealed that 90% of the population didn't even speak the national language.

'*La montagne aux montagnards* – the mountains belong to those who live there' is the rallying cry, a slogan which is resuscitated for every social conflict in which local interests seem threatened. In 1979 it united the opposition to a project to create a National Park covering the area round Valier. National Parks provide the administrative structure for protecting and managing a natural environment, an idea which at first sight might seem to be a guarantee of the future *authenticité* of the area. It was rejected by the vast majority of the 59 communes concerned.

In 2005 a new project was born: a Regional Natural Park. The name suggest that this too will be an instrument for preserving the environment. Yet the idea is popular, with over half the *département* participating in its construction. Why? Partly because the initiative came from Ariège and not from outside, but mainly I suspect because its primary aim is presented as sustainable economic development, not nature conservation.

Later, at home again and sitting in front of my computer, I apply a litmus test to the Park's website. What is its position on the reintroduction of bears? The most telling document is a SWOT analysis where bears appear as a strength, a weakness, an opportunity, and a threat! The only thing which unites the protagonists it that they don't want to argue about the issue.

Nevertheless, with the right therapy for its schizophrenia, the Park (now functioning) could present a way forward for local development.

Still in St Lizier d'Ustou, I open the door of the shop and enter a realm where everyday items have acquired a different meaning. The cavern is just big enough for two aisles and a central reservation. The shelves are packed and the tunnels between them correspondingly narrow. Customers can circulate, as long as they keep their elbows strictly under control, and as long as they all go in the same direction.

Feverishly, I stuff my basket with luxuries: a kilo of golden, honey-smelling grapes, two very large, very orange carrots, some slices of freshly cut ham, smelling of salt, a *pain au chocolat* oozing its soft treasure, three Mars bars, three Lion bars, three Nuts bars, a packet of biscuits, a packet of olives – dried Greek ones, nice and salty, and a large can of ice tea. I add several other items and then remove them. On my second time round, in the gloom at the back of the shop, I see an apparition, in the form of a blue woman. She wasn't there the first time and there are no doors through which she could have come. She is blue from head to foot: blue hair, blue lipstick, a blue tee-shirt, blue jeans, and blue toenails.

I leave quickly. Back in the ordinary insanity of the outside world I consume a second breakfast sitting on a bench. Half an hour later I am struggling up a slope with a bloated stomach and leaden feet, regretting not having bought the flying carpet. I calculate that my rucksack is 5kg heavier than it was before my shopping spree, taking into account the two litres of water I added. I stop and throw away the remaining grapes, all the olives, the two carrots, and empty out half of my water. I eat a Mars and a Lion bar. Even so, it doesn't make much difference to my energy levels so I take off my tee-shirt. (Approximately half the energy consumed in mountain walking goes in keeping cool. So any other means of refrigeration helps.)

By the time I arrive at the Col d'Escots at the top of the Guzet-Neige ski slopes I have eaten two breakfasts, lunch, and several snacks. The weight which was once in my rucksack is now blundering around in my gurgling stomach. My feet are complaining as well. Worse still: there is a restaurant here; I am furious. I force down a couple of ice teas for the sake of it.

Now well above the tree line, my path flanks the mountain and I walk progressively faster as the clouds gather, blacken, and start to relieve themselves of their load. Very exposed and still a long way from shelter, I speed up some more, hoping to reach the relative safety of the forest before the lightning strikes. Then, a long, long clap of thunder rolls from horizon to horizon and, although I don't see the lightning, I fear that the storm is about to start in earnest. But instead of announcing the end of the world, the celestial belch seems to have resolved the meteorological indigestion. A sudden wind, and the clouds begin to disintegrate.

In the forest – except for the victim of a previous cataclysm, its contorted, sea-washed-white branches piled up like flotsam around a vain stump – the trees also are reassured. But they have suffered over the centuries, and not just from natural forces.

From 1829 to 1832 this area was the focus of the *Guerre des demoiselles* or, as I prefer to call it, the Fancy Dress War. The 'warriors' – men – only pulled their shirts out of their trousers but this was considered sufficiently outlandish in an area so steeped in tradition that it became their defining characteristic. They were wearing dresses!

In addition, to disguise themselves, they blacked-up their faces with charcoal or covered them with scarves or animal skins. Just as they might have done for the annual carnival, when the normal rules of society were relaxed, and minor transgressions went unpunished. But these transgressions were not minor, and the psychological consequences are still evident. For the inhabitants of Ariège, the *Guerre des demoiselles* remains a victory over Paris. So much so that in 2006, an anti-bear march in Luchon saw their return to the streets.

It all started in 1827 when the government, concerned by a degradation of the nation's forests, passed a law restricting access to them. But the Pyrenees were suffering from the effects of a growing population – it doubled between 1741 and 1846 – and every scrap of land was vital. The woods were used for building, for firewood, for food, and even for pasture – they were often not very dense. The peasants had come to think that they owned them.

For the government, one of the bones of contention was the way the locals managed the forests. A few trees would be left to grow to maturity but the others would be culled young, often damaging the remaining stands. Self-seeded trees would be left to grow wherever they sprouted. The state foresters disparaged this as *jardinage*, gardening. For them, the only way to manage a forest was to plant a zone, let it grow to maturity, and then raze it all at one fell swoop.

For the peasants the enemies were the state, bourgeois landowners, and industrialists, the first two trying to keep the forest for themselves, and the last destroying it for charcoal for their iron furnaces. So on 27 January 1830, 400–500 demonstrators – a huge number in a rural environment – marched on Massat just down the valley from here, crying 'Death to the foresters'. A month later there were twice as many. The month of May saw an assault on the house of a forester who killed one of the attackers in self-defence. On 15 August the inhabitants of the Ustou valley I have just crossed besieged the mayor's house and burnt it down.

The government capitulated, granting an amnesty and temporarily restoring grazing rights. But the dissatisfaction – and sporadic outbursts of violence – continued, with pastoralists sometimes going as far as to endanger their own communities, as in the village of Arac which suffered frequent winter avalanches as a result. The lessons of Barèges had not been learned.

By the 1930s, however, peace had returned to the forests because, quite simply, the human population had declined. Paradoxically, although the forest was now largely managed by state-trained foresters, *jardinage* and related practices had been rehabilitated. As Tamara Whited says, *jardinage* was now considered to be

> a remarkable way of allowing sufficient shade and protection for young beeches and firs, preventing erosion, and mitigating damage from livestock… it produces the impression of a devastation; and yet this method, practised for centuries along the entire range of the Pyrenees has assured the conservation of the beech forests.

Imagine, in the 1940s, a long-retired forester and a wiry old peasant sitting side-by-side on a bench overlooking the valley. For a century they have been looking at the same landscape, but the forester saw the woods whilst the peasant saw the trees. Now, finally, they are beginning to see the same thing.

As for me, I am still walking through the woods, but the trees are no longer hiding the village in the valley. The Pyrenean Way turns right but, needing supplies, I continue straight on. The road sign at the entrance to the village proudly proclaims 'Aulus-les-Bains, the cholesterol spa'. I understand from this that Aulus, like most Pyrenean spas, has been reinventing itself. The road sign used to read 'Aulus-les-Bains, the syphilis spa'. Probably not. But venereal diseases were a speciality, and the arrival of penicillin was one factor in the spa's temporary closure. The reopening confirms Hippolyte Taine's predictions: in cholesterol it has found itself a different disease to cure. The new spa building opened in 1989. It has also found itself an additional vocation: there is now a leisure pool and a sauna.

At the same time that the syphilitic patients were flocking to Aulus and the shepherds were fighting a rearguard action against the foresters, the village – along with neighbouring Ercé and Ustou – was also famous for a different activity: bear taming. In the 1880s, with a burgeoning population, any source of income was welcomed, and bears were literally part of daily life for 200 households in the valley, practically living with the family. They were trained to dance and perform tricks, and then taken throughout Europe and across the Atlantic. In Central Park, New York, the Rock of Ercé is a reminder of the American connection. When there were no longer enough bears left in Ariège they were imported as cubs from the Caucasus.

The village is pleasant – even in the rain, for the storm has returned – the hostel Le Presbytère excellent, and the company at table friendly. Apart from me, there are eight Dutch people and one Frenchman. I learn that in Amsterdam if you wish to hire a bicycle, and even if both you and the bicycle's owner are Dutch, you will conduct the transaction in English. Even so, I am told, the Dutch do not feel they are being swamped by Anglophone culture.

Julie, from the Lac d'Araing hostel, was here last night but went on this morning. Maurice, on the other hand, hasn't arrived.

Aulus to Marc

A graffito on the road out of town reads: Mushrooms, wood etc. Collect them on your own property.

A little higher up, I make out another graffito, reading 'Private property', with an arrow pointing to the right. I interpret this as an assertion of property rights aimed at latter-day *demoiselles*.

In the woods above, still dark, I can hear a wild but distinctly human voice crying: 'Eyow, eyow,' repeatedly. And behind it, a waterfall crashing down the hillside. The waterfall can't be the famous Cascade d'Ars because it is on the other side of the valley. No, the waterfall is in the same direction as the voice, its inarticulate sound confused by its passage through the branches. As I move, and the light begins to penetrate the woods, the waterfall and the voice seem to move as well. Then, without warning, the waterfall disintegrates into its constituent droplets: a hundred quivering bells intermingled with the sound of hooves on rock. Now I can see them. The cows are being brought back from their somnambulant wanderings to their daytime pasture. I arrive at the Coumebière at the same time as the herd, which spreads out, preparing the meadow for its morning shave.

In places the mountain's skin is pock marked, its bones exposed, not through an excessive zeal on the part of the cows, but as the result of old injuries, not yet quite healed, from the mines.

At the Port de Saleix, a few hundred metres above, the Pyrenean Way turns to the south, bouncing up and down across rocks seemingly claw-marked by giant eagles, the limestone also speckled with myriad tiny lakes. At each one I fill my hat and pour the water over my head, shivering deliciously for a few seconds.

As I approach the edge of the plateau, the limestone is replaced by red-brown schist and the silence penetrated by a pneumatic drill. Down below, the Bassiès hostel, isolated at the end of a long valley two hours' walk from the nearest road, is being remodelled. A small mechanical digger and a trio of workers are laying waste to an area behind the building.

Once inside it, I sit down at a table. There is a printed menu! I have never before seen a menu in an isolated hostel. It is difficult enough to put together a set meal in these conditions, never mind trying to cater for individual whims. I am stunned.

The manager, a small, stiff man with short-cropped hair, marches up to me and asks:

'Your order, sir?'

'I'll have the sea bream, please'

'Yes, sir. Straight away.'

He barks at a thin, nervous-looking woman in the kitchen.

When I ask about the building works, he tells me that the hostel is being renovated.

'I've just taken it over, this year. Today's walkers demand better quality food and proper bedrooms. I'm replacing the dormitories with smaller rooms.'

He'll have to do something about the toilets, then. Yesterday's walkers can understand that they can be completely out of order, but today's walkers won't want to expose their backsides behind a bush.

Digesting comfortably, I squelch unhurriedly across the reedy lake shore back to the trail. The waymarks have been repainted with military precision but, apart from a couple of unobtrusive reservoirs, the valley remains unconquered. At the end of it, my path descends steeply and then strides along an unexpectedly level concrete-covered path which has been carved out of the hillside. From time to time, gaping tunnels to one side exhale their refreshingly cool mountain breath, dribbling a few more drops of saliva into the aqueduct below my feet.

The end of the aqueduct is marked by a road sign offering the delectable alternative directions of Les Toutous d'en Haut or Les

Toutous d'en Bas – literally the High Doggies or the Low Doggies. I choose the Low Doggies and pass through them to Marc.

Marc is an old hamlet, but surrounded by thoroughly new chalets. Bikini-clad teenage girls are walking back from the swimming pool. On the other side of the road, boys of their age are milling around, studiously ignoring the girls. Neither group believes that there is a hostel here. A holiday centre, yes. But nothing as down-market as a hostel. Eventually I find the holiday centre reception and despite my incongruity, I am made to feel welcome. Yes, there is a hostel, just next door.

It was evidently built for the purpose. For those who are doing their own cooking, the kitchen has a fridge, cooking equipment, and Formica surfaces everywhere. 'Choose whichever bedroom you like,' I have been told, 'there is nobody else yet'.

Later, a man and a woman of my age arrive and then flit out again, taking their microcosm with them. So I go down to the bar, where one of the staff is trying to break the ice with a general knowledge quiz. In the evening I am placed at a table on my own in the restaurant and served efficiently.

The room fills up with families and small groups who keep themselves to themselves. They are all dressed in clean clothes, conspicuously ironed. From overheard conversations I gather that quite a few people are going walking. I have, indeed, seen posters for organised trips with guides – don't go walking on your own, it's not safe, they imply. These holidaymakers must be 'today's walkers'.

All the same, I am really looking forward to the bed with its wonderfully silky, laundry-fresh white sheets.

Marc to Goulier

I walk in the murky gloom to the hamlet of Mounicou, and then under a volcanic sky up through the forest ablaze with the first shafts of sunlight. Yet, as the morning advances, the clearing sky belies the dawn's humid prediction. It is going to be hot again.

After diving down to the postcard-village of Arties and then scaling the other side of the Vicdessos valley, the path discovers the languorous virtues of contours, snaking along a mule-track balcony. I think I hear a first cicada. It is as if the Mediterranean has advanced inland along with the sun.

Down below, in Auzat the long red necks of mechanical vultures are stretching out over the concrete carcass of what was once an aluminium smelter. Their beaks tug at its entrails, extracting the last lifeblood from the valley. A huge resource for the valley of Vicdessos for nearly a century, the departure of the aluminium smelter in 2003 with the loss of 270 jobs has left the area impoverished.

The industrial carnage at Auzat marks the end of a long association with mining and metallurgy. The unions correctly blame *mondialisation*, decisions made in offices far away. But even where industry was in local hands the results were the same: nearby Rancié was the biggest single iron ore mine in the whole of the Pyrenees but it closed definitively in 1929.

The operation was anarchic, resulting in much wastage and numerous accidents. 'They have death balanced on their heads,' reported one critic after a visit to the mine. Yet, like Bentaillou, in its 19th-century heyday the mine provided work for 400. Up to six million tonnes of iron ore were extracted. But the co-operative organisation became a liability. Attempts to modernise fell on deaf ears, because jobs would be lost: for example, the construction of a cableway to transport the ore, it was argued, would make the mule drivers redundant. So a cableway was only installed in 1896, 17 years after the one at the much smaller Bentaillou.

By the end of the 19th century it was no longer possible to run a mine as a social service and it became increasingly uncompetitive. The 1929 Crash finished it off.

I leave the remains of the Auzat foundry behind me and head for

Goulier, arriving in the middle of the afternoon. The outskirts of the village are well kept but the disparate interior presents a different picture. A terraced row of two-storey houses seems to encapsulate it.

The first cottage is covered with excruciatingly uniform, rectangular mechanical tiles. A modern roof light reflects the sun, drawing attention to itself. The shutters, however, are firmly closed. Holiday house.

The next house is covered with small *lauzes*, traditional rounded tiles made of schist, in a multitude of shades of grey and brown. Undulations in the roof suggest a collapse not too far into the future. The rendering is cracked and large parts of it are missing completely. Future ruin.

The owner of the third house has obviously taken to heart the advice that any renovation work should begin with the roof. It is made of new, half-moon shaped mechanical tiles and has a new gutter. But there is nothing below the gutter. Literally nothing: I can see through the house to the trees on the other side; a couple of rusty acrow props are doing their best to hold up the roof. Future holiday house.

The roof of the fourth house is rusty corrugated iron but the guttering is new and the rendering intact. A sun umbrella is leaning against the door. Resident.

In the centre of the village, carefully tended geraniums, ivy, and honeysuckle climb up the walls. Despite the heat, water is everywhere, trickling along the channels at the side of the narrow streets, pouring out of fountains. Although cars could theoretically pass through, albeit at the risk of scratching their bodywork, they are banned.

Frequently, the houses are pierced by cobbled *passarots* leading through to another street, each neatly labelled with a wooden plaque: one of them, the passarot Micoòu, was created in 1832. Although there are some passages through houses in other Pyrenean villages, Goulier seems to have an exceptional number of them. I realise, finally, that *passarot* is a misnomer. They are not so much passages dug through existing buildings, as the opening left when a neighbouring house was extended over the street at the height of the 19th-century mining-driven population boom.

The 'Friends of Goulier' Association
Do you have a project for activities, exhibitions linked to our village? Would you like to publish an article or a photo in our 6-monthly journal? Don't hesitate to tell us about your ideas, by letter, email, or when we meet in the streets of Goulier.

The address of the president is in Toulouse, 120km away. And then there is the mayor's New Year message:

The soil of our ancestors, though engraved in our hearts, does not belong to us. Wherever you may have been born, wherever you may have lived, if – respecting our traditions – you have decided to put down roots here, you have the right to do so. You have chosen Goulier, Vicdessos, and Ariège and from now on, like us, with passion and affection, talk, write, be active: make them live.

In the evening Veronica, my wife, comes to join me, bringing dehydrated supplies and warm cuddles from the Corbières where we live. I decide to have a day's rest at the Relais d'Endron.

Goulier

In the morning, after Veronica's departure, I meander lazily around the village, following the road which leads up to the ski resort. At the first bend there is an *orry*, which I take to be an evocation of a rural way of life which no longer exists. But perhaps I haven't understood everything.
Orrys are dry-stone huts. Built like igloos and covered with stone and

Orry on the outskirts of Goulier

turf, reeking of smoke, sweat, and lanolin, like *cayolars* in the Basque country they provided shelter for shepherds in the *estives*. In the better class of *orry* a raised stone platform served as a bed; otherwise heather provided the only comfort. Their construction is so rudimentary that it is impossible to tell how old they are: dry-stone buildings like these first appeared in the Neolithic. Indeed, some of the surviving ones may have been in use, every summer, for centuries. Then husbandry practices changed: for the last 50 years they have remained empty.

Made of newly hewn stone, clean, and out of place, the Goulier *orry* is a parody of its ancestors. But perhaps I am missing its deeper artistic significance? Is it a subtle combination of performance art and sculpture? A reflection on the changing world of shepherds? There are still *patous* and sheep gathering around the *orry* but the new *patous* sit behind the steering wheels of excursion coaches, and the new sheep have two legs. Meanwhile real *orrys* are decaying, neglected on the hillside.

Further up the road, two megaliths straddle a spring. A notice explains that they are cup and ring stones, each stone being marked by three hollows and a crudely incised ring. The notice also explains that they don't belong here. They probably come from a prehistoric site further up the valley known as the *camp de las breiches*, the witches' field, where there are other cup-and-ring stones 'some of which have been, alas, destroyed during the construction of the road'.

There is a third tourist attraction a little further along. This too is out of context, but in this case the town council can't be blamed. The 'Roco de Goutelhe' is an enormous glacial erratic.

I sit down on a bench outside the Swiss-chalet-style town hall. On the gravel esplanade in front of it, four teams are playing *pétanque*: a second swallow-sign, after the cicadas. Maurice limps up and slumps down onto the bench. He has walked all the way from the hostel at Bassiès today, a stupendous feat. He is looking for somewhere to pitch his tent and, although I suggest that he sleeps in the *orry*, decides to camp outside the village.

I have booked Maurice in for dinner at the Relais and we are both standing at the bar drinking mead when a local resident enters. Maurice is very good at striking up a conversation with strangers and when we sit down to eat he asks Arthur to join us.

I ask Arthur to interpret the mayor's homily to newcomers 'The soil of our ancestors…'

'He has a poetic turn of phrase. But there is a problem with second homes. Not only do they put the prices up but the owners don't understand what is good for the village. They don't even understand village politics. It's not a matter of ideas. It's not even a matter of personalities. It's all a matter of clans. It is the same in all villages. They don't understand that.'

'House prices have gone up enormously,' he carries on. 'I reckon mine is worth eight times what I paid for it. But this isn't a good thing.

Youngsters can no longer afford to buy property in the village where they were born.'

I ask him about another item on the village notice board:

Letter of support for the mayor,
published in the Dépeche du Midi newspaper, May 2006

The town councillors of Goulier, whatever their individual position on the reintroduction of bears in the Pyrenees, unanimously and unconditionally support its mayor, Claude Théron. They strongly condemn the insults and death threats made against him and his family in an anonymous letter from the group 'kill the bears'. The council considers that such methods are unacceptable in a democracy. It hopes that the writers will be identified rapidly and made to realise the gravity of their actions.

Arthur leans towards me, conspiratorially.

'I don't want to speak too loud, because I'm friendly with the people who run the hostel and I don't want to start an argument. The manager and his wife are outsiders, not only because the hostel is on the edge of the village, but also socially. So they don't cause any problems, and they don't have any problems. They are perfectly well accepted like that ... as long as they don't talk about bears,' he whispers. 'I can't see how you can live in a village like this and be in favour of the reintroductions. My shepherd neighbours fear that they will discover a massacre each time they go up to the *estives*.'

The debate over the bears is complex. It is a pity that it has been reduced to the simple yes or no of the pros and antis.

I am reminded of the possibly apocryphal story of the death of Gaston Fébus as related by a guide at the Foix château, here in Ariège. Gaston was one of the greatest Pyreneans of all time. A renowned diplomat and a redoubtable warrior, he carved out a sphere of influence which spanned two-thirds of the length of the Pyrenees in the 14th century. He was also a passionate hunter, writing a hunting manual which still commands respect today. Unsurprisingly, perhaps, he died as the result of a hunting incident.

But the manner of his death was unpredictable. He wasn't mauled by a bear or crushed in its unloving arms. He was simply startled by one appearing unexpectedly nearby, the fright provoking a cerebral haemorrhage, or so the guide said. The bear left him untouched. Will Pyrenean sheep farming die like Gaston Fébus, I wonder, not because of the damage caused by the bears themselves, but from fear of them?

Arthur changes the subject, pointing out a small statue of a bear on the mantelpiece.

'Look carefully and you will see that it's made of two sorts of talc, one bluish, and the other pure white. I used to work in the quarry where the talc is dug up.' And so we talk about the quarry instead.

'When you get to the Plateau de Beille, you can't miss it,' he predicts.

Goulier to Col de Sasc

I walk for three and a half hours before I meet anybody, a typical early morning experience.

'I've seen lots of shepherd's huts but I didn't notice any for walkers,' a man coming the other way tells me.

The *FFRP Guide* says that there is a hut at the Col de Sasc: '1798m. Spring… shelter possible mid-slope, four places, without amenities.' This is where I am aiming to sleep tonight.

The clouds are low today. They almost touch the tops of the trees but the path is dry as it climbs up to the pass and down into the valley of Siguer. Just before the village, a large poster announces an all-day *pétanque* contest. Just after it, a hang-glider circles on a thermal. The sun has melted the clouds and I am beginning to roast.

Then, approaching the Col de Sasc, I see a herd of cows, eying me up. Yann, whom I met at Rouze, warned me about these very beasts, just here.

'We were walking along the path when the cows started to follow us, and then started to run after us. We started to run too. In the end, we only escaped by jumping into a ravine. The cows were at the very edge with their front hooves in the air! I was terrified but not half as much as my friend. She was brought up on a farm with cows. She couldn't believe that they could behave like that. Later, we met a local and explained what had happened. He asked me to turn round, and pointed to the black plastic bag for rubbish tied to my rucksack. "It's your bag," he said. "The cowhand has just gone down into the valley to get some salt because it has run out. Your bag makes a rustling sound like a sack of salt being opened. Cows go mad for it."'

Today, the cows must have already had their fix. They ignore me, and shortly afterwards I reach my destination. I have been guzzling water in anticipation of filling up at the spring but when I find it, the water is weeping rather than flowing out of the ground. Not only that, but the tears emerge at ground level. There is no way of putting my mouth, a bottle, or even my hands under it. After a few languid centimetres the water disappears into spongy, muddy peat. I get out my plastic spoon – the only digging implement I possess – and start patiently scraping to create a hollow.

From the Col de Sasc I can see, down below on the east side, what must be the hut described in the *FFRP Guide*. The Cabane du Besset d'en Haut, as it is called, is as adequate as the spring. The size of a garden shed, it is built of breeze blocks and has gaping holes where there might once have been a door and a window. Inside, the walls are decorated with graffiti graphically evoking the pleasures of cannabis, or possibly the horrors of delirium tremens. The evidence of drug consumption, however, is limited to a single empty bottle of *vin de pays* and two beer bottles. The floor is concrete, with a stained piece of foam rubber pushed into one corner. Apart from a burnt-out Baby Belling and an empty gas cylinder, that's it. I unroll my sleeping bag and take a siesta.

I am woken up by Maurice.

'I'm going to camp a couple of hundred metres away. There's just a little bit of flat ground, next to the spring.'

'A real spring?' I exclaim. All that effort for nothing!

'With a cistern and a tap.'

I pour out the brownish fluid in my bottle and go to fill it up.

Later, whilst waiting for my dehydrated rations to reconstitute, I look over the valley to the east. The grass and shrubs, the soft verdant contours nearby, give way to banks of black conifers spilling over into the gulf carved out by the river Ariège. Beyond, the sharp grey angles of St Barthélemy are accentuated by the low sunlight.

Every one minute and thirty seconds precisely an aircraft passes silently high overhead on its way to Barcelona. Two, three, four. My dinner must be ready by now. Tomorrow, at least I will be able to eat a proper meal in the restaurant on the Plateau de Beille.

The sun dips behind the ridge, although it won't set properly for several hours. Instantly the heat is sucked out of the air and the cooling process begins. I go to see Maurice, who is already in his sleeping bag in his tent. He shows me the video he has taken of a herd of *isards* – 30 or so – which he came across first thing this morning. His mobile phone rings. Near ski resorts, and rarely elsewhere, mobile phones work. Afterwards he says:

'To hide nothing from you, I will probably go to the Rulhe hostel tomorrow evening. So I will arrive at Mérens on Monday and have a chance to rest before my friends arrive.'

I go back to my cold-store hut telling myself that I will go up to the ridge to see the sunset, but by 8 o'clock I am shivering. I get into my sleeping bag and doze fitfully, woken up by aches in my feet spreading out from my toes and heels. I am also too hot – it *is* a good sleeping bag.

The sun climbs over the horizon. Cold at first, it turns from purple to crimson and then melts and flows down the slopes of St Barthélemy. My giant shadow walks across the heath. At the Cabane de Courtal Marti, the horses and cows are already at work but their foreman is still slumbering. Even his two barking dogs don't bring him out.

I steer well clear of his hut, its white van, and the dogs, but I see that there is a second hut. Opening its door reveals the mountain nest of my dreams. Clean mattresses, wood for a fire – clearly, it has recently been converted for walkers. And it was empty last night: a spider has had the time to spin a web between the bedposts, now refracting radial rainbows in the crack of light coming through the door. Needless to say it doesn't feature in the *FFRP Guide*.

Down in the first valley of the day I struggle through ferns on a neglected section of the Pyrenean Way. At the top of the next hill, Maurice catches up with me and we walk a while together, getting lost and found again, until my right knee lets out a sharp pain, and I sit down to give it a rest.

Water is running out and I am correspondingly dried out when I start the final ascent to the Plateau de Beille, through the woods in the stifling heat. I don't appreciate the climb at all, even though the sun's ardour is diminished by the foliage. The path has become a multitude of possibilities, each as contrary as its neighbour, between waymarks spaced too far apart. When I emerge into the full sun at the edge of the plateau, the only thing I really want to do is to lie down with my eyes shut. I press on because the restaurant promised me when I rang up that I would be able to eat a proper meal at a real table, with cool beer, *if* I arrived before 14:00.

I have a few minutes to spare. Maurice is sitting at a table outside, and is just about to get up and go on.

'It's full. I've been here about half an hour but it was already too late. They might be persuaded to do you a sandwich.'

I eat several half-baguettes and drink many cans of ice tea. There are perhaps 20 people sitting at tables on the terrace, under red and yellow sun umbrellas, nibbling sandwiches or sipping beer, sucking Coca-Cola through straws, mostly family groups. A cowhand ushers his herd in front of us and within seconds the terrace empties.

'Look. Wild cows!' exclaims one woman.

I count 16 adults and children, cameras clicking, striding towards them.

I ask one of the waiters if I can sleep at the Cabane de Beille d'en Haut, which is a hut for walkers according to the *FFRP Guide*.

'Yes, there are three parts. One for the shepherd, one for walkers.' He doesn't specify the use of the third part.

Here I could buy postcards, knurled walking sticks, whistling *marmottes*, or sweets. But not food to take away. The Plateau de Beille is primarily a ski resort, doing its best to promote a summer season.

I waddle out of the building dragging my rucksack and then try to put it on. My stomach bulges out between the straps. I have just bought a litre and a half of bottled water to supplement the three litres that I took from the tap – there are no springs between here and the Refuge du Rulhe. With all this extra baggage, I am carrying eight kilos more than I was when I arrived. I walk past a hut labelled 'Base Angaka: dog sledding' pining for snow, a pack of willing huskies, and a sleigh to whisk me off comfortably up the hill to my hut.

An hour later, on a dirt track, I am passed by a white four-wheel drive vehicle, with three collies yelping in the back. When I arrive at the hut five minutes later, the car is parked next to it but there is no sign of the shepherd or dogs. I knock on the door.

'*Putain de merde* – fucking hell!' shouts the cowhand as he explodes through the door in his underwear, followed by his three growling dogs.

'I'm sorry to have disturbed you,' I reply, 'but I have been told there is a part for walkers.'

'No!' he spits at me. 'There isn't. In any case it's occupied. And it's only for when it's hailing.'

'It was the waiter at the restaurant who told me. If you don't want to be disturbed you'll have to see him.'

'That's bullshit. Bullshit. In any case, it will be fine this evening. Everyone under his own roof.'

He ushers the dogs back inside and slams the door.

I walk another two kilometres to an *orry* marked on the map. This is a step *down* from yesterday's accommodation. It is definitely not a Goulier built-for-tourists high class *orry*. There is no shelf for a bed. The only place to sleep is the floor, a mixture of damp mud and sheep shit. The roof doesn't look too stable either. Its earth covering has washed away leaving gaps open to the elements.

I am beginning to see why the motto of the *département* until recently was '*Ariège: terre courage* – land of courage'. (Curiously the motto was changed in 1997 to become '*Ariège, les Pyrénées avec un grand A* – the Pyrenees with a big A' which makes a great deal more sense, of course, and apparently discourages tourists less.)

I decide to sleep in the open air and start cutting heather, still partly in flower, and sweet-smelling pine branches. Lighting a pine cone fire, I force down some re-hydrated mush, rinsing the pot with water to clean it and then drinking the swill, so that I don't waste any.

Opposite me, the slopes of St Barthélemy are an open wound, the layers of skin showing white: the terracing of the Trimouns talc quarry. At this distance, set against the scale of the Pyrenees, it looks insignificant. Yet it produces 8% of the world's talc, for pharmaceuticals, for making paper, paint, plastics, and car tyres. At over 1700m above sea level, quarrying is only possible in summer but the refining takes place all year round, employing 300–400 workers. In short, it is the single biggest remaining extractive industry in the French Pyrenees.

Looking at the quarry reminds me that I have a problem. On a six-month old it would be called nappy rash, the result of dicey digestion. Despite the immense quantities of talcum powder visible on the opposite side of the valley, I only have two possibilities: sun cream or anti-inflammatory cream. Sun cream doesn't seem very appropriate since that area rarely sees the sun, so I try the anti-inflammatory cream, and regret it immediately. It stings like hell. Trousers still round my ankles, I jump up and down. I try rubbing it off. In desperation I try washing it off, wasting precious water. But it does no good and it takes ten minutes before the fire has settled down and I stop hyperventilating.

As the sun sets I spread my perfumed mattress out and get into my dew-damp sleeping bag. The plateau is completely empty, except for the animals. Nearby, cow bells are tinkling; in the valley the sheep are echoing them. Then I hear a helicopter far off, approaching. Then the noise is all around me. It is not a helicopter; it is bees or wasps, hundreds of them, thousands perhaps. They are collecting something in the small pine trees which are protecting me from the breeze. They arrive with the dusk and depart with the dark as the first stars begin to appear.

The cows seem to be coming nearer. Will they lick my face in the middle of the night? At least their bells will warn me if any wild animal approaches. The sheep settle down and I drift off to sleep, briefly. In my nightmare I am at home, upstairs in bed, and a burglar is trying to break in through the back door. I wake up with a start.

The bells are tinkling. Something is disturbing the cows. It isn't that they are very agitated but nor have they settled down to sleep. I sit up and look, but can see nothing. I listen for a long while, but I can't hear anything either. Eventually I realise that the cows are right. There *is* a strange animal in the vicinity. I'm not supposed to be here.

Plateau de Beille to the Rulhe hostel

In the morning I soon reach the Col des Finestres, where plateau turns into ridge. I strip down to shorts and tee-shirt and slather sun cream over all the exposed surfaces, working it into my ever-thinning hair. Either side of the ridge, the valleys are hidden in cloud but further away islands peek out.

The path temporarily leaves the ridge and descends the slope passing a hut and a spring, neither of which is mentioned on my map. Soon, it climbs sharply to the pass at the Col de Didorte, a strategic viewpoint. Back in the valley I have just left, a man is assembling his cows, aided by dogs. They are already in a tightly packed formation, complaining, tossing their heads, sounding their bells, but moving slowly towards the hut. On the ridge opposite me a long straggly line of sheep is making its way down, pushed by a shepherd and his two dogs. Behind me, on a different high ridge, another line of sheep, this one more disciplined, is outlined against the sky. Walking head to tail, this flock has another general behind it.

The route is well marked, but I am unaccountably nervous. The residues of last night's anxiety are still lurking in some corner of my unconscious.

Heather is everywhere, still in pinkly lilac flower, criss-crossed by sheep tracks like the estuary of a river as the tide recedes, dividing into a hundred creeks. When I get to the top of the hill, I can see a third flock of sheep, in a different valley. Only about 50 of them this time, but tightly packed together. All is quiet. Then the shepherd says something. The flock moves a few steps to the left. Another order and the flock moves to the right. It becomes a triangle and moves resolutely forward only to stop abruptly, and then revert to a circle: in training for the next exercise.

Finally I meet a family of walkers coming from the Rulhe hostel. They tell me that there is a water crisis and advise me to fill up my bottles if possible. A few hundred metres from the hostel I meet the manager digging with a pick and shovel at the side of a small stream.

'You can go in,' he tells me, 'but don't use the toilets.'

So I sit on the terrace, on the leeward side of what turns out to be another corrugated metal box, sunning myself, looking at the lakes and the broad glacial valley below, then up to the rocky heights of the Rulhe mountain.

By evening the hostel is bustling with walkers arriving from all directions. The Refuge du Rulhe still has that special conviviality now disappearing from more accessible establishments. I am at a table with an oldish couple who have already completed the Pyrenean Way and a younger couple who have just overtaken me. We talk about rucksack weight, distances, times, and, inevitably, getting lost in the fog. Various methods of dealing with fog are mentioned: hitching a lift on a mechanical excavator, cowering in a sheepfold until the shepherd comes to tend his flock, or playing leapfrog with the waymarks (you need to be at least three to try this).

Paul, I discover, passed through here two nights ago. Tomorrow I will finish for this year, at Mérens, so I won't quite catch him up.

Rulhe hostel to Mérens

In the morning, the waymarks on the path are so close together that sometimes I can stretch my hands from one to another. Yet at every one I have to stop and look for the next. When I can't see it I strike out in one direction, hopefully, frequently to return to base a few seconds later. But it isn't foggy – the sky could hardly be clearer. It is the scree. Not just any scree. Not the sort of scree one can glide over. Here, the loose stones are a metre, two metres across and the path is nothing more than faint scratches on the surface of the blocks. There are cairns as well as waymarks but they too melt into the rusty unweathered moonscape, which reminds me of the summit of Aneto. Jumping, slithering, stumbling, I am soon exhausted.

The map and the waymarks disagree but in the end I make it over the pass into the Mourguillou valley, frightening a bootlace-obsessed Spaniard on the way. Walking down the valley, I come across several herds of horses. Most of them are jet black, but some have attractive

Crête de la Lhasse, 2439m

chestnut tinges to their coat. I am no expert, and at the other end of
the Pyrenees wasn't sure if the horses I saw were true Pottoks, but
these are easy to identify, particularly given the name of the village at
the end of the valley: Mérens. The black ones are *mérengais* (commonly
known as Mérens) and the chestnut-tinged ones, their lesser-known
cousin, the *cheval castillonnais*.

Like Pottoks, Mérens were in danger of disappearing because they
are no longer any use to the army, foresters, or butchers, but their
salvation came with the on-going conversion of the Pyrenees from a
place where people work in primary, production industries to a place

where – increasingly – they play. Mérens horses have successfully adapted themselves to the changing times, now working in the leisure industry. Hardy and versatile, they are ebony black with a long mane and a Rasta haircut and beard. They like nothing better than being left to fend for themselves all summer in the high pastures.

Although the horses have adapted themselves to the new economic reality, the village which organised their retraining singularly failed to profit from its input. Despite its name, the National Mérens Horse Centre is not in the valley but 50 km away at La Bastide de Sérou. Yet it was the communes of Mérens and neighbouring Le Hospitalet which took the first steps to save the breed from decline creating, in 1933, the Syndicat Hippique d'Élevage de la Race Chevaline Pyrénéenne Ariégeoise dite de Mérens (SHERPA) – the Union of Breeders of the breed of Pyrenean horses from Ariège called Mérens. It now has the snappier title: Association Française d'Élevage de la Race Pyrénéenne de Mérens. Like Pottoks, Mérens have been saved from extinction if not from verbosity.

The eponymous village itself is grubby, from the passage of the thousands of cars which daily wind their way up to the tax-haven of Andorra. In the centre, a rotating advertising panel vaunts, in turn, the leather goods on sale at a boutique there, a motorbike accessory shop, and a supermarket. A train clatters through. But there *is* a bar for a celebratory drink.

The hostel, La Soula, well away from the main road, is quiet and after my beer, I sit in the garden and wait patiently for it to open. At five o'clock the manager, Stéphane, drives up. A Dutch couple and a Spanish man arrive seconds later. They are followed by an Irish couple, Veronica, who has come to pick me up, and Maurice who has decided to quit the campsite and stay in the hostel for the night. His friends are late and he is going to continue alone.

Later, Stéphane tells me that Paul left this morning.

'He tired himself out on the rocks after the Rulhe, so he stayed two nights to recover.'

'I saw him yesterday,' says Maurice, 'but I didn't have a chance to talk to him. I was in the grocers and he was walking along the street. By the time I had finished, he had disappeared.'

'When you catch up to him, say hello from me,' I request.

Stéphane invites everyone to sit down at a table in the wood-panelled dining room with a massive bay window overlooking the valley. The conversation meanders between English and French.

The Irish couple, Aileen and Patrick, are here by chance, because petrol is 20% cheaper over the border.

'A year ago, going to Andorra, our car ran out of petrol so we were obliged to stay in the village. We only stayed overnight,' Aileen explains, 'but we liked it so much we came back. Short walks only, though. We're wimps.'

I go over to the bar and ask Stéphane to suggest an aperitif. He proposes Banyuls, a sweet wine made in tiny terraced vineyards at the end of the Pyrenean Way. It seems appropriate to me and I order a bottle to share.

Back at the table, I ask Maurice, who hasn't heard me ordering: 'Would you like some Banyuls?'

'Thanks but I've being promising myself a bottle when I get to the Mediterranean, as a kind of incentive and I don't want to drink any before I get there. It wouldn't be right.'

'What can I get you then?' I ask. But before Maurice has had the time to reply Stéphane reappears.

'Here's your bottle,' he announces, presenting me with one.

'Oh, never mind,' says Maurice. 'I can still buy myself a bottle when I get to the coast. I didn't buy this one so it is all right. Cheers.'

The Spanish man, David, is walking the GR 107, the Chemin des Bonshommes, which most people do from north to south. Only, he is doing it the wrong way round.

'I meet people coming in the other direction, but I never see them again. I'd hoped walking would be more sociable,' he tells me. 'I'm not really enjoying it but I'm nearly there now,' he adds wearily.

I'm glad to be walking with the flow.

The Dutch couple, two days into their abbreviated Chemin des Bonshommes, are going in the right direction, and enjoying themselves: their baggage is being transported from hostel to hostel for them.

Maurice has dumped his rucksack on the floor nearby. I pick it up to see how much it weighs and then invite the others to do the same. It isn't 22kg. It must be at least 25kg.

Picking up the sack has a dramatic effect on everyone who tries it.

'You carried that from Hendaye!' exclaims Veronica, examining him carefully. 'He's got muscles on his muscles,' she whispers to me, admiringly. I ask him about the journey from the Col de Sasc to the Rulhe hostel.

'I was knackered at the end. I can do 450m of climbing in an hour but still it took me 12 hours altogether.'

'You walked for 12 hours!' is the chorus. Like me, the other walkers can rarely sustain more than six or seven.

'And he does parachuting,' I add, consciously stoking the fever. Maurice explains that he will be taking part in a national championship in September. He has his own parachute. Out of 800 jumps it only failed to open three times.

'What's the attraction?' I ask.

'The weightlessness. In freefall you drop from 4000m to 1000m in a minute.'

David interrupts: 'If you can descend 3000m in one minute, how come you can only go up 450m in an hour?'

Aileen turns to me: 'What's it really like, the Pyrenean Way? Can wimps do it? Or do you have to be a hero, like Maurice?'

'What counts is the head,' I reply.

At home, two weeks later I receive two postcards, one from Maurice, who has arrived at Banyuls nine days after he left Mérens, making 51 in total. Paul, however, has been obliged to give up for this year:

Maurice told me that you arrived in Mérens a day after I left. A pity… I had to stop at Batère. I slipped in the shower of the hostel, cut my head open, and was taken to hospital. Nothing serious but still a bit dazed. Fatal imprudence: never take your boots off!

IV

Chez les Catalans –
Mérens to the Mediterranean

Mérens to the Bésines hostel

Back in Mérens a year later, Veronica and I stay at the same hostel overnight. The bear Boutxy, son of Mellba, has been spotted in the area and talk at the dinner table once again turns to defensive techniques.

'I have been told that you should always carry an anvil in your rucksack,' says Benjamin.

'Why?' we ask.

'To throw at the bear. It may not work, but if you've been carrying an anvil, you'll run a hell of a lot faster without it.'

Obsessed as we are with bears and the weight of rucksacks, it gets a good laugh, but what pleases me most is that finally, as we approach the sea, we can start to joke about them both.

In the morning Veronica and I stroll up the peaceful valley above the hostel under the grey cool of the clouds and I explain the *pas de Mahomet* to her. Not the ridge which guards the summit of Aneto, but a way of walking all day long without needing to rest.

'Lift your foot off the ground and hold it in the air for a fraction of a second before putting it down again. Don't push too hard. Alice learned it from an Arab guide who took her up Toubkal, last summer. If you are heading for Mecca on foot it is the recommended technique.'

Ruined romanesque church at Mérens-d'en-Haut

Before I have finished we blunder into a war zone. The roof has gone but, like the Berlin Gedächtniskirche, the four walls and the bell-tower are still intact. The church, another reminder that the surrounding area has not always been peaceful, was burnt by the Spanish in 1811. The church and the village which surrounded it never recovered. The village gravitated down the slope into the valley, and was renamed Mérens-les-Vals.

In the forest, higher up, heavy, sulphurous fumes cling to the trees, invading our lungs. Their origin, an acrid spring, trickles out of the hillside into the first of two pools, mere hollows in the rock. The top pool of this natural spa is just a little too hot but the lower one is a more reasonable temperature and we dangle our hands in it, swirling the viscous water between our fingers.

I kiss Veronica goodbye and she goes back down to the car in search of a Mérens to ride. Now in mist, I can hear water crashing down the mountain side, but of the nearby river I can see nothing. Brushing through the ferns, my trousers are soon sodden.

As I approach the pass, I see the cotton wool being sawn up by a jagged dark green mountain ridge, exposing an indecently blue sky. But the water in the lake is icy cold and the frogs prefer to bask on the shore.

From the pass at the Porteille des Bésines, the highest point on the walk today, I can see down into the next valley, still partly hidden. So I decide to slow down, let the sun dry out my trousers, and have lunch in a mountain meadow, watching the clouds billowing below me. It is mid-afternoon when I arrive at the hostel, having seen nobody else all day. The Refuge des Bésines is still enveloped in cloud. Benjamin is already there.

'*La finlandaise*, the Finnish woman passed through an hour ago. She's going to camp somewhere further on in the wilderness,' he explains. 'She was still looking stressed. I don't think she has managed to relax yet… I got here at 10:30. Have you seen the sun?'

We all have the same destination – Banyuls – and roughly the same timetable. *La finlandaise* has come for a soothing holiday, away from the stresses of work, but she still can't sleep properly.

The Bésines hostel (like the Rulhe hostel and the one at the Lac d'Araing) is one of those space stations which the Club Alpin Français (CAF) has dropped on to some of the most natural and isolated mountains of France. Yet the CAF is not completely insensitive. The first hostels it built were much more in harmony with their surroundings, constructed largely in wood and stone. But they had a limited life in the harsh climate and the CAF was forced to rethink. The new hostels are comfortable, clean, energy efficient and, above all, affordable because they can be made in kit form in the valley and then assembled on site. Solar panels and radio-telephones are also part of the way of life of the modern hostel manager.

Bésines hostel

At the Bésines hostel there is a warm welcome and a considerable selection of herb teas. This evening, there will only be four of us, we are told. We hear a helicopter coming up the valley but, unable to land, it flies on over the clouds to supply shepherds' huts higher up in the mountains. It will try again tomorrow.

Later on the mist clears, unveiling a sumptuous view over a lake towards l'Hospitalet. Glancing out of the window, I see two roe deer calmly walking along a path on the other side of the valley.

Bésines hostel to Bolquère

By common agreement we breakfast early. We all leave at the same time but Benjamin quickly outdistances me and the others take a different route. I spot Benjamin's pink tee-shirt against the snow drift blocking the path up the side of the valley ahead of me. He is trying to cross it horizontally some distance above the valley floor. If he slips he won't be able to stop on the icy slope. He is nervous and not making much progress.

I decide on a different approach and start at the bottom of the snow and climb upwards, laboriously hacking footholds with a stick and enlarging them by kicking violently at the hole until I can get a purchase on the ice-covered snow. I get to within stretching distance of the top edge of the snow but my dead branch no longer penetrates the hard crust. I look across. Benjamin has disappeared. I look down. I descend ignominiously backwards down the steps I have created. Regretting having left my ice axe at home, I spend the next half hour circumnavigating the problem, clambering over giant granite blocks which, like those between Rulhe and Mérens, have not moved since the last Ice Age.

Later I catch up with the others and together we tackle a huge sloping snowfield. Alone, I would have walked around it, but once the difficulty is behind us, we split up again. A few minutes later I step out of winter and into spring: near the Étang de Lanoux the wild daffodils and blue gentian are in flower. But I hear thunder, though the cloudless sky gives no indication of its origin.

The Portella de la Grava pass in the shadow of the Carlit massif, reached soon after, marks the watershed between the Atlantic and the Mediterranean. It also marks the beginning of the Pyrénées-Orientales and the unofficial border of Catalonia, a country which no longer exists, except in the collective imagination of its inhabitants.

At first there is nothing to tell me I have entered a different zone, but soon I start to notice new waymarks at the side of the Pyrenean Way. Previously exclusively red and white, they are now frequently red and gold, like the stripes of the Catalan flag. I still expect to have feet covered in blood, but instead of walking with my head in the clouds I am can now walk with my mind focussed on golden sands.

My home is in the neighbouring *département* of the Aude. Living not far away means that I have walked in these mountains and also have a friend who lives here, so I know some of the history of the area.

Although Catalonia started life as a united medieval kingdom, today three-quarters is in Spain, one-quarter in France. The language is spoken by 9 million people, most of whom live south of the border. One thing is clear: there is a huge difference between southern and northern Catalonia, just as there is between the Spanish Basque country and its French counterpart. Barcelona, the capital of southern Catalonia, is a flashy modern city. Franco's clumsy repression of Catalonia and particularly its language inevitably ensured their survival. Since his death in 1975, southern Catalonia, like the Spanish Basque country, has been reasserting its identity.

Northern Catalonia is noticeably less dynamic. Only a surrealist – Dalí – could imagine that Perpignan railway station was the centre of the world.

I have asked my Catalan friend how he feels about his homeland.

'I am part of the fifth generation to live in the same house in Vinca,' Luc explained. 'Being Catalan is important to me. I help organise the *troubade*.' The *troubade* brings together thousands of Catalans in a summer celebration on the slopes of Canigou. It is *the* big Catalan get-together.

'My grandparents only spoke Catalan,' he continued, 'and I spoke it with them. But I am French first, then Catalan. With my parents I only spoke French...' He shook his head: 'My son will sell the house.'

For the moment on the GR10, apart from the blood-red and gold waymarks, there is nothing else to tell me that I am in Catalonia. On the long descent to the Lac des Bouillouses the cows are eating the first grasses exposed to the sun by the melting snow. The grass is rather short and not very green but the flowers are increasingly abundant, yellow broom sweeping across the northern side of the valley. The southern side is yellow and purple, the broom alternating with clumps of rhododendron. It is getting increasingly hot. In the space of a morning's walking, winter has melted into summer.

The Lac des Bouillouses itself – an artificial lake created to provide hydro-electricity – is a sparkling blue, reflecting an increasingly Mediterranean sky. After walking round it, the last few kilometres to Bolquère turn out to be a monotonous trudge, eyes glued to the ground, relieved only by escaped lupins and the screaming sirens of a squadron of police motorbikes. A helicopter descends to look at me. Not knowing what is going on, I point one arm to the sky and the other to the ground, the best I can do to look like the letter N: no, I don't need any assistance. The helicopter swerves away.

Veronica arrives in Bolquère later, drags me out of a bar, and drives me to a hostel in nearby Odeillo. 'The advantage of riding a horse,' she says, 'is that the horse looks where to put its feet so that you can look at the countryside.'

The hostel is set into the hillside which keeps it cool in summer and warm in winter. It is run by a couple who have exchanged the claustrophobia of Paris for the wide open landscapes of the Cerdagne. At the Cariolettes – named after the edible mushrooms which grow in the garden – the owners eat at the same table as their guests and talk about the area with an easy familiarity which belies the fact that they have only lived here for a few years.

Sleep in a comfortable bed is interrupted by aching feet. I bought some expensive new boots six months ago and have been breaking them in ever since. My old pair leaked and the soles had worn smooth, but they were wonderfully comfortable. Now, every time I go out, I come home with sore feet and blisters. One pair of socks – as advised by Aimé – two pairs, double-layered, thin, thick, it makes no difference. It is too late to buy different boots; I will just have to put up with them until I get to Banyuls. When I arrive I will walk into the Mediterranean, unlace them, and leave them there.

Already, my big toes are tender from kicking at the ice and the toe nails are just beginning to colour. I predict that they will fall off in three months' time. My bones feel a lot older than they did at Mérens, two days ago.

Planès to the Ras de la Carança

When I get out of bed, the legs are raring to go but the feet are somewhat less willing. Veronica drives me to Planès, skipping an hour of dull walking along roads and across flat meadows.

Above the village the shamrock-shaped church is shut so we content ourselves with walking around the outside of the three lobes which make up this unusual structure. Middle-eastern, mosque-influenced Father, Son, and Holy Ghost can wait for another day. Veronica goes to look at the solar furnace in Font Romeu, 'the sunniest town in France'. I head off up the hill, on a familiar path: I have already walked several stretches of the Pyrenean Way between here and the sea.

Veronica, not being a walker, is following me in the car this year, spending lazy days seeing the tourist sights, meeting me from time to time when the path crosses a road or descends into a village. Our next rendezvous is in two days' time, in the village of Py.

Across the valley I can see a train climbing up the hillside. Painted, inevitably, in red and gold, this is the 'petit' Train Jaune, which is powered by electricity from the Lac de Bouillouse. Initially an economic lifeline, it transported minerals and cattle, but now tourists fill the carriages.

Like the rack railway at Luchon, this line had its share of problems. It was about to be inaugurated in 1909 when the brakes failed. Six people were killed, including the engineer who had designed it. An extra brake had to be added before the official opening a year later. It is not strictly a rack railway as the third rail doesn't have teeth: the adhesion is magnetic. This also means that the rail is a live conductor.

Church at Planès

It may not have teeth but it certainly has a bite: the nickname for the railway in Catalan is *mata gossos* – the dog killer.

I am walking in the forest when Benjamin catches up with me. He started early and didn't cheat. He promises to reserve a place for me tonight at the hostel.

At the Refuge de l'Ori I meet a young man walking with a donkey.

'It takes me about one-third longer than it would if I were alone,' he says, looking at the donkey, 'because he needs to stop and eat. So I walk eight or nine hours a day instead of six.'

He asks me about the Bésines and I confirm that a donkey wouldn't be able to cross the snow.

'Apparently, even without the snow a donkey wouldn't be able to get through. I have been told that I can use another pass, to the north. I'll ask when I get a bit nearer.'

Fresh puffball mushrooms are waiting to be picked by the side of the path, but I leave them to grow some more as I have no way of cooking them.

Finally, I descend to the hostel at the Ras de la Carança, surrounded by cows, bells-a-tinkling, gorging themselves on the pasture; also a colony of flies attracted by the new season's cow pats.

Benjamin leaps up to tell me that he has spotted *la finlandaise*. She was just leaving when he arrived. She had camped in splendid isolation at the Étang de Lanoux two nights ago and is pressing on this afternoon at a feverish pace. He has also seen a family of *isards* licking at a salt cake put down for the cows. He is making notes.

'I did the walk fifteen years ago, and I can hardly remember anything about it. That's why I'm doing it again,' he explains.

A donkey nuzzles up to me and sniffs at my sack. Today, he is lazing around but normally it is Petit Pois' job to transport fresh bread and other necessities from the nearest road, a six-hour return trip. The helicopter only visits at the beginning and the end of the season.

In the evening, there is an empty place at our table. The hostel manager explains that a young scientist who has gone to look at the plants and animals up the valley will arrive shortly. We are told not to wait for him, so we share out his soup. We then share the spaghetti carbonara and we are just finishing the last helping of chocolate mousse as I look out of the window into the dusky half-light. A flash of blue and yellow is bounding down the hillside. As it comes nearer I can distinguish a man, his arms flapping wildly as he tries to keep balance. No rucksack; he has a waistband stuffed with canisters and technical equipment. I tell the others, 'I think our young scientist has just come back.' We look around sheepishly. When he crashes through the door, panting, the hostel manager doesn't even give him time to catch his breath. 'You said you'd be back in time for dinner, an hour ago. If you hadn't arrived shortly I'd have had to call out the rescue services.' Nevertheless he scrapes together some more food and we all relax a little.

Before turning in for the night, I walk the fifty metres to the toilet shed. As I approach, I hear the noise of a braying donkey coming from inside it but the door opens and only a man comes out. There is no sign of the donkey as I open the door again and the décor is clean and surprisingly under-perfumed, a novelty as far as mountain-side toilets are concerned. The secret of this innovation is to separate the solids from the liquids, which is where the donkey comes in. The braying comes from the wooden plank which scrapes the metal sheet and sends one's digestive extracts into well-earned oblivion. Operate it three (crossed out), five times please.

The dormitory, taking up the whole of the first floor of the hostel, contains just two large bunk beds. There are 28 unwashed walkers already sardined into them but still a few spaces left, so I position myself where the body count is less dense. Luckily the quadraphonic snoring is drowned out by the sound of the nearby river.

Ras de la Carança to Py

I grab a plastic bag out of Petit Pois' mouth, pat him on the back, and stride off across the river and up the hillside into the woods.

A rustling in the undergrowth startles me. A bird flies off cawing its warning. A few steps further and there is another rustling close by. An unmistakable snort tells me that I have just missed a close encounter with a disgruntled wild boar. I'm surprised how calm I am: boars can be dangerous and people are regularly killed by them. Their principal concentration is in the Aude but somehow I have never been apprehensive about meeting one. They are almost familiar. Bears, on the other hand, represent the unknown...

When I reach the top of the hill at the Col del Pal, the pine forest gives way to pasture and I can see the characteristic peak of Canigou clearly for the first time. Looking back, Carlit stands out against the sky. At the Refuge de l'Alemany I fill my water bottles from the spring.

Linguistic confusion. Alemany means 'big wing' in Catalan and not 'German', as I thought at first. Nevertheless, in the Second World War, there really was a German headquarters near here, controlling access to the Spanish frontier, an hour's walk away. Customs officers are said to still keep a discreet eye on the mountain passes. I have never seen any, but then, if I notice them they aren't doing their job properly, are they?

My knees tell me to walk more slowly and I pick my way carefully down to Mantet where the path fords the river and clambers up to this little paradise-in-waiting, clinging lovingly to the steep hillside. Flat pasture is a valuable resource in the Pyrenees – too valuable to be used for human habitation – so the houses are dug into the slope, with the grey slate sliding down the back of the roofs almost to ground level. On the exposed side of the buildings, the stonework is flattened by the intense sun. The streets are paved with large irregular stone blocks. Flowers, more or less domesticated, vie for attention with the harsh breeze blocks and steel mesh of unfinished restorations. Heaps of worn stone rubble await their turn.

I look back at the pasture on the river bank. Yes, his goats are still there. Mottled brown-and-white, black, or long-haired Angora, the goats are owned by Richard, one of the two dozen permanent residents. Although he looks as if he has always lived in the mountains, he was brought up on the plain and spent ten years working in a Social Security office before leaving Perpignan. When I was last here, his white hair and full beard were long and straggly, but when I pass by to say hello, I notice that he has recently been shorn. He is short but stocky, with strong legs. In the daytime he has a quiet measured voice. But in the evening he talks passionately and knowledgeably about local political and financial scandals, village intrigues, and life in the valleys in general. He looks after the animals. His wife, Angeline, looks after the hostel. When she smiles there is a curious shyness to it, but she smiles a lot. She frowns when she disagrees with what Richard is saying, but doesn't interrupt. She busies herself in the garden and the kitchen. The food is excellent but I won't be able to eat here today because they can only serve food to people who are staying overnight. It is a fragile community and commerce is strictly regulated. If there are too many restaurants fishing for the same customers none of them will net a decent living. Mantet is not a place for free-market liberals.

It may now be fragile, but in 1901 the village was a thriving community with 157 inhabitants. Its nemesis came in the Second World War when the Germans suspected the residents of helping the Resistance and evicted them. The village remained deserted, apart from a few shepherds with their flocks in summer, until the 1960s. The difficult access over the pass and rising expectations discouraged newcomers. The old track, suitable only for donkeys, was replaced with a tarmac road in 1964. Even now Mantet is a 30-minute drive from its nearest neighbour. It wasn't until 1983 that electricity was installed.

When Richard and Angeline moved there at the end of the 1970s, Mantet was just beginning to revive. Making a living still isn't easy. The hostel and the livestock have been through several permutations. Each time there are new skills to be learned, new challenges to be faced.

'The only predator in this valley is humans,' Richard complains. 'I've lost four goats in recent years because people have let their dogs off the lead. Last year I heard a commotion outside and looked down from the terrace. There was a dog chasing my goats. One of them jumped off the cliff. My son picked up his gun and rushed out and caught up with the walkers. "Don't worry, we are insured," they said. They didn't give a damn. But it isn't just a matter of money. My son aimed his gun at the dog and pointed out that he had the right to kill it. It was only then that they started to look concerned. "You can't do that!" they said. "Don't worry," he replied, "I'm insured."'

'But I'm still learning myself. I managed to kill one of my own goats because I didn't know what I was doing. I was coming back down from tending to the horses on the Col del Pal. When I got to the Refuge de l'Alemany I saw that the herd was working its way up the valley, away from me. I wanted to bring them in for the night but the closer I got the higher they went. Normally I wouldn't let the dogs out of my sight but I was tired and it was getting late. So I sent the dogs off to round them up.'

Richard has two dogs, a male and a female.

'When I caught up to them, one of the goats was dead. The bitch had attacked it. I couldn't understand why because she is normally so well behaved. The male dog had gone round the herd and brought most of them back, no problem. But there were six of them which were a bit wilder than the others. They were born on the mountains and it was several weeks before I brought them home. They would never keep together with the rest. We were always having trouble with them. They had climbed up onto a bluff and the bitch had grabbed one of them by the leg. It was much later when I discovered why. You know the shepherd who did that show in Paris?'

'Yes,' I replied. He had previously told me how the shepherd had come to Mantet to prepare his sheep and dogs for their Parisian début.

'He told me that you should never use a couple – male and female – for herding. Two males or two females but not a couple. In the wild, when a dog and a bitch go hunting together she waits, hidden, whilst the dog goes round the prey and brings it back for her to kill.'

'Will she do it again? Did you have to get rid of her?'

'No. I'm just more careful and I never let them out of my sight. My son has another technique. You can tell when he is bringing the goats home. First you see a cloud of dust in the distance. The ground starts to vibrate and then you hear the sound of pounding hooves, getting louder and louder. Finally the goats appear, charging down the valley at a furious pace. It's like the Alamo. I don't really like it, but he is my son. What can I do? He has to do things his own way.'

Since I can't eat with Richard and Angeline, I go up to the restaurant at the top of the village. I am tired, and looking at the map I see that the second half of the path to the village of Py and my rendezvous with Veronica is on a tarmac road. This is not an inviting prospect so I settle down to eat a hearty meal. I know I'm going to regret it later but my only concession to the crushing heat is not to drink the cool refreshing beer that I had promised myself.

In the afternoon, even without the dehydrating alcohol, and despite my efforts to pace myself, I feel rather faint at the end of the climb up to the Col de Mantet.

However, the *FFRP guide* is wrong and for once I am pleased. The Pyrenean Way does *not* follow the now-melting road which bootlaces its way down from the Col de Mantet to Py. Instead I find myself on the old cobbled track which was abandoned when donkeys gave way to motor cars. It is steeper but shorter and shaded by trees. A lizard darts across from one dry stone wall to the other. A few steps later another stops abruptly, trying unsuccessfully to melt into the rock. These are browner than their cousins in the Aude. Suntan?

I pass abandoned gardens and reach up to collect the just-ripe cherries overhanging the path. Today is 21 June. In the nearby valley of the Tech the cherries are famously ripe from the beginning of May, but at 1600m above sea level everything is later.

Between the Col de Mantet and Py there is a plaque which marks the *méridienne verte*, an imaginary line stretching north–south down France. I arrive there just after the solar mid-day on the day of the solar mid-year, by chance. I smile to myself, take my rucksack off and sit down for a rest. Space and time have always been important to me and the *méridienne verte* celebrates them perfectly.

When I was an archaeologist, I used to commute daily into the past, and time and ways of quantifying it were a constant preoccupation. When I was working in Orkney, I once went to see how it was measured in the Neolithic. It was mid-winter's day, and sitting in the central chamber of the Maeshowe tomb I watched as the last light of the setting sun crept down the entrance passage to illuminate the stones. Discovering the *méridienne verte* is not quite as moving, but it is a delightful coincidence. And the *méridienne verte* is not just a question of time, it is also a question of space, and lately I have become obsessed by space: longitude and latitude (and height, of course).

Whilst Britain spent over £800m on its Dome, celebrating the new millennium, the French government spent a mere £5m on the *méridienne verte*. The idea was to plant a line of trees stretching from the Channel to the Spanish border. 'Above all, I didn't want something fixed, nor a kind of Eiffel tower 3000m high dreamed up by architects in need of Viagra.' explained the architect Chemetov. There was to be a giant picnic to celebrate planting the trees, at different points all along the line. Thankfully, the authorities didn't insist on celebrating the millennium on 1 January 2000 with the rest of the world, but left it to 14 July.

If the idea caught the public imagination it was partly because the *méridienne verte* has a considerable historical significance. It follows the line of the original Paris meridian. Like its ultimately more successful cousin, the Greenwich meridian, it was the starting point for measuring longitude, the zero degrees for French sailors.

In addition, the basic unit of length, the metre, had been defined using the meridian. For the French Academy of Science, it had to be something *universally* acceptable: 1/10,000,000 of the distance from the poles to the equator. Unfortunately this is rather difficult to measure but Messieurs Delambre and Méchain were asked to do their best. They decided that it was not necessary to leave mainland Europe to do the work. So instead of setting out for the North Pole they headed for Dunkirk, France's nearest equivalent. Striking a line due south they passed through Paris and where I am now standing, and ended up in Barcelona. Thus, although the Greenwich meridian became the standard for seafarers, it is the Paris meridian which shapes modern scientific measurement.

Leaving space and time behind me, I pick up my weighty rucksack and hobble into Py, feet aching, knees wobbling. As in Mantet, the stone-built houses crowd the narrow streets. Here, in contrast, they are capped with red-orange clay tiles brought up from the Roussillon plain.

In the distance I see two people waving at me. As I approach I recognise one of them as Veronica. *La finlandaise* is also there. She explains that she has blisters on her 'pinky toes'. I suggest glibly that she cuts them off.

'It's not really a very good idea. I've done it once and I don't want to do it again. I made a complete mess of it.'

'What?'

'I'm a surgeon. The bloke had frostbite. But I can tell you, amputation hasn't advanced greatly since butchers used to do it with a saw borrowed from the carpenter down the road.'

Tomorrow she will go to a bookshop in Perpignan, followed by a beach on the Mediterranean. She will come back and finish the Pyrenean Way another time. We never did discover her name.

Veronica drives me to Vernet-les-Bains. In the 19th century and early 20th century it was a genteel spa town, much favoured by the English. Rudyard Kipling called it the 'Paradise of the Pyrenees'. It is no longer genteel. In summer the population swells from 1,400 to 10,000.

We are staying in a hotel named, confusingly, *Le* Princess, though as far as I know princesses are required to be feminine. Like *le vache*, and *le grande randonnée 10*, the name seems to be designed to trip up foreigners. The hidden words which determine the gender are, respectively, *hôtel, fromage de* and *sentier de*.

In the bathroom I remove my socks and gently ease off the remains of the Compeed plasters. Second skin it calls itself, and as long as it stays in place, that is what it is. In the mornings I have the impression that my heels are baby-soft. But after a few hours the plasters begin to slip, leaving a disgusting semi-liquid goo on my socks. I put on new plasters every lunch time.

I examine my feet under the harsh illumination of the light above the bathroom mirror. There are tender suppurating red patches covering half of each heel. A yellowish liquid drips into the wash basin. Tomorrow, I must see if something can be done, otherwise I will never reach the sea.

Py to Mariailles

The next day, Py to Mariailles is an easy 3-hour stroll along a natural balcony overlooking the valley, then up through the forest. Veronica arrives in the car just before me and I book us in for breakfast at the hostel at Mariailles the next day, though we are staying down in the valley in Vernet again for the night.

I telephone around and discover that there is a pharmacy in Font Romeu. We arrive before it opens and look longingly through the plate glass windows at the cool imitation-marble. Finally the lights come on, though the shop appears to be completely empty. We open the door and walk in. Instantly, music starts playing – jazz music, swing. We glide across the floor and stand timidly by the counter expecting the pharmacist to emerge from behind a curtain, arms in the air, crooning, as in the wonderful *Les Parapluies de Cherbourg* which helped to launch the career of Catherine Deneuve.

The pharmacist tells me that he has seen worse. He floats around the shop, selecting spray-on antiseptic, something he describes as 'dry water', lint eye pads, especially big Compeed plasters, and sticky elastic bandages. According to the instructions the 'dry water' is designed to clean out babies' noses. According to the pharmacist it will dry up the antiseptic. This, in turn, is removed by the absorbent eye pads.

The plasters are held on by the bandages. With a certain subtlety, he throws in some liquid soap samples to wash my socks.

Mariailles to the Chalet des Cortalets

After breakfast at Mariailles, Veronica drives herself back down to Vernet for a rendezvous with a four-wheel drive which will take her up to the Chalet des Cortalets on the upper slopes of Canigou.

I take a track which descends at first, climbs steeply through a mixed forest, and then stumbles into a meadow. Below, half way up a steep ravine, I can see the terracotta roofs of the abbey of St Martin du Canigou.

I have visited the 1000-year-old abbey previously. It is a real treasure,

Salome and musicians in the abbey of Saint-Martin-du-Canigou

particularly the decorated capitals in the cloister. Today, one of them comes to mind, the one that tells the story of St John the Baptist. The connection with Canigou is that tonight a bonfire will be lit on the summit, in celebration of mid-summer's eve, a tradition which started as a pagan rite, was captured by Christianity on behalf of John, briefly celebrated a rugby victory, and now has become a major event in the Catalan year.

That is something to look forward to, but for the present on the mountainside it is hard going. The rough grass has given way to a barren rock-strewn slope, only relieved by the occasional *joubarbe*, with its star-shaped purple flowers, and the exuberant yellow sunburst spikes of gentian flowers.

I drink from my water bottle spilling some on the stones. It sizzles. The cairns which mark the passage are indistinguishable amongst all the other boulders and soon there is no sign of the path. The ferns and brambles, initially knee-high, are now waist-high as I force my way through into the forest. In a small clearing I extract the GPS from my rucksack. It tells me that I really am on the path. So I strike off, following the contours until I come to a larger clearing and see the path only a few paces away, plainly visible now that there are no trees obscuring it.

I am pleased with the results of my visit to the pharmacy. My feet still ache but a lunch-time inspection shows that the layers of bandages are still in place. After lunch, however, my feet decide to revolt. Instead of the constant dull ache that they have been putting out since the beginning, my left foot comes up with a sudden stupefying pain which stops me dead in my tracks. Tendonitis again. I sit down and curse. I tentatively try a few more steps – with the same result. I get out my collapsible stick without much faith and step gingerly forward, putting all my weight onto it, persuading myself that it is less painful.

A man striding down the path greets me. '¡*Hola!*' he says, continuing without stopping. A few minutes later it is '*Bonjour,*' again with a heavy Catalan accent. I am approaching the top of *their* mountain.

I can see the hostel at the other side of a couple of lakes, girdled by Swiss mountain pine. The Chalet des Cortalets consists of two block-houses – made in local stone, it is true, but still unremittingly, heavily, rectangular. In front is a circular arena defined by ranch style fencing. Four-wheel drive vehicles chase each other around the periphery, snarling. For them this is the end of a gruelling 90-minute drive from Prades, only 9km away as the crow flies.

I am soon sitting on the covered terrace in front of the main building. The manager serves me a beer. He is in his fifties, solid, and no-nonsense, like the building. Yes, Veronica has arrived – at 9 o'clock in the morning. No, he doesn't know where she is.

On the terrace a plaque records that Les Cortalets was burned to the ground by the Nazis in July 1944 – Henri Barbusse, a Resistance fighter, had sheltered here. At the same time, according to Rosemary Bailey, Canigou was officially renamed Pic Pétain, an incident not mentioned in any of the numerous French books and articles I have read.

Today, a good-natured patriotism fills the air. More and more groups of people appear, some on foot, but most in four-wheel drives. They are Catalans, southern Catalans, identifiable – even before I can distinguish the words – by the babble of voices competing with each other, all talking at once.

A flickering paraffin lamp sits on a blood-and-gold flag draped over one of the tables on the terrace. A Catalan brings his own lamp, lights it and then returns to his car and drives off. The paraffin lamp on the table goes out. Unconcerned by this symbolic disaster, somebody re-lights it with a cigarette lighter. I wander through the woods and pastures. There are tents pitched all over the place but none of the usual cows are present. Apparently, they became ill and had to be taken down to the plain. Eventually I discover Veronica. She has been reading, wandering around, eating lunch, drinking an occasional beer, and reading. We snuggle up together on a bed of pine needles cushioned by spare clothing, in a small clearing padded with flowering rhododendrons. Veronica picks up her book. I look up at the light sparkling through the tree tops, and doze.

The menu this evening is lettuce and onion salad, *escudella* with macaroni, cheese, and *crema catalana. Escudella* is a Catalan version of *garbure. Crema catalana* is a kind of *crème brûlée* thickened with cornflour and flavoured with cinnamon, the latter being a classic Catalan ingredient. Perfect walking food with regional overtones. Lots of liquid for rehydration, carbohydrates for sustained effort, minerals and vitamins in the salt and vegetables. I sip parsimoniously at my glass of wine; Veronica finishes the jug.

I like the Chalet des Cortalets. Despite its size and the number of people who arrive in cars, its entire ethos is geared towards walkers, as indeed it should be at a hostel run by the CAF. When I ask for breakfast at 5:30, the waitress simply takes note and asks me where I am going.

I had intended to climb up to see the fire but I just don't have enough energy so I go to bed at 9 o'clock. In any case, I tell myself, I was there exactly two years ago.

Bonfire on Canigou

On that occasion I walked over from Mariailles in the afternoon and up the last bit of the slope in the evening to see the fire. This is the second annual celebration of Catalan identity after the *troubade*, which took place at the Chalet des Cortalets the previous weekend. This evening, fires will be lit simultaneously throughout the region and beyond, metaphorically spreading Canigou's glory as the highest peak at the western end of the Pyrenees. But what might now seem an ancient rite was only invented in 1955.

From the summit you can see: to the east, a golden arc of sand curving into the distance, separating the dark Mediterranean from the silver coastal lagoons and the regimented vineyards. From the

Taking wood up Canigou, as part of the trobade

summit you can see: to the north, the rolling heath of the Corbières stretching almost to the turreted walls of the medieval city of Carcassonne, 100km away. From the summit you can see: to the west, Madres, Carlit, and a long inventory of Pyrenean peaks. From the summit you can see: nothing. You can hardly even make out your feet. It depends.

I arrive at sunset. This time, I can see the top of Carlit but its base and the plain are hidden in haze. Although theoretically at the height of its powers, this evening the sun dissolves ignominiously into the murky grey, hardly colouring it.

Tomorrow, 24 June, is the traditional midsummer's day, three days after the true solstice on the 21st. It has always been a time of festivals and magic to mark the apogee of the sun, a time of bonfires in the streets to keep it burning. Enrolled by the Catholic church, the festival became the feast day of John the Baptist. The church's explanation for the choice of date is that, before he ended up on a platter, John had baptised Christ, saying, 'He must become greater; I must become less.' Just as the sun begins to decline after midsummer's day, from then on John's authority was waning.

This is the first reason for the celebrations. The second lies in another, older tradition of gathering herbs on the slopes of the mountain on midsummer's eve. Herbs are at their most pungent at this time of year and folklore and chemistry combined to endow them with special powers. St John's Wort was one plant favoured for its medicinal properties. And all along the Pyrenees, carline thistles with their sun-drenched flowers were collected and nailed to doors to protect against evil spirits.

The summit of Canigou is a jumble of rocks. The area that might be called flat is about the size of a large living room. At one end of the living room is an orientation table. At this time of night it is useless for showing local landmarks but it nevertheless indicates the orientation of the evening: bottles of fizzy *blanquette de Limoux* (from the Aude), whisky, and other drinks and snacks are being pulled out of rucksacks and placed on top of it. At the other end of the room a large metal cross, constructed like an electricity pylon, is surrounded by a pile of combustibles brought here during the *troubade*. Instead of walls, the room has cliffs dropping away into the growing blackness.

Sixty people have been invited, or invited themselves to the party. Being a *gavatx* (a non-Catalan), I qualify as a gate crasher, but nobody cares. We move the wood from around the cross to the middle of the room. Helmut and Yvonne, 11-05, have bound their destiny to a

Vine trimmings piled around the cross at the summit of Canigou

bundle of neatly cut chipboard with black wire – it looks like a gigantic wine bottle cork. But the rest of the faggots are vine trimmings tied into bundles with Catalan ribbons. The pile is draped with Catalan flags and a home-made pennant with a sketch of a *burro* (donkey), another Catalan icon. The labels on the faggots name nearby villages like Sahore, ones from further away, and other organisations: the Narbonne Natural Park, for example, has sent a faggot even though it lies outside Catalonia.

    'Good evening everybody,' says a man in a blue anorak, standing up. 'For those who don't know me, my name is Daniel. Today is special for me, because I am going to light the fire for the twentieth time.'

Night is closing in around us. The feeling of being on a summit fades at the same time as the distances disappear. We are floating in space, an increasingly windy, increasingly cold space. Progressively, I empty my rucksack and put on more layers of clothing.

'The first time,' Daniel continues, 'everything went well. The second time everything went well. The third time everything went well... The tenth time, we were about to leave the Chalet des Cortalets when it started to snow. We said to ourselves, are we going or not? Then I saw the Catalan flag. We must be up there for the fire! So we set out and the further we advanced the more it snowed. We were within five minutes of the top when we were forced to turn around. We came back the following Saturday and lit it in the middle of the day... And now it is the twentieth time.'

He is given a present, a tee-shirt, and reads out the motif, in Catalan.

'Tell us what it says. Translate,' demands a woman behind me, but nobody does.

The speech was entirely in French as is nearly all the conversation around me. I can identify only three people who are exclusively speaking Catalan and they are patently from Spain. Of the others, some slip into Catalan for a few words but soon revert to a language in which they are more comfortable.

'The first fire was organised by François Pujade,' Daniel continues. 'He decided to light the fire on the summit of Canigou because, on the one hand it was his birthday and at the same time it was to celebrate the victory of the Perpignan rugby team. A group of friends. Just like that. That lasted several years.'

The fire was seen in the neighbouring villages and the tradition was born. In subsequent years wood was stacked near ancient watchtowers and at other high points in the area. The lighting of the Canigou bonfire became a signal which was to be passed from fire to fire. One year, a radio link was established with Perpignan, and the Catalan song *Muntanyes regalades* was sung at the summit to commemorate the event.

Muntanyes regalades	Bountiful mountains
són les del Canigó	Are those of Canigou,
que tot l'estiu floreixen,	Covered in flowers all summer,
primavera i tardor.	Spring and autumn, too
Jo que no l'aimo gaire,	*And I, who don't like it much*
jo que no l'aimo, no.	*I, who don't like it, no.*
Jo que no l'aimo gaire,	*I who don't like it much*
la vida del pastor.	*The life of a shepherd.*
El pare m'ha casada,	My father has married me,
m'ha donada a un pastor,	Given me to a shepherd.
ell se'n va a la muntanya,	He goes off up the mountain,
jo resto al Rosselló.	and leaves me on the plain.
Jo que . . .	*I, who...*
Ell beu de l'aigua clara,	He drinks the clear water,
jo bec vi del millor;	I drink the best of wines;
ell dorm damunt la palla,	He sleeps on straw,
jo en llençols de cotó.	And I, on cotton sheets.
Jo que . . .	*I, who...*
El menja pa moreno,	He eats coarse bread,
jo em menjo del flecó;	I eat from the bakery;
ell cull brotets de menta,	He picks sprigs of mint,
jo floretes d'olor.	I, scented flowers.

In 1958 more than 50 singers from the association A Cœur Joie clambered up the slopes. But by 1962 interest was flagging. The weather was not always clement and fire on the summit not always visible. And if the mountain was not visible, the necessary symbolic link was lost. The problem was that the flame had to come from the mountain *and* all the bonfires had to be lit at the same time on mid-summer's eve. It required a feat of physical and intellectual gymnastics to resolve it.

Jean Iglésis, president of the Perpignan *Cercle des jeunes* (youth club) thought up the idea which would ensure the future of the event.

Daniel explains: 'In 1964 an old lady, Marguerite Mestre-Grando, captured the sun with a magnifying glass and lit a fire in the kitchen of the house where she had spent her youth. By that time, the kitchen was in the Catalan museum in Perpignan. This flame has become the Canigou flame. It burns all year in the museum. At 10 o'clock on the morning of 22 June it is taken by three members of the *Cercle des jeunes*, who bring it to the summit of Canigou. That was yesterday. Just after midnight, they regenerate the flame like this: they take it from the lamp and light a single faggot at the summit. The three walkers then rekindle the flame in the lamp and bring it down to the Chalet des Cortalets and leave it for me to bring back up to the summit. From that moment on, the flame is shared. There are lots of Catalans from the south who come for the flame and distribute it.'

So the flame which lights the fire on the summit on the evening of 23 June can simultaneously light fires on the plain, in Perpignan, and further away: in Paris, in Japan even. Thousands of fires. The technical problem had been solved and the centre of the celebrations displaced from an inaccessible summit to Perpignan where the festivities last well into the night.

'You have the text of the songs? Pass the photocopies around,' Daniel instructs.

A few words in Catalan, the fire is lit, and we sing from the song sheets – *Muntanyes regalades, Canigou, Se canto, Les montagnards sont là,*

La Santa Espina – in Catalan, French, and Occitan. The bottles are passed round, as we toast by the fire.

There are many odd things about this celebration of Catalan identity. It was invented to celebrate a rugby victory and a birthday. It is mostly conducted in French for a French audience. The lighting of the fire has been sidelined in the sequence of events, which mainly take place elsewhere. Even the fizz is French *blanquette* rather than Catalan *cava*. But all the same it makes for an enjoyable evening.

The fire burns rapidly down to glowing embers and people start to make their way back, the glow-worm trail of head torches stretching down the slope. For those who remain, there are grilled sausages and melted camembert.

Finally I am alone. Away from the fire, to avoid the sparks, I move a few rocks to make a v-shaped slot and wedge my sleeping bag into it. The wind has cleared the sky and I can see the lights of Perpignan and the coastal villages. The stars are here too. I am no longer enclosed by the night but part of it.

Chalet des Cortalets to Arles

Back at the Chalet des Cortalets two years later, it is just light when I fill up my water bottles at the spring. It is going to be a long hot day but for the present the air is coolish. I warm up carefully, avoiding straining my muscles. I climb easily, but then trip over a lump of metal. A little further on, the path is strewn with the tangled skin and dismembered sinews of an aircraft: all that remains of a Dakota travelling from London to Perpignan with 31 passengers and three crew on 7 October 1961. There were no survivors. At the time, the magnetic influence of the mountain, long mined for its iron ore, was blamed for upsetting the plane's instruments but in reality the problem was that the radio transmitter in Toulouse was too far away to work properly.

Strolling comfortably along the Balcon du Canigou, everything seems to be on schedule for arrival in Arles-sur-Tech this afternoon. I smile to myself: it was a good idea not to go to the summit but to conserve my strength. In the thick of the woods, I meet a young man, his dirty tangled hair exploding around an unwashed face, two sparklingly clean collie dogs scampering around his grubby trousers. No rucksack. He is living in a hut, though he is not a shepherd, he tells me. I am envious.

My path winds down through the ONF-managed forest and up again to the Col de la Cirère, the watershed between the valleys of the Têt and the Tech. I emerge into the open pasture overlooking a strangely irregular landscape. Below me, where there was once an industrial ant heap, nature is smoothing the contours, pencilling in the hillside.

The mines, the last on the Canigou massif, closed in 1977. The company itself limped on selling its stockpiles for a few years until it finally collapsed in 1987. The workers' hostel at Batère was taken over by the CAF, and the cable system which transported the ore to Arles-sur-Tech was dismantled. In 2001 the mines were sold for the symbolic franc to the Arles town council.

One by one the industries of the French Pyrenees have closed down over the last century. The valleys are changing. With the exception of talc, the mineral resources are either exhausted or uneconomic. The timber industry still exists, but wood is no longer as important as it once was. Hydroelectricity, though significant, employs few workers. Pastoralism is a sideline. Tourism is hardly an *industry*, in any real meaning of the term. The Pyrenees are no longer *productive*.

I stride down the slope from the pass, full of energy, but within a few paces the mechanism judders sharply to a halt. My left knee has given way. I experiment. Every time I take a step forward it sends out a sharp pain. I take off my rucksack and pull up my foot behind me, stretching and twisting my muscles. I straighten my leg against a rock and tension other muscles. This works for a few steps and then the pain comes back again. I try walking like a duck; I try turning my toes inwards. Nothing seems to make any difference. I turn round and try walking uphill and discover that here lies the solution. If I can just walk uphill, I can keep going for as long as I like. However, my destination Arles-sur-Tech is 1500m lower down. Eventually I discover that the pain is bearable if I don't bend my leg more than a few degrees and stop every few minutes. So I peg-leg awkwardly down past the concrete platforms, avoiding the holes left by subsidence, tripping over the sprawling steel hawsers, through the ruins of the abandoned mine.

I limp on to the hostel at Batère taking two hours for a section which should have been done in less than one. The hostel is closed and knocking on the door fails to produce any reaction. But it looks as though it might be open at lunch time so I sit at a long wooden table in the shade of an umbrella.

A notice defiantly proclaims, 'No water, we don't have any to spare.' Nobody appears, so I can't even buy a can of sickly brown bubbles. Instead, I sip carefully at my remaining litre of tepid liquid and slurp up a melted Mars bar. By 11 o'clock I am feeling sufficiently restored and decide to attempt the three-hour walk into Arles. The first section along the almost flat tarmac road flanked by pine forest is easy enough. Then the path turns off into a luxurious grassy green cleavage between two ferny hillocks. A small stream feeds shady pools, but there are sheep and cows around and I don't dare take the risk of drinking polluted water: 'purifying' tablets have their limits. The grass gives way to heath, small kermes oaks, waist high bushes, broom, brambles, an uneven path, and an extremely painful knee. Two hours later I am still less than two kilometres from the hostel. I sit on a broken concrete block which once supported the aerial cable transporting ore down to the valley, and cry.

I try to rationalise my situation. There will come a point when I cannot move at all. I have only seen two people on the path all day and I would be surprised if anyone was foolish enough to be climbing up from Arles in the heat of the early afternoon sun. My mobile phone can't find the network.

On the other hand, the nearest road is not too far away. Even though this will mean a much longer haul down to Arles, at least it will be less steep, and it is better to be crippled and incapable on a road than in the middle of the heath. So I follow a track leading to it and reach the road without too much difficulty.

Sitting at a bright blue folding picnic table where the track meets the road is a prim young couple just starting lunch. He is unfolding the sunshade; she is opening a bottle of wine. There are real glasses and china plates on the table, and a new wicker picnic basket displaying enticing foodstuffs.

I analyse the situation again. They have a shiny new car. This road doesn't go anywhere apart from the hostel and they don't look as if they are going to stay there. There must be no more than half a dozen cars a day. Arles is 14km away.

I straighten my back, swing my arms nonchalantly, smile radiantly, and say my best '*bon appétit*'. Do I look wholesome enough, the kind of person you would be happy to have in your brand new car? Have I managed to disguise the dribbling, sweat-stained, limping tramp, with smelly feet oozing pus and probably a beard full of lice and yesterday's food? The longer I stay in their vicinity, the more likely they are to realise that they would prefer not to get to know me in the intimacy of a small metal box.

I continue on down the road, feeling wobbly from the effects of the sun. I have now completely run out of water and am not thinking straight, so that when I see a stream, instead of filling up my water bottle, adding the tablets and waiting for an hour, I decide to try the Captain Bligh method of rehydration. The stream trickling down the hillside is only a thin reminder of what it must be in winter so I cannot possibly submerge myself in it. Instead, I dunk my tee-shirt in the none-too-clean liquid and put it back on without wringing it out. Then I fill my hat and pour it over my head. I drip, like a shower.

There is no possibility of hitching a lift now, so I eat lunch by the side of the road.

Afterwards I carve a second stick out of a branch. Although the road isn't steep, the hard tarmac still jars my knee. At the first farm, I knock on the door. Five bushy men come rushing to the door and glare at me, but one of them takes my bottles and fills them up, chatting pleasantly, if a little nervously. Back on the road, dry by now, I am making slow progress when a Dutch car drives by, ignoring me. Much later, I hear a second car. I take my hat off, smooth my hair down, and … the car stops. It is the couple who were eating lunch earlier. I arrive in Arles on schedule, but rather less smug than I was this morning.

I check into the only hotel in town, the Glycines, named after the wisteria which covers its magnificent wrought iron terrace. The thermometer on the pharmacy says 31°; the doctor says, 'Inflamed tendon. I'll give you some anti-inflammatory tablets, which will get you to Banyuls.' Veronica will be there waiting for me. Tired of chasing up and down mountains, she is spending the rest of her holiday lazing on the shores of the Mediterranean.

Here in the Vallespir, the last major dip on the Pyrenean Way before it tumbles into the Mediterranean, I am beginning to see the mountains more clearly. The range is not just a long spine with ribs sticking out. Certainly the rocky structure is important. But it is not just the bones which count, there are also the spaces between them: the valleys, with their histories, their communities, their individuals. The Pyrenees are mountains *and* valleys. Mineral, vegetable, and animal, of course. But above all human.

Arles to Moulin de la Palette

This morning I put the *pas de Mahomet* into practice, with a light day's walking. The climb up to the Col de Paracolls is steep and although the sun is now veiled behind a haze, the temperature does not seem to have dropped at all overnight, and the humidity has increased. Half way up I wring out the handkerchief I have been using to mop my brow. The vegetation is increasingly Mediterranean: sweet chestnuts, kermes oak, and spiky-leaved holm oak, fig, and rosemary. The sweet chestnut is garlanded with starbursts of white flowers.

The navigation is tricky as the path no longer follows the line marked on the map. The owners of Can Soler, a large farm, have decided that they no longer want walkers passing by their door, although the path has been there for many years and follows a traditional route through the woods. A few years ago they put a notice saying 'Private' at the edge of their property and forced walkers to make a long detour. By May 2003 the courts had ruled the action illegal and a new route with a much smaller detour was set up, leading directly to the hostel. But the gangrene had already spread and two other owners in the area have put up similar signs.

I arrive at the hostel at the Moulin de la Palette with a few twinges but nothing show-stopping, and spend much of the afternoon paddling in the river. I am the only guest and eat alone at a long wooden table outside. A heavy, slightly sickly perfume fills the air: the hostel manager, Roger Chinaud, is also a bee keeper. Later, I sit on the terrace, alone, feeling melancholy.

Moulin de la Palette to the Salines

Following Roger's advice, I turn right instead of left to head straight for the frontier and the Roc de France, ignoring the 'official' detour.

I have been walking slowly all morning and trying to avoid jarring my knee but as soon as I start to descend from the Roc de France I rediscover my inflamed tendon. However I walk, whatever I do, every step is painful. Even an unusual waymark in the form of a pink pig fails to lift my spirits. At 10:30 I stumble down to the Col du Puits de la Neige. I don't even bother to look for the building after which the pass is named. I ring up Veronica.

'I'm in the aquarium. The fish are fantastic. All kinds of colours, it's like a painting. The more you look at it the more you discover. And the hotel is superb. Wonderful food,' Veronica exclaims.

'Come and sweep me up. I need a *voiture balai*. I'm giving up. It's no fun anymore.'

We arrange to meet at Les Salines, a chapel on the Spanish side of the border. The chapel is a short distance away through the forest but twice as far on the track. I choose the track. It is less steep, and above all it allows me to walk backwards, tricking my knee into thinking that I am walking uphill. An hour later I am at the chapel, defeated.

On the map there is a white dotted road leading from the nearest village to the chapel. The reality, as Veronica discovers, is a dirt track roughly hewn through solid rock. Five hours after my phone call we arrive in Banyuls.

The next day I look regretfully at the plaque on the town hall on the sea front marking the end of the walk.

Las Illas to Col de Ullat

Two weeks later, however, Veronica drives me back to the mountains. We stop in Céret in the foothills to eat and are immediately swept up by the bacchanal surrounding the annual bullfighting. Yesterday's victim is being served up on plates at the improvised restaurants which line the streets. On the edges of the *féria*, the air smells of spilt wine and sick. In the centre, frying *churros* and fresh sweat create a distinctive atmosphere. Every stall seems to have its own pulsating sound system, with marching bands adding to the cacophony.

As an appetiser to this afternoon's entertainment in the arena, young bulls are being raced up and down the main street by a man on horseback. Their human equivalents, a red bandana tied round their necks or ankles, try to wrestle the bullocks to the ground. When one is brought to its knees the crowd roars its approval. The scene could come from a Minoan bas-relief. But we have evolved in the last 3500 years; there are now barriers to protect the crowds.

I pick up the baton at Las Illas, on the French side of the frontier and much more accessible than Les Salines. In the enchanted wood above the village I trail my fingers in the still, cool ponds which punctuate the cascading stream. Here, under the tree cover, everything is still dark green despite the continuing heat wave. Water is in its element.

Veronica has abandoned me again. I will have to get to Banyuls under my own steam this time. As yet, I am the only person at the hostel in Las Illas but the owner tells me that a group of Belgians rang up from Arles-sur-Tech at 10 o'clock booking in for the night. Neither she nor I believe that they will make it.

By 8 o'clock in the evening, the restaurant at the top of the village is full despite the half-hour drive up the winding road from Céret, and many of the customers appear to be regulars. The food is *correct*, but nothing special. I cannot work out where the clients have all come from, certainly not from the huddle of houses which makes up the hamlet.

When I get back to the hostel dormitory, the beds are covered with sleeping bags and rucksacks but their owners are nowhere to be seen. They certainly weren't at the restaurant. A tall, angular man leaps out from the shadows, frightening me. He has come from Arles-sur-Tech today; 20 kilos, Mérens.

'I left at seven this morning and I arrived just five minutes ago,' he looks at his watch. 'Nine o'clock. Twelve hours on my feet and only two hours' rest. I'm done for.'

I am suitably impressed.

'The path goes all over the place. The guide book is useless.'

No, he has not seen any Belgians.

He is visibly shaking from the effort of the day, his muscles unable to relax properly. Leaving his wife and family in the Ariège, he started a week ago. 'I've got to eat something,' he mumbles and disappears into the growing darkness. I get into my bed and finally doze off after the other fourteen hikers have flopped into theirs two hours later.

Next day, stealing quietly out of the dormitory at dawn, I sit on the terrace, easily warm enough in shorts and a tee-shirt, eating a very skimpy breakfast. The hostel doesn't provide food and the hotel-restaurant isn't yet open. I slather both knees with anti-inflammatory gel and take two anti-inflammatory tablets but refuse the *Ariégeois'* offer of anti-burn cream. He is agitated, muttering that he intended to be underway already.

I am a long way down the street when I hear shouting and see him waving his arms wildly. He has found a soap bag in the shower and thinks that it might be mine. He seems excessively disappointed when I tell him that it isn't.

The road out of the village passes under umbrella pines, immense villas widely spaced on either side. The houses are numbered with figures which jump by fives or tens or more up to 175, as if the village plans to destroy the green isolation which has attracted these first new residents. The number of houses does, however, explain the popularity of the restaurant yesterday evening.

A sign of the climate: fig trees can grow here at 700m above sea level and in sufficient quantity for a small plateau to be named after them – the Col del Figuier. Occasional wild asparagus and more frequent cork oaks add their confirmation: the sea is not far away.

A notice on the path tells me that I am about to enter a nature reserve and warns me not to disturb the inhabitants, who have their summer quarters here during July and August. They appear to be living in some kind of symbiotic relationship with a flock of geese. Cackling a warning, the birds chase me away as I approach too close to the nest building. The inhabitants must still be curled up, asleep. A pity. I would have liked to have seen them in their

Cork oak bark

natural state. A few minutes later, at the other boundary of the reserve, a second notice indicates that I can put my clothes back on again.

Further on, I enter a plantation of cork oaks. They have stripped off too, leaving the newly exposed trunks to tan in the sun. Piles of peeled skin wait to be collected, stacked against the trees, reminiscent of the curved tiles which have covered local roofs since the Roman era.

Cork oaks belong here on the edge of the Mediterranean. The trees can live for centuries but they are highly susceptible to frost and can only be harvested once every twenty years. In certain circumstances they can be prolific: one exceptional tree near here had a recorded circumference of 5.65m, but specimens of this kind of size no longer exist. Competition from the big producers in Spain, Portugal, and North Africa, the introduction of plastic substitutes, and forest fires have ravaged the industry. Although there are roughly 10,000 hectares of cork oak in the region, much of it is overgrown.

At a turning in the path I discover frontier post no 565. Only another 37 to go. These stumpy, worn stone blocks have become so familiar that it is easy to forget the significance of the line which they represent. But a little further on there is a more disturbing relic, a tall concrete post wrapped in a shroud of tattered barbed wire, dating to the time when crossing the frontier could be a matter of life or death. The border has sometimes been a vague dotted line, sometimes sharply defined.

I now realise that the line on my map is illusory. It isn't just a question of the two ends where the Basque and Catalan linguistic, cultural, and social communities have smudged the political discontinuity. Nor a question of the influence of the *lies et passeries* and other local recent cross-border agreements. Governments in far away Madrid and Paris have also perceived the border in a variety of ways, adjusting their telescopes over the years so that the border has floated in and out of focus.

In 1700, Louis XIV reportedly said, '*Il n'y a plus de Pyrénées* – the Pyrenees are no more' when his grandson became the first Bourbon king of Spain, but the War of the Spanish Succession soon put paid to the political tectonics. More recently the frontier was closed in the bitter winter of 1939 to prevent half a million Republican refugees pouring into France at the end of the Spanish civil war, and only opened *in extremis*. Then it was sealed again under Franco until after the Second World War. But now it has again dissolved to such an extent that vehicles can zoom through on motorways at 90km/hr. Smugglers can also zoom through, but this is nothing new.

Over the centuries *trabucaires* (the catalan name for *contrabandiers*), like their Basque counterparts, have frequently taken advantage of the ease of access to Spain. The frontier here, like the bark of the forest which covers it, has nearly always been porous. Initially, the *trabucaires* were locals out to make a few francs to supplement their income. But then the first drug barons moved in.

By the 1770s, contraband trade in tobacco was growing to such a degree that it posed threats of 'social disorder' as much as a loss of fiscal revenue. In May 1773, a band of 140 smugglers 'took' the town of Puigcerda while officials stood by helplessly, and the smugglers emptied the prisons of convicted colleagues.

Even when the frontier was theoretically closed, as during the Second World War, some brave souls managed to filter through: the French Resistance.

Officially 33,000 people – French refugees, Jews, and British and American pilots shot down by the Nazis – passed across the Pyrenees during the war. Jean-Claude Billes, from near Perpignan, was one of them. With a guide, he hiked across the fields and scrambled through the forest to the Puig Neulos, a little further along the Pyrenean Way. A German patrol caught wind of them but a liberal sprinkling of pepper put the dogs off the scent. In Spain he was soon arrested and like most escapees spent several months in prisons. He was then packed off to Casablanca where he joined the Free French.

Curiously, after the Second World War the situation was reversed for a while. Many Spanish men had left their homes, fleeing Franco at the end of the civil war in 1939, and the only way for their families to rejoin them was to pass across the mountains, from Spain into France.

I am approaching the most important crossing point at the eastern end of the Pyrenees. At Panissars, I climb up from the Pyrenean

Panissars : cart-ruts

Way to frontier post no 567. The trees have been cut back here and the view encompasses both the French and the Spanish sides of the watershed. To the north, badly maintained stone terracing cuts through the pale green rows of vines. Vines! Vines everywhere. I'm beginning to feel at home. To the south, the Mediterranean oaks and pines cascade down the hillside towards the coast and dissolve into the haze.

The hill crest itself is an astonishing memorial to the passage of time and peoples. It is here that the Roman general Pompey decided to commemorate the (re-)capture of 876 Spanish towns in the 1st century BC by erecting a monument. Known as the Trophée de Pompée and mentioned by many classical authors, only the foundations now remain. But the most impressive vestige of the past is neither the priory nor the monument. It is the ruts engraved into the solid rock by the passage of thousands of wooden cartwheels over tens of centuries.

It is little quirks of circumstance like this that make archaeology meaningful for me nowadays. I spent twenty years as a field archaeologist, mostly directing excavations on Roman sites in Britain. I slowly discovered that I was no longer interested in the words 'probably' and 'ritual'. It is fifteen years since I decided that archaeology was a thing of the past. Looking at this dig confirms to me that I have become a rank amateur.

Like William Golding I am 'digging for pictures'. Professional archaeologists, he wrote: 'are very efficient. Their published minds never run away with them. They are austerely proof against the perils of exercising an imagination which might assume too much.'

But now I can see carts laden with stone crawling up the slope, the reluctant oxen wheezing from the effort. Masons are carving the hundreds of names which will feature on the sides of the monument. Roman soldiers, stationed at the checkpoint between the two provinces, look on indifferently, bored. Their thoughts stray to the potential delights of Narbo Martius, the capital of southern Gaul, LX miles away. Well-dressed merchants canter down the slope, destination Tarraco. As yet there are no ruts in the rock surface. Narbonne and Tarragona are in their infancy.

Continuing along the Pyrenean Way, within a few hundred paces I have changed centuries. The watershed has taken on another meaning. Communication and common identity have been replaced by discord. Forlorn ironwork crosses in the 17th-century military cemetery record individual destinies caught up in the storm. And the nearby fortress of Bellegarde, dominating the hilltop, demands respect for the French government and the burgeoning power of the increasingly centralised state.

It is now 1688. After eleven years, the work on the fortress has just finished. The medieval castle which stood in the way of the new structure has been demolished. The 1659 Treaty now has a solid foundation. Vauban, the king's military commissioner, has done his job well. The multiple walls will withstand the worst assaults of modern flintlocks and cannons. The well, 65m deep and 6m across, will provide water during a siege. The projecting towers on the outer defences may look like decorative ornamentation but they provide for raking fire along the outside of the walls.

Vauban's solid, forbidding, spiky pentagon finds its echo wherever there was a frontier to be defended. In the Pyrenees he constructed or improved forts in Prats-de-Mollo, Villefranche-de-Conflent, Mont-Louis, and St-Jean-Pied-de-Port, not to mention the coastal ports.

Even so, the treaty failed to put an end to war between France and Spain. Several disputes broke out over the next century and a half, with Spanish possessions in the Netherlands being one of the prizes at stake. The French revolution of 1789 destabilised an already fragile peace and four years later France declared war on Spain. Bellegarde was taken by Spanish troops and it was only recaptured after a four-month siege. The church and village in Mérens were later victims.

Leaving the fort behind me, I suddenly realise that the mysterious clap of thunder I had heard on the path down to the Lac de Bouil-louses was not actually thunder but artillery fire from Mont-Louis, one of the few Vauban forts still in military hands.

There are other sounds in the air: I can hear the insistent sst … sst … sst … of the cicadas for the first time this year. And the noise of heavy traffic. Doomed to compete with the roar coming from the motorway linking France and Spain, the cicadas can be making little headway in their amorous quest.

Ten minutes later, I pass through a flaking council housing estate worthy of some of the depressed suburbs of Paris. I try to phone Veronica but the phone box has been vandalised. Graffiti asserts '*sem catalans*', we are Catalans, and '*Catalunya lliure*', free Catalonia.

On a nearby wall I also read: 'THT TNT – very high voltage, trinitro-toluene.' It was a threat which worked in the Basque country, when ETA declared itself against the planned electric pylons connecting

France and Spain. Since then the proposed site of the interconnection has moved progressively along the Pyrenees, only stopping when it could go no further, on the beaches of the Mediterranean.

Although the suburbs of Le Perthus are run-down, the town centre is buzzing: a zone of feverish contact, this time a contemporary one. The relationship between France and Spain is turning full circle. Two thousand years after the first carts began to etch their passage into the exposed bedrock at Panissars, the A9 motorway carries more than 50,000 vehicles a day over the Pyrenees. The European Union has replaced the Roman Empire.

The town (population 626) is overlooked by huge car parks (with space for 3000 cars) for French shoppers desperate for Spanish prices. Le Perthus is the Basque Col d'Ibardin writ large. This is not ordinary shopping. This is seven-day-a-week consumer worship. Today being Sunday, the church is full. Cigarettes are exceptionally cheap. Overweight heart-attacks struggle to push trolley loads of lung cancer back up the hill to their cars.

I walk down the high street. The contrast between the thriving commercial centre and poor housing estates seems inexplicable at first and it takes me some time to understand the schizophrenic personality of this wild-west town. All the big supermarkets are on the left hand side of the high street and all the staff are chattering in Spanish or Catalan. On the other side, from the open windows I hear the unmistakable nasal vowel sounds of the language of Molière. The customs post is plainly visible at the bottom of the high street at the very edge of the town, but this is misleading. One side of the high street is in Spain, a part of the commune of La Jonquera, and the other side is in France. The shops are all in Spain, the cafés in France. The French town council gets little benefit from the pilgrimage to Our Lady of the Consumer, even though there are many believers.

Coming out of the town, I pass under the motorway stilts. Above me, a monstrous pyramid topped by a post-modern evocation of a classical temple marks the frontier. The pyramid makes no attempt to integrate itself. Like the motorway, it simply asserts its right to be there.

I trudge along the tarmac for the next hour, climbing slowly, crossing over the road at each bend to stay in the shade of the trees. Somewhere down below my feet, engineers are tunnelling the rock for the TGV which will link Perpignan to Barcelona in 2012, but I cannot see or hear anything which betrays their presence.

The other sounds also disappear: the cicadas, the motorway too, but the tarmac is as hard on my feet as the sun is on my scalp. I fill up my water bottles at the Font del Molinas, the Spring of the Mills. At the Font Sant August I kneel down in the grotto and let the water dribble into my hair and over my shirt. The Font Miqueta, the Driblet of a Spring, is dry. Finally the route leaves the road, and tunnels into the forest. This is the beginning of the Albères, where the Pyrenees tumble into the Mediterranean. The name is derived from the pre-Roman *alp*, meaning mountain or mountainside, but they have no resemblance to their namesakes.

Picnic tables, cows, and cedar trees mark my passage through St Martin de l'Albère, where there is another diversion from the official route. I struggle up through the rough pasture hiding under the few trees, suffering from the relentless sun. At least my knees are holding out.

At the Col de Ullat, the hostel looks as though it has been imported from the Alps. A chalet made mostly of wood, at least it is appropriate to its setting. The surrounding park is occupied by families out for the day, picnicking, their cars waiting patiently. Inside, a giant television screen is showing the Tour de France cycle race, on its second day in the real Alps. Life-size cyclists drip sweat into the bar but few people are paying any attention.

Although the couple who run the chalet have been here for several years, they don't seem to understand the needs of walkers. The evening meal has several varieties of grilled meat but little in the way of carbohydrates. And when I say that I want to leave at half past five in the morning they are visibly shocked.

'But the sun won't have risen,' they protest. Perhaps they could get up for half past six, they suggest. I propose that they leave me breakfast and a packed lunch somewhere with a thermos of coffee.

At least the rising sun will wake me up, I think, leaving the shutters open in case I don't hear my alarm clock. But I sleep badly in any case. During the night, I am woken up by the full moon shining through the window. I look at the clock, anxious not to sleep through its signal. Not only would I miss the cool of the early morning but also I would have to face the scorn of the owners. I dream that my left knee collapses as I am walking along and I fall sideways over a cliff. In the end, my stomach knotted, I am thoroughly awake well before five.

Col de Ullat to Banyuls

I push on the door of the room opposite, where my breakfast is waiting for me. It seems to be stuck. I push harder, but it is locked.

Outside, the moon casts a reddish light over the chalet; the terrace, where I ate yesterday, is eerily abandoned. I can't bring myself to wake the owners up but I can't leave without provisions for the day.

I finish packing my rucksack grumpily and come across the tiny bottle of Atlantic seawater, now nearly empty: the water must have permeated through the polythene. Then I wander around the chalet again looking for any signs of life. Finally I realise that the manager must have left my breakfast in a different room. Wolfing it down, I attach my lamp to my forehead. Outside, clambering up the hill, I trip over the tangled roots of giant Corsican pines. The moon is setting to the west as I enter the beech plantation. Soon, I can see the first signs of the new day beginning to appear.

At the top of the hill, I slip surreptitiously through the bars of a gate which marks the frontier, and down through the yellowing ferns to the *pou del glaç*. A large cairn with loose iron bars vaguely protecting a dangerously wide opening marks the top of the structure. The entrance is further down the slope. I switch my head torch on again and crawl along the tunnel which leads into the flank of the mountain, narrowly avoiding falling into the pit at the end. In France this would be called a *glacière* but the Catalan translates literally as ice well. Like an iceberg, it is mostly submerged below the surface of the mountain. In winter, ice and snow were shovelled through the hole in the top, and in summer ice was extracted from the tunnel at the bottom. The ice house is 400 years old, a pretty good age for a refrigerator still in perfect working order.

At the Puig Neulos I can see the hazy Mediterranean of my dreams, even though it is hidden behind a television transmitter and an ugly mesh of barbed wire.

A few minutes later when I arrive at the Refuge de Tanyareda, a head pokes out of the door. I recognise the *Ariégeois*. He complains about the number of wine bottles littering the floor. When he arrived yesterday evening a clutter of young people was already in residence. A few minutes later they were falling into their car, visibly displeased that they couldn't smoke their joints in peace anymore.

We set off together but the *Ariégeois* soon outdistances me. My phone has packed in and I have six hours of walking before I reach the next road. Unfortunately, most of the route is downhill. I realise that if my knee decides it has had enough there is little hope of immediate rescue.

As yet, the sun is still timid and low mist obscures the Spanish foothills as I follow the ill-defined frontier ridge. At the Puig des Quatre Termes where I catch up with him, the *Ariégeois* is drinking greedily from his water bottle.

'There's a spring marked on the map just down the hill, at 970m above sea level,' he says, getting out his digital altimeter. 'Look, I've climbed 6,517m since I set off.'

We agree to search together but he races ahead and when I reach the spring he is nowhere to be seen. Half an hour later I catch up with him, still frenetically searching the undergrowth, still hoping to find the water. I offer him some of my liquid wealth but he declines. I would like to walk quietly, alone, but he keeps on waiting for me to catch up.

At the final pass before the long descent to Banyuls there is a crèche tucked into a niche in the rock. In a small Perspex box, the pottery *santons* play out the Nativity scene once again. The inscription reads 'Happy Christmas 2000. Peace – wisdom – love for the third millennium.'

Then, halfway down the rocky ridge I meet the first person coming from Banyuls, soaked in sweat from the climbing to get to this point. My right knee begins to hurt and I decide to stop for an early lunch. An enormous ham sandwich seems to solve the problem – sympathetic magic, perhaps.

Finally, I can *really* see the Mediterranean – the yellow-brown strand of Argelès-Plage stretching out northwards before curling up for its afternoon siesta – but I'm not yet capable of relaxing. The *garrigue* is also tense, waiting for the thunderstorm which would normally punctuate the afternoon. But it has been waiting for two months now. Earth, wind, fire, and water in nervous equilibrium, almost smouldering, are waiting for the slightest spark. There are no more trees to provide passing shade and the sun is still rising, but the first signs of civilisation appear in the distance: the healthy vivid green of a vineyard stands out against the dull grey-brown of the surrounding heath.

Gradually I become aware of the sound of gurgling water, although there are no streams here. At first I think that I am suffering from some kind of audible mirage, as the sound ebbs and flows, but then I notice a loose rough stone pad by the side of the path. I lift it up and see water. There is an underground conduit following the line of the path, with intermittent access holes for cleaning. It is not clear where all this water is going but even 'purification' couldn't make it drinkable.

Finally, I reach the road and the Tour de Madaloc on the hill watching over the coastal plain. A young couple sitting at the pass ostentatiously waits for me to pass by so they can continue with whatever they were doing before I appeared. The heath has now definitively been replaced by vines, cultivated cactuses, and flowers. The cicadas are stage-whispering again. Artfully trained olive trees decorate onetime farmyards, now populated by polished four-wheeled ruminants, driven down from the north for the quality of the summer pasture. The houses have new windows, the shutters wide open, letting in the afternoon heat and betraying the presence of *gavatx*.

Below, Banyuls sprawls along the coast with modern tower blocks guarding its flanks but it still manages to look seductive. The end is in sight. My maps tell me I have walked almost 1000km, including 50km up and 50km down. I can't quite believe it. It has taken me 62 days, including rest days and extras.

Why did I do it? My fellow walkers have proposed many reasons for undertaking the Pyrenean Way. For some it is the physical experience: the exhilaration of muscles functioning, of lungs filling with fresh air, of being outside, battered by wind and rain, only to be later caressed – or burnt – by the sun. There is the silent emptiness of the heights. The beauty of the valleys. The smell of new-mown grass and damp sheep. That delicious hunger brought about by physical exercise, soon to be rewarded.

And then there is the pain. No question about it, we must all be seeking it out. It isn't just something we tolerate because we have to. It is something we *want*, something we *need*, because it validates the experience. Without the pain, the GR 10's *credencial*, the walk would be trivial.

Some walkers talk about the social aspects: meeting people, and above all the camaraderie of shared experience which keeps them going.

And then there are those who highlight the mental aspects. Far away from everyday concerns, the Pyrenean Way is set in a different world, imposing its own constraints. It is a challenge which occupies the spirit. At the same time, it allows you to think about things. Or to think about absolutely nothing and let new ideas infiltrate, opening new doors.

Mostly it is about personal boundaries, both physical and mental, and going beyond them.

For me there is truth in all of these suggestions. But have I discovered *my* reason for walking day after day? Perhaps, but not in the Pyrenees. Before I set out this year I went on a walk in the Calanques, near Marseille. One of the participants, Michèle, said: 'Walking is a primitive activity. Not only have we been doing it since childhood, but it has also been programmed into us genetically. We spend so much of our lives thinking, analysing, and coping with new situations that it is good to return to doing something instinctive.'

Yes, that's it.

The *Ariégeois* is waiting for me in his underwear at a spring just before the town.

'It's too hot.' he says. 'This is the first drinkable water I have found. I tried drinking from the underground conduit but it was disgusting. I'll just finish my lunch, then I'll be with you.'

'Don't hurry. I'm sure you'll catch up with me anyway. You walk much faster than me,' I say. But now that I am within sight of my goal I speed up, virtually sprinting the last few kilometres.

In the town centre, my first objective is a clothes shop. The only one which is open has racks of tie-dyed skirts outside, with mock-designer tee-shirts crowding the doorway. Inside, it is small and dark, with tiny electric lamps highlighting brightly coloured cottons. My rucksack brushes against the hangers on either side. The main clientele must be young women in their twenties but there are some men's swimming trunks on one of the shelves. The assistant emerges from the background of which she was part – she is wearing the same garments as are on display in the shop. Slim, with long black hair, elegant and poised, I expect her to recoil at my visibly unwashed state but she treats me as if I am exactly the kind of customer she was hoping for. She asks me if I would like to try on the trunks, but I feel that this is taking politeness too far. I hold a promising pair in front of me and ask if she thinks they would fit. She acquiesces. As I am leaving the shop, she fishes a paper bag out from behind the counter and insists that I take a plum. I'm not quite sure why.

My next objective is a bar. I choose the darkest and quietest I can find and hide myself in a corner. Two beers and a quick change in the toilets and I feel almost respectable. I see my reflection in a mirror, wide-eyed, disbelieving. I have done it!

Finally on the beach, I open the pocket of my rucksack to look for my talisman, the tiny bottle of seawater from the Atlantic, but it isn't there. I empty the pocket and then the rucksack onto the beach, carefully sifting through my belongings, turning the rucksack upside down and shaking it. The bottle has vanished: perhaps I lost it when I filled up at the spring. There is nothing to be done. I can't make a contribution to the Mediterranean.

Removing my boots, I stow them carefully with my clothes. I am not going to throw them into the sea. We get along just fine, now. Either they have worn my feet down or I have broken them in.

The swimming trunks are somewhat skimpy but I don't care; I walk into the sea as if it wasn't there, only stopping when it is up to my chest. Turning round, I see another rucksack next to mine. The *Ariégeois* has rediscovered me. He comes down to the shore, takes out his mobile phone, and rings his wife, putting the mouthpiece to the waves so that she can hear the sea. Finally, we shake hands and swap names. Christian and I take each other's photos in front of the plaque on the town hall marking the end of the Pyrenean Way and settle down for a large beer. I am really pleased to see him. We are both grinning like Cheshire cats.

Afterword

A few days after I arrive home, it rains during the night leaving the morning sky clear and the air dry, so I climb the hill behind our house to get a good look at the Pyrenees. Canigou seems closer than usual, with a slightly purple tinge, I fancy, but apart from that it hasn't changed. I put my binoculars to my eyes and can distinguish the outlines of Madres, Carlit, and perhaps Rulhe. The mountains seem solid, natural, eternal... at least at this distance.

But I have also seen them in close-up. Close enough to distinguish the blades of grass. And I have been able to listen to their uneven heartbeat through my Pyrenean Way stethoscope.

No, they are not eternal. They are not even natural. We humans have constructed them both physically and in our minds. The process started two centuries ago with their 'discovery' by Paris society, led by Ramond. Just as Columbus' 'discovery' of America was destined to revolutionise the lives of the inhabitants, Ramond and the visitors who followed him were to transform the Pyrenees, in a process which is continuing today.

The mountains are changing physically, the animals which inhabit their slopes and the humans in the villages are changing and, most importantly, our perceptions of them are changing.

Physically, rhododendrons are replacing grass, to be replaced in turn by scrub and trees, even before global warming takes its toll. New tunnels are being gouged through the foothills and new roads are climbing the slopes.

The animal population is in a state of flux with the arrival of the *mouflon* and the *marmotte*, the disappearance of the ibex, and the continuing efforts to improve local breeds, like the Pottoks.

And the humans are not the same either. Once a population in decline, subsisting on the fruits of the land, those who have stayed have seen their way of life influenced by miners and foresters, winter skiers and summer walkers, who have brought with them not only the opportunity of new sources of income, but also a threat to the traditions which have bound the *montagnards* to their mountains.

New perceptions of the mountains are being imposed from outside. The unfinished battle over the reintroduction of the bears is only part of the story, a story of human intervention at all levels. Where once nature held sway, at best we now find a 'managed wilderness'. At one time isolated, with more in common with their mountain neighbours on the other side of the watershed than with the inhabitants of the plains, the French Pyrenean *montagnards* are turning round to look the other way, towards France. Reluctantly or willingly, depending on the individuals, faster or slower depending on the area, the Pyrenees are changing.

Annotated bibliography

I have learned a great deal from: Pierre Minvielle (1980) *Les Pyrénées des Quarante Vallées*, Paris: Denoël, an indispensable guide to life in the Pyrenees up to 1980. I have quoted him on the French–Spanish border, superstitions, the Chemin de la Mâture, the Mines d'Arre, extinct species, Bentaillou, the failed project to create a National Park in the Ariège, and Rancié.

Another excellent overview of the Pyrenees is: A. Lévy (ed.) (2000) *Le Dictionnaire des Pyrénées* (2nd edn), Toulouse: Privat.

The references below are listed in the order they first appear.

- One of the most extensive websites on the Pyrenees is http://www.balades-pyrenees.com/.
- Basque houses and culture are discussed in Peio Etcheverry-Ainchart and Alexandre Hurel (2001) *Dictionnaire Thématique de Culture et Civilisation Basques.* Urrugne: Pimentos.
- The official site of the Friends of the Chemin de St Jacques is: http://www.aucoeurduchemin.org/
- On the different ways of seeing the mountains, see J. Cubero (2019) *L'Invention des Pyrénées* (p. 185). Cairn: Pau.
- For bears: Olivier de Marliave (2000) *Histoire de l' Ours dans les Pyrénées* (p. 153). Bordeaux: Sud Ouest.

- For the place names of the eastern part of the Pyrénées-Atlantiques see Marcellin Berot (2002) *La Vie des Hommes de la Montagne dans les Pyrénées Racontée par la Toponymie*. Éditions Milan.
- Leytés are described in: Terranoos (2008) *Pyrénées, l'Aventure Botanique: Sur les Traces d'Augustin Pyramus de Candolle* (p. 88). Terranoos.
- For guides, including Barrau, and the Vignemale race, see Antonin Nichol (2002) *Les Grands Guides des Pyrénées*. Oloron-Ste-Marie: Monhélios.
- For an entertainingly personal view of the exploration and literature of the Pyrenees in the 19th century see the seven volumes by Henri Beraldi (2001) *Cent Ans aux Pyrénées* (originally published 1898–1904). Pau: Librairie des Pyrénées et de Gascogne
- Several travellers' accounts of 19th-century voyages through the Pyrenees are collected in André Gabastou (ed.) (2001) *Voyage aux Pyrénées*. Urrugne: Pimientos. This collection is the source of the various quotations on Cauterets.
- The Pyrenean Romantics are dissected in J. Fourcassié (1990) *Le Romantisme et les Pyrénées* (2nd edn). Toulouse: ESPER.
- The greatest Pyrenean of the last two centuries, Henry Russell does himself justice in: Henry Russell (1999) *Souvenirs d'un Montagnard* (1st edn 1878, revised 1888 and 1908). Pau: Pyré Monde. But there are also some interesting insights in R. Bailey (2005) *The Man Who Married a Mountain*. London: Bantam.
- For a plausible explanation of why Russell married a mountain rather than his girlfriend, and much more, see Monique Dollin de Fresnel (2009) *Henry Russell*. Éditions Sudouest: Bordeaux.
- Statistics and other information on the National Park are available at http://www.parc-pyrenees.com/
- For avalanches, the Service for the Restoration of Mountain Terrain, and Barèges see Christophe Ancey (1998) *Guide Neige et Avalanche. Connaissances, Pratiques, & Sécurité* (3rd electronic edn). On WWW at http://www.toraval.fr/livre/guide.php.

ॐ St-Lary-Soulan: http://www.saintlary.com/

ॐ Although scathing of any other views, the pro-bear http://www. loup-ours-berger.org/ contains much useful information.

ॐ The first book about the Pyrenees from the man who 'invented' them is: Ramond de Carbonnières (1813) *Travels in the Pyrenees* (trans. F. Gold). London: Longman, Hurst, Rees, Orme, and Browne. The original *Observations Faites aux Pyrénées* was republished in 2000 by the Librairie des Pyrénées et de Gascogne, Pau.

ॐ On Luchon see: Philippe Francastel (2004) *Le Pays de Luchon.* Biarritz: Atlantica.

ॐ For the bear cubs at the Hospice de France see: *Pyrénées Magazine*, 113 (p. 49). The magazine is a useful source of current information.

ॐ Glaciers: Association Morain, www.moraine.fr.st and the *Revue Pyrénéenne* (2007), no 119.

ॐ For a dispassionate pro-bear view of the reintroductions see: F. Benhammou *et al.* (2005) *L'Ours des Pyrénées.* Toulouse: Privat.

ॐ On the other hand, for a passionately anti-bear stance, see: V. Berot (2006) *Pourquoi Nous Disons non à la Réintroduction de l'Ours dans les Pyrénées.* On WWW at http://www.nonalareintroduction. com.

ॐ The Biros valley: http://biros.free.fr/biros_histoire.html.

ॐ Broutards: Corinne Eychenne (2006) *Hommes et Troupeaux en Montagne: La Question Pastorale en Ariège* (p. 238). L'Harmattan.

ॐ For an academic study of the relationship between peasants and foresters in the Ariège (and the Alps) see T.L. Whited (2000) *Forests and Peasant Politics in Modern France.* New Haven and London: Yale University Press.

ॐ The Ariège Natural Park has a website at www.projet-pnr-pyreneesariegeoises.com.

ॐ Auzat: http://www.liberation.fr/economie/0101440776-auzat-village-isole-prive-de-pechiney (published 20 Feb 2003)

- Rancié: http://auzatvicdessos.free.fr/rancie.htm and Robert Simonet et al. (2008) *Ariège* (pp. 118–120). Bonneton.
- 'The Pyrenees are no more', and tobacco smuggling: Peter Sahlins (1989) *Boundaries: The Making of France and Spain in the Pyrenees*. Los Angeles: University of California Press.
- *Muntanyes regalades* and more on Canigou: Bernard Rieu, Patrice Teisseire-Dufor et Paul Palau (2009) *Canigó*. Le Boulou: Objectif Sud.
- Canigou bonfire: www.acg66.org/focs%20de%20Sant%20Joan.pdf
- Pyrénées-Orientales: Marc Calvet *et al. Pyrénées-Orientales Roussillon*. Bonneton.
- Resistance in WWII: Pierre Cantaloube (2002) *Évades de France Internés en Espagne*.

For more information on the GR10 and the Pyrenees see my blog www.pyreneanway.com/blog.

Printed in Great Britain
by Amazon